Removing Obstacles

Removing Obstacles

A Mutual Learning Experience Towards Good Practices in Competition Law Enforcement

Anna Gerbrandy
Wouter-Jan Berends (eds.)

eleven
international publishing

Published, sold and distributed by Eleven International Publishing
P.O. Box 85576
2508 CG The Hague
The Netherlands
Tel.: +31 70 33 070 33
Fax: +31 70 33 070 30
e-mail: sales@budh.nl
www.elevenpub.com

Sold and distributed in USA and Canada
International Specialized Book Services
920 NE 58th Avenue, Suite 300
Portland, OR 97213-3786, USA
Tel: 1-800-944-6190 (toll-free)
Fax: +1 503 280-8832
orders@isbs.com
www.isbs.com

Eleven International Publishing is an imprint of Boom uitgevers Den Haag.

ISBN 978-94-90947-79-8

Printed in The Netherlands

Contents

Introduction

A. van den Brink

The enforcement of EU competition law relies to a great extent on national courts and tribunals. They are, thus, faced with a challenging responsibility given the dynamic nature of this area of law. Also, the interplay of EU competition law and national law, especially national procedural law, poses them with various challenges. The decentralised enforcement of EU competition law is a relatively new field of law for the recently joined Member States and prospective Member States. Although courses on competition law may remedy a possible gap in academic knowledge, it is felt that what is (also) needed is an exchange of practical expertise: how to deal with the fast-paced developments in European competition law in practice. The exchange of solutions to competition law problems for the judiciary, set in an overarching structure of sound scholarly knowledge, is a good way to provide the judiciary of the new and prospective Member States with this practical knowledge.

It is in this light that the European Commission has financed a project to set up a training program for national judges in EU competition law and to stimulate judicial co-operation between national judges. The project focuses on a bottom-up approach to avoid going beyond the necessary but often lofty academic aspirations. This bottom-up and multi-national approach of the project ensures that the needs of national courts and tribunals are central. However, to accurately assess practical needs, an academic knowledge of competition law is required. It is an optimum of this mix that this project strives for. The main goal is to improve the national enforcement of EC competition law by:

a. identifying problems and other issues related to the enforcement of EU competition law in the Member States.
b. identifying, sharing and evaluating national good practices related thereto.
c. stimulating processes of mutual learning among competition law judges, both transnational and national.
d. dissemination of knowledge through publication of the conference proceedings and conclusions.
e. strengthening transnational and national co-operation between judges.

To reach this goal, a two day conference entitled 'Removing Obstacles: a mutual learning experience towards good practices in competition law enforcement' was held at the Europa Institute of Utrecht University on 21 and 22 October 2011.

The participants in this conference were competition law judges from a selected group of countries: Hungary, Croatia, Slovakia, Czech Republic and Slovenia. From each of the new Member States and Croatia a total number of five judges were selected and invited to participate in the conference. Since competition law is a relatively new area of law altogether, the dissemination of knowledge and processes to stimulate mutual learning are of particular interest to these countries.

It is therefore that apart from these new Member States and candidate country Croatia, participants from the Netherlands, Luxemburg (including judges of the Court of First Instance), Germany and Austria were invited. The group of judges from the selected Eastern European countries, (Slovenia, Czech Republic, Slovakia, Hungary and Croatia), were mixed with members of the judiciary from Member States which have been part of the EU for a longer period of time (the Netherlands, Germany and Austria). In this set-up, the judges from countries with a longer-running experience in the enforcement of EU competition law could share their experiences and the problems they encounter with judges who are relatively new to this legal area. Moreover, leading experts in the legal area were invited to participate and deliver key note speeches.

The conference focused on five themes relating to the enforcement of competition law. To ensure a bottom-up approach, these themes were prepared and elaborated in collaboration with the national expert organisations, the partner in Slovenia included, in the selected Member States. For the purpose of establishing the themes, the participating judges in each of the countries were approached to make an inventory in the first stage of the project. On the basis of this preliminary inventory, which was drawn up in November 2009 for the purpose of this proposal among the Dutch judiciary, the following themes were conditionally proposed:

- organisation of competition law adjudication;
- competition law in civil proceedings;
- the recovery of unlawful state aid;
- parallel application of European competition law and national competition law;
- economic evidence, *e.g.* in Article 102 procedures.

On each of these themes, several background papers have been written by key note speakers and other scholars in order to inform the participants of the conference beforehand. Moreover, country papers have been written to assess national competition law in the new Member States and Croatia.

The conference consisted of several plenary sessions with international experts of high standing as well as workshop sessions which served as a forum to exchange and evaluate good practices. The plenary sessions focused on informing the participants of the background of the themes and their development at the European level. The focus of the workshop sessions was on practical solutions, aimed at sharing knowledge and formulating good practices.

The conference impacted the target group of competition law judges by enhancing the substantial understanding of topical issues in legal procedure. By stimulating the evaluation of their own and other national legal systems and promoting the substantive insight in these issues and the formulation of good practices, the selected judges were given the tools to disseminate their knowledge further to other judges upon their return to their respective countries. The national judicial academies participating in this project will oversee that this occurs. Furthermore, in the long term, it is expected that the informal networks created at the conference enhance judicial co-operation and create coherence and consistency in the enforcement of European competition law.

To ensure further dissemination of knowledge obtained at the conference, the background papers and country papers of the conference are published in a book to ensure the project results in a long-lasting and influential product. The book, thus, contributes to a broadening of the target group and its sustainable effect. It is this book that now lies before you.

Claims for Damages in European and National Competition Law

R. Bolhaar

1. Introduction

Claims for damages in European and national competition law have been a much debated topic during the past decade.[1] As part of the effectiveness of decentralised enforcement of competition law, the European Commission (hereafter: the Commission) has proposed legislative instruments in order to achieve a more effective enforcement of the reparation of damages, resulting from infringements of competition law.[2] Although these instruments have not yet come into being, they are part of a trend that shows a shift towards civil proceedings to provide for a 'legal forum' for claims in competition law, including damages.

In its 2008 White Paper,[3] the Commission, in accordance with the European Court of Justice (hereafter: the ECJ), stated that:

> any citizen or business who suffers harm as a result of a breach of EC antitrust rules (Articles 101 and 102 of the Treaty on the Functioning of the European Union[4]) must be able to claim reparation from the party who caused the damage.[5]

The Commission derived this conclusion from case law of the ECJ; more specifically the *Courage* case and the *Manfredi* case.[6] However, the same White Paper notes that:

1 Hereafter European and national competition law will be referred to as "competition law".

2 *White Paper on damages actions for breach of the EC antitrust rules*, Commission of the European Communities, Brussels, 2.4.2008, COM(2008) 165 final.

3 *White Paper on damages actions for breach of the EC antitrust rules*, Commission of the European Communities, Brussels, 2.4.2008, COM(2008) 165 final, p. 3, para. 1.1.

4 With effect from 1 December 2009, Arts. 81 and 82 of the EC Treaty have become Arts. 101 and 102 of the Treaty on the Functioning of the European Union. In this chapter, in citations from judgments the numbering has also been changed in order to reflect the new Treaty numbering.

5 *White Paper on damages actions for breach of the EC antitrust rules*, Commission of the European Communities, Brussels, 2.4.2008, COM(2008) 165 final, p. 3, para. 1.1.

6 Case C-453/99, *Courage and Crehan*, [2001] ECR I-6297, and Joined Cases C-295-298/04, *Manfredi*, [2006] ECR I-6619.

> despite the requirement to establish an effective legal framework turning exercising the right to damages into a realistic possibility, and although there have recently been some signs of improvement in certain Member States, to date in practice victims of EC antitrust infringements only rarely obtain reparation of the harm suffered.[7]

The initial and final enforcement of competition law takes place within Member States rather than on a European level.[8] Taking into account the principle of effectiveness, European rules of competition law are to be effectively applied and enforced within EU Member States.[9] Furthermore, the principle of equivalence obliges the Member States to ensure "that the rules governing the enforcement of Community rights are not less favourable than those governing similar domestic actions".[10] Meanwhile, these same European rules often leave Member States and National Competition Authorities with discretionary space.[11] It is for national governments and authorities, usually in civil law suits, to ensure the practical and effective compensation and reparation of damages which are the result of infringements of European (and national) competition law. In practice however, Member States often struggle in balancing their discretionary freedom with their obligation to effectively enforce European competition law on a decentralised level. The Commission sees this struggle – also relating to claims for damages – as an impediment to the actual effective enforcement of European competition law.[12]

This chapter will discuss the topic of claims for damages in competition law. In doing so, it will provide an overview of the 'law-as-it-stands', on the European level considering these claims for damages. Subsequently, it will provide insight into problems and questions that have been raised relating to this topic. Obviously, the problems mostly arise both on the national level where competition law is enforced and claims for damages may be filed. In order to provide a deeper insight in the problems and issues that arise in the decentralised application and enforcement of this specific topic in competition law, this chapter will further asses this topic from a comparative perspective. This comparison will be an intra-European overview of the legal framework and its enforcement mechanisms within some EU Member States, and the implications of those individual, decentralised legal frameworks for the European legal framework on this topic. Finally, some conclusions and recommendations are drawn and some further questions to be answered considering this topic will be posed.

---

7 *White Paper on damages actions for breach of the EC antitrust rules*, Commission of the European Communities, Brussels, 2.4.2008, COM(2008) 165 final, p. 3, para. 1.1.

8 Case C-106/77, *Simmenthal II*, [1978] ECR 629 and Case C-213/89, *Factortame I*, [1990] ECR I-2433.

9 Case C-213/89, *Factortame I*, [1990] ECR I-2433.

10 Commission Staff Working Paper accompanying the White Paper on damages actions for breach of the EC antitrust rules, Brussels, 2.4.2008 SEC(2008) 404 [COM(2008) 165 final], paras 77 and 78.

11 In accordance with the principle of procedural autonomy. See on this principle for example J. Jans *et al.*, *Europeanisation of Public Law*, Groningen: Europa Law Publishing, 2007.

12 Commission Staff Working Paper accompanying the White Paper on damages actions for breach of the EC antitrust rules, Brussels, 2.4.2008 SEC(2008) 404 [COM(2008) 165 final], para. 10.

2. The *Manfredi* Case and the European Legal Status Quo

2.1 *Legal Basis for Bringing an Action for Damages*

For setting out the legal basis which provides for the possibility of bringing an action for damages done by, and harm suffered as a result of, infringements of competition law, the *Manfredi* case is of utmost importance.[13] In this case the ECJ formulated guidelines for Member States and national courts to ensure effective reparation of the harm suffered as a result of infringements of competition law.[14]

> The *Manfredi* case was about an agreement between automotive insurers, that, according to the Italian Competition Authority (*Autorità Garante della Concorrenza e del Mercato*), infringed Italian and European competition rules. More specifically, it concerned an agreement between automotive insurers, *inter alia* consisting of an unlawful exchange of information, which on its turn resulted in an average twenty percent inflation of insurance premiums charged to consumers.[15] Clearly, the damage done by the competition infringement in this case was the overcharge suffered by Italian insurance 'consumers'. Being one of these consumers, mr. Manfredi and others brought an action before the Italian court to get their damages repaired by their insurers. Eventually this case led to five preliminary questions being addressed to the ECJ.[16]

As to the right to claim damages for harm suffered as a result of an infringement of national and/or European competition law,[17] the ECJ followed the lines it set out in the *Courage* case.[18] This means that in assessing the practical applicability and enforcement of competition law, the ECJ focuses on the 'practical effectiveness' of, in this case, Articles 101 and 102 TFEU, by stating that:

> Next, as regards the possibility of seeking compensation for loss caused by a contract or by conduct liable to restrict or distort competition, it should be recalled that the full effectiveness of Article 101 TFEU and, in particular, the practical effect of the prohibition laid down in Article 101(1) TFEU would be put at risk if it were not open to any individual to claim damages for loss caused to him by a contract or by conduct liable to restrict or distort competition (*Courage and Crehan* (...) paragraph 26). It follows

13 Joined Cases C-295-298/04, *Manfredi*, [2006] ECR I-6619. The *Manfredi* case was one of the four cases the Court decided on in a preliminary ruling on the 13 July 2006.

14 G. Oosterhuis, 'Manfredi: respect voor deze rechter! Private enforcement in de praktijk', *NTER*, Nr. 3 March 2007, p. 1.

15 De Smijter & Denis O'Sullivan, 'The Manfredi judgment of the ECJ and how it relates to the Commission's initiative on EC antitrust damages actions', *Competition Policy Newsletter*, Nr. 3 Autumn 2006, p. 1.

16 Some specific issues will be discussed later in this chapter.

17 In *Manfredi*, the ECJ first stressed the national applicability of European competition law by stating that "it should be recalled that Articles 101 and 102 TFEU are a matter of public policy which must be automatically applied by national Courts". Moreover, the ECJ indicated that a practice which impairs competition can be an infringement of both national and European competition law at the same time, Joined Cases C-295-298/04, *Manfredi*, [2006] ECR I-6619, paras 3-52.

18 Case C-453/99, *Courage and Crehan*, [2001] ECR I-6297, paras 26.

> that any individual can claim compensation for the harm suffered where there is a causal relationship between that harm and an agreement or practice prohibited under [Article 101 TFEU].[19]

Next, the ECJ again emphasises the right to effective redress for those harmed by infringements of national and European competition law:

> Secondly, it follows from the principle of effectiveness and the right of individuals to seek compensation for loss caused by a contract or by conduct liable to restrict or distort competition that injured persons must be able to seek compensation not only for actual loss (*damnum emergens*) but also for loss of profit (*lucrum cessans*) plus interest.[20]

One of the remarkable aspects of these paragraphs is the causal connection that the ECJ 'creates' between an infringement of competition law and the harm that is caused as a result of that infringement. The ECJ decides that the existence of this causal connection in a specific case is sufficient to accept a claim for damages to repair the harm done by the infringement of European competition law.[21] Further on in this chapter the implications of this causal connection in cases where an actual claim for damages emerges is discussed.

In accordance with the *Courage* case, the ECJ ruled that effective redress would be nullified when claims for damages – in any kind of infringement of European competition law cases – would be practically impossible before national courts. Moreover, the ECJ ruled that where European law does not provide procedural rules, it is for national governments and judges to provide for these rules and procedures, while the principles of equivalence and effectiveness are to be taken into consideration.[22] European law itself therefore provides for the general legal basis for any claim for damages; national procedural law will have to make such a claim realistically realisable.

In the *Manfredi* case, the ECJ therefore also confirmed the Commission's purpose to achieve effective redress of harm resulting from infringements of competition law, as described in the Commission's Green Paper of 2005.[23] In reality, it is the *Manfredi* case that shows us the objective of the Commission to achieve effective redress and minimum harmonisation of claims for damages in competition law. More specifically, this case illustrates the issues that national courts have to deal with concerning these claims for damages. The current question is how to deal with these issues, and whether European Community legislation is needed to create Europe-wide legal certainty on a relative short term. The Commission's proposals in this area are the subject of the next chapter.[24]

19 Joined Cases C-295-298/04, *Manfredi*, [2006] ECR I-6619, paras 60-61.
20 *Ibid.*, para. 100.
21 De Smijter & O'Sullivan 2006, pp. 1-2.
22 Oosterhuis 2007, pp. 2-3.
23 *Green Paper on damages actions for breach of the EC antitrust rules*, Commission of the European Communities, Brussels 19.12.2005, COM(2005) 672 final, p. 7, para. 2.2, option 11.
24 De Smijter & O'Sullivan 2006, p. 4.

2.2 Problematic Issues at National Courts

In the *Manfredi* case the Italian Courts struggled with several questions concerning the claims for damages made by mr. Manfredi and others. In order to solve these questions, the Italian Courts posed several preliminary questions to the ECJ.[25] As examples of the issues national courts deal with, some of these preliminary questions will be discussed.[26] The issues relate to the jurisdiction of national courts and their role in the effective safeguarding of legal rights derived from European law; time constraints considering actions for damages; and the scope of 'damages' that can be awarded.

2.2.1 Jurisdiction of National Courts

The first issue to be discussed is phrased in the second preliminary question, as put forward by the Italian court to the ECJ in Case 298/04. This question (together with the third question), concerns the principle of effective safeguarding of legal rights:

> Is Article 101 TFEU to be interpreted as meaning that it precludes the application of a national provision similar to that in [the Italian legislation] under which a claim for damages for infringement of Community and national provisions for anti-competitive arrangements must also be made by third parties before a Court other than that which usually has jurisdiction for claims of similar value, thus involving a considerable increase in costs and time?[27]

This question mainly focuses on the jurisdiction of different courts within a Member State. In answering this question the ECJ emphasises the principle of procedural autonomy: whenever Community law does not have a provision, the issue should be dealt with by the national laws of the Member States and the national courts. It is then for Member States to determine which court has jurisdiction to assess claims for damages as a result of infringements of competition law.[28] Two further remarks are made by the ECJ concerning this issue:

> ...provided that the provisions concerned are not less favourable than those governing actions for damages based on an infringement of national competition rules and that those national provisions do not render practically impossible or excessively difficult the exercise of the right to seek compensation for the harm caused by an agreement or practice prohibited under Article 101 TFEU.[29]

These remarks obviously refer to the application of the principles of equivalence of national and European law, the principle (or prerequisite) of practical possibility

25 As to provide a structured overview, I will stick with the order of questions as put forward in Case 298/04 (*Pasqualina Murgolo v. Assitalia SpA*).
26 Oosterhuis 2007.
27 Second preliminary question in Case C-298/04 (*Pasqualina Murgolo v. Assitalia SpA*), para. 21.
28 Case C-298/04 (*Pasqualina Murgolo v. Assitalia SpA*), paras 70-72.
29 *Ibid.*, para. 72.

and the principle of effectiveness concerning the implementation and application of European law in the Member States.[30] The *principle of equivalence* aims to ensure that remedies for violation of rights of European law are not less favourable than those relating to similar domestic claims. The *principle of practical possibility* aims to safeguard the quality of such remedies; the remedy concerned should not be impossible or excessively difficult to realise.[31] These principles are well-known and applied fairly consistently by the ECJ. However, this does not mean that the application in a national context is always clear: which domestic claims are supposed to be 'similar' to the European claims? When are circumstances 'not less favourable'? When is the remedy 'excessively difficult to realise'? Although the case law of the ECJ does provide clues, as will be shown below, the actual determination of these issues is in the hands of national courts. The *principle of effectiveness* furthermore, obliges Member States to make sure that European law is applied effectively and that remedies for breaches of European law ensure this effective application.[32] This principle is also at issue in the next preliminary question, considering effective safeguarding of the legal rights accruing from Article 101 TFEU. The referring court asks:[33]

> Is Article 101 TFEU to be interpreted as meaning that it *entitles* third parties who have a relevant legal interest to rely on the invalidity of an agreement or practice prohibited by that Community provision and claim damages for the harm suffered where there is a causal relationship between the agreement or concerted practice and the harm?[34]

In answering this question and taking into account the *Courage* case, the ECJ emphasises again the principle of effectiveness of European law (in this case Art. 101 (1) TFEU). The ECJ judges that the useful effect of this European provision would be nullified when actions for damages for any kind of infringement of European competition law would not be possible.[35] Therefore, indeed Article 101 (1) TFEU entitles third parties, as specified in the question, to claim damages. But then again, it is for the Member States to provide for legal rules for the enforcement of this right to claim and receive damages. Also in this situation, the remarks considering equivalence and practical possibility are to be taken into account by the Member States.

2.2.2 Time Constraints Concerning Actions for Damages

Another issue raised by the referring Court concerns the time constraints considering actions for damages as a result of infringements of European competition law:[36]

30 It can be debated whether a principle of practical possibility exists, or that it is subsumed by the principle of effectiveness.
31 Case *Comet B.V. v. Produktschap voor Siergewassen*, C-45/76, [1976] ECR 2043, ECJ and Case *Rewe-Zentralfinanz e.G. v. Landwirstschaftskammer fuer das Saarland*, C-33/76, [1976] ECR 1989, 1997.
32 Case *Factortame I*, C-213/89 [1990] ECR I-2433, ECJ.
33 The question put forward by the Italian Court as phrased in para. 21, and answered by the ECJ in paras 56-64.
34 Emphasis added.
35 Case C-298/04 (*Pasqualina Murgolo v. Assitalia SpA*), para. 60.
36 *Ibid.*, para. 21.

> Is Article 101 TFEU to be interpreted as meaning that for the purposes of the limitation period for bringing an action for damages based thereon, time begins to run from the day on which the agreement or concerted practice was adopted or the day on which the agreement or concerted practice came to an end?

The question obviously relates to a real concern: if the limitation period were to start at the beginning of the infringement, the agreement or concerted practice usually functioning below radar, how would those suffering the damage be able to know about the infringement? Concerning the time limitations, the ECJ states, similar to the Advocate-General, that once again, in case of a lack of Community law, it is for Member States to determine time limitations for these actions for damages. Again, the remarks concerning equivalence and useful effect apply.[37] These requirements are furthermore put into perspective as the ECJ states:[38]

> A national rule under which the limitation period begins to run from the day on which the agreement or concerted practice was adopted could make it practically impossible to exercise the right to seek compensation for the harm caused by that prohibited agreement or practice, particularly if that national rule also imposes a short limitation period which is not capable of being suspended.
>
> In such a situation, where there are continuous or repeated infringements, it is possible that the limitation period expires even before the infringement is brought to an end, in which case it would be impossible for any individual who has suffered harm after the expiry of the limitation period to bring an action. It is for the national Court to determine whether such is the case with regard to the national rule at issue in the main proceedings.

In conclusion to its answer on the question of time limitation, the ECJ judges that it is for national courts to determine the actual start and end of the term in which an action for damages should be made. Furthermore, it is for these national courts to decide on a case-by-case basis whether a specific national time limitation rule makes it "practically impossible or excessively difficult" for those suffering from an infringement of competition law to effectively claim compensation for the harm suffered. Especially when national law implies short time limitation periods that cannot be extended, it is for the national court to secure the effectiveness of this right to seek compensation for the harm suffered.

2.2.3 The Scope of Damages that Can Be Awarded

A last issue the Italian court faced concerned the scope of 'damages' that can be awarded. More specifically, the Italian court, *inter alia*, wanted to know whether

37 *Ibid.*, para. 81.

38 *Ibid.*, paras 77-82.

so called *punitive damages*, as additional redress to *compensation damages*, are included in the definition of 'damages'. The question put forward to the ECJ reads:

> Is Article 101 TFEU to be interpreted as meaning that where the national Court sees that the damages that can be awarded on the basis of national law are in any event lower than the economic advantage gained by the infringing party to the prohibited agreement or concerted practice, it should also award of its own motion punitive damages to the injured third party, making the compensable amount higher than the advantage gained by the infringing party in order to deter the adoption of agreements or concerted practices prohibited under Article 101 TFEU?

After repeating the principles of equivalence and effectiveness, concerning the possibility to impose punitive damages the ECJ rules that, in absence of a European provision, it is for the national legislator to include the possibility to impose these fines in the national legal framework. More broadly the extent of damages is to be set by this national legislator, under the constant condition of the principles of equivalence and effectiveness.[39] In practice, this means that there is *no* obligation to provide for punitive damages, but if the national legislation provides for such damages for equivalent national claims, then these would also have to be made possible for infringement of European competition rules.

2.3 Conclusions

In conclusion, concerning the issues national Courts have to deal with it can be stated that the practical (in)effectiveness of actions for damages in competition law is the main issue. In Italy, as in most EU Member States, there are legal provisions of claims for damages in competition law. These provisions are – so far – absent on the European level. Although national legislation thus does exist on this issue, a great amount of legal uncertainty appears to still exist. The questions discussed above are the result thereof. The question now is, whether a European legislative framework, harmonising the laws of Member States on claims for damages in competition law, should be on the agenda.[40] As mentioned above, the Commission has put forward several possibilities.[41]

3. The Commission's Proposals

Struggling with, and trying to find an answer to the difficult questions relating to claims for damages, the Commission has presented several quite far-reaching instruments that, although they have not yet come into being, might form the future

39 *Ibid.*, paras 89-100.

40 Joaquín Almunia, Vice President of the Commission, responsible for Competition policy Common standards for group claims across the EU, University of Valladolid, School of Law Valladolid, 15 October 2010, SPEECH/10/554.

41 *White Paper on damages actions for breach of the EC antitrust rules*, Commission of the European Communities, Brussels, 2.4.2008, COM(2008) 165 final, pp. 2-3.

portal to European legislation on this topic. This, in turn, might lead to legal harmonisation and implementation throughout the European Union. The proposals were presented in a *White Paper* on damages actions for breach of the EC antitrust rules, which the Commission published in 2008 (preceded by the *Green Paper* of 2005). The White Paper suggests specific policy options and measures. These should provide all victims of EU antitrust infringements with access to effective redress mechanisms, so that they can be fully compensated for the harm they suffered. Although there is some doubt as to the political viability of the direction the White Paper takes, it is the starting point for a discussion in this chapter.

3.1 The White Paper on Damages Actions for Breach of the EC Antitrust Rules

As we have seen in the *Courage* and *Manfredi* cases, the ECJ has explicitly recognised that each and every individual or undertaking must have the right to claim damages for harm suffered as a result of competition law infringements. Preceding these 'breakthrough' judgments, the Commission had published a Green Paper in 2005. In summary, in this Green Paper the Commission came to the conclusion that individuals or undertakings, which have been harmed by infringements of competition law hardly ever succeed in getting their damages reimbursed. According to the Green Paper the lack of successful actions for damages is "largely due to the obstructive nature of the Member States' rules and procedures governing antitrust damages actions".[42] In April 2008, the Commission published a White Paper in order to follow up its conclusions in the Green Paper. The main objective of the White Paper was "to improve the legal conditions for victims to exercise their right under the Treaty to reparation of all damage suffered as a result of a breach of the EC antitrust rules." In order to achieve effective improvement the Commission aims at "full compensation" of harm done by infringements of competition law.[43]

In the White Paper the Commission has come up with several proposals for legislative measures in order to provide for effective redress of damages as a result of competition law infringements. The Commission proposed a set of minimum rules that would ensure the efficiency of rules and procedures considering such damages actions.[44] In balancing the objectives and practical issues the Commission presented nine proposals in its White Paper.[45] Obviously, the Commission is dependent on the effective cooperation of the Member States and therefore recognises that "compensation of victims can only be obtained via national courts, in accordance with national procedural rules".[46] Not all nine proposals are discussed

42 *Commission Staff Working Document, Executive Summary of the Impact Assessment*, White Paper on damages actions for breach of the EC antitrust rules, COM(2008) 165 final, p. 2, para. 2.

43 *White Paper on damages actions for breach of the EC antitrust rules*, Commission of the European Communities, Brussels, 2.4.2008, COM(2008) 165 final, p. 3.

44 *Commission Staff Working Document, Executive Summary of the Impact Assessment*, White Paper on damages actions for breach of the EC antitrust rules, COM(2008) 165 final, p. 2, para. 2.

45 *White Paper on damages actions for breach of the EC antitrust rules*, Commission of the European Communities, Brussels, 2.4.2008, COM(2008) 165 final, p. 4 *et seq*.

46 *Commission Staff Working Document, Executive Summary of the Impact Assessment*, White Paper on damages actions for breach of the EC antitrust rules, COM(2008) 165 final, p. 2, para. 2.

here, but five that directly relate to access to and effectiveness of compensation-procedures are briefly discussed in this chapter.[47]

3.2 Proposals in the White Paper

3.2.1 Standing: Indirect Purchasers and Collective Redress

As mentioned above, the main objective of the White Paper is to facilitate access to procedures and provide for the possibility of effective and practical compensation. It is important to note that this right to damages does not exclusively aim to protect *direct purchasers* but also those individuals who are, along the distribution chain, *indirectly* harmed by – for example – infringing prices that are being passed on down the supply chain. Further down this chain, damages are likely to be relatively small compared to the damages done to 'first purchasers'. More importantly, individuals at the end of the supply chain are often deterred to bring claims for their damages due to the relatively high costs of procedures and delays, as well as the legal uncertainties and business risks that are inextricably connected to such claims.

In order to enhance the opportunity for all individuals, including those at the end of the supply chain, to effectively seek redress for the harm suffered, the Commission put forward two proposals. In summary, these two proposals allow for (1) representative actions to be brought by consumer and trade associations and state bodies,[48] and (2) opt-in for collective actions.[49] These proposals enable victims of infringements of competition law to jointly bring their claims in a single claim if they explicitly opt to be included.[50]

3.2.2 Access to Evidence: Disclosure Inter Partes

The White Paper emphasises the fact that competition law cases often are very much dependent on information and facts gathered and put forward as evidence by both claimants and defendants. Due to the amount of information that is held by the defendant, and which is therefore most of the time unknown to the claimant, this claimant might experience difficulties in gathering essential information and consequently fail to meet its burden of proof. In order to rebalance this "structural information asymmetry" between the defendant and claimant,

47 This is not to say that the other proposals are irrelevant for the determination of effectiveness.

48 "Representative actions, which are brought by qualified entities, such as consumer associations, state bodies or trade associations, on behalf of identified or, in rather restricted cases, identifiable victims. These entities are either (i) officially designated in advance or (ii) certified on an ad hoc basis by a Member State for a particular antitrust infringement to bring an action on behalf of some or all of their members". *White Paper on damages actions for breach of the EC antitrust rules*, Commission of the European Communities, Brussels, 2.4.2008, COM(2008) 165 final, p. 4.

49 "Opt-in collective actions, in which victims expressly decide to combine their individual claims for harm they suffered into one single action." *White Paper on damages actions for breach of the EC antitrust rules*, Commission of the European Communities, Brussels, 2.4.2008, COM(2008) 165 final, p. 4.

50 See also E.-J. Zippro, *Privaatrechtelijke handhaving van mededingingsrecht*, Deventer, Kluwer 2009.

the Commission states that a minimum level of disclosure *inter partes* should be ensured on the European level.[51]

On the practical level of enforcement of these European standards on disclosure, national courts should have the power to order parties to disclose precise categories of relevant evidence. The Commission proposes several safeguards and conditions to this rather extensive power of national courts.[52] In providing national courts with this additional power to demand disclosure of relevant information, the Commission emphasises the fact and information-dependency of competition law cases and stresses the importance of a balanced access to this information. In this 'balancing' the Commission recognises the concern of avoiding negative effects of excessive disclosure obligations which might result from this extensive power.[53]

3.2.3 Binding Effect of National Competition Authorities' Decisions

Another proposal that would enhance the effective redress of harm resulting from infringements of competition law relates to the evidentiary value in civil proceedings of final decisions taken by National Competition Authorities (NCAs). In the White Paper the Commission expresses its desire that in every Member State final decisions taken by NCAs finding a breach of Article 101 or 102 TFEU, which are upheld by a final judgment of a reviewing court, should be unconditionally accepted as indisputable evidence of an infringement of competition law in civil proceedings concerning damages.[54] The Commission states that when it finds a breach of European competition law it can rely on the decision that results from that finding as binding proof in civil proceedings for damages. In its White Paper the Commission suggests that this should also be the case for NCAs decisions on European competition law.

The Commission argues that a harmonised application of this rule will result in increased legal certainty and will enhance "the effectiveness and procedural efficiency" of claims for damages in competition law. Furthermore, the Commission considers, for other reasons, that it is not the task of a court deciding on a claim for damages to re-examine the investigational work done by "a specialised public authority (and a review Court)".[55] Concretely, as a result of these considerations, the Commission proposed the following:

> National Courts that have to rule in actions for damages on practices under Article 101 or 102 on which an NCA in the European Competition Network has already given a final decision finding an infringement of those Articles, or on which a review Court

51 See on this issue also the contribution by Bekkering.

52 *White Paper on damages actions for breach of the EC antitrust rules*, Commission of the European Communities, Brussels, 2.4.2008, COM(2008) 165 final, p. 5, para. 2.2.

53 Zippro 2009.

54 The Commission based this conclusion on Art. 16(1) of Regulation 1/2003 (Council Regulation No 1/2003 of 16 December 2002, on the implementation of the rules on competition laid down in Articles 81 and 82 of the Treaty, Brussels 16.12.2002) and established case law, which considers the uniform application of Community competition law.

55 *White Paper on damages actions for breach of the EC antitrust rules*, Commission of the European Communities, Brussels, 2.4.2008, COM(2008) 165 final, pp. 5-6, para. 2.3.

> has given a final judgment upholding the NCA decision or itself finding an infringement, cannot take decisions running counter to any such decision or ruling.[56]

An important note is that this provision holds only to the binding effect when NCA decisions are indeed final, which implies that there is no national legal remedy left for the defendant, provided the national term for appeal has expired. Furthermore, this rule can only be applied by the civil court on the same case as on which the NCA and reviewing court have decided there is an infringement of competition law.

3.2.4 Damages

Another question addressed in the White Paper is which *types of harm* suffered by victims of antitrust infringements are eligible for compensation. In answering this question the Commission emphasises that the concept of "full compensation" is the main objective of providing for effective redress procedures. According to the Commission, victims of infringements of competition law should be eligible for full compensation of the actual harm, the real value of the loss, they suffered. The concept of full compensation therefore not only includes the actual loss suffered as a direct result from the infringement, but also the indirect loss of profit and corresponding interest. The Commission states that it is its intention with regard to the precise calculation of damages to "draw up a framework with pragmatic, non-binding guidance for quantification of damages in antitrust cases, *e.g.* by means of approximate methods of calculation or simplified rules on estimating the loss".[57]

3.2.5 Passing-On Overcharges

The Commission notes that, as a result of downward passing-on of anti-competitive overcharges within the supply chain, legal uncertainty abounds in civil proceedings on claims for damages in competition law. This issue is especially problematic for victims of infringements of competition law whenever an infringer (the defendant) defends himself on the ground of passed-on overcharges. In case the claimant – for example, the wholesaler claiming damages from a producer - passed on to his consumers the overcharges that were initially 'imposed' on him by the infringer (the producer) and the infringer will argue that the claimant did not actually suffer from the infringing overcharges and therefore has no right to receive damages. The Commission agrees with this notion and emphasises the concept of sufficient *causality* between the infringement of competition law and the *harm* suffered by victims of this infringement.[58] The Commission states that this will prevent unjust enrichment of those who are affected by the infringement but did not actually suffer any harm because they passed on this 'harm' to their customers. The Commission has presented the following proposal on passing-on of overcharges in its White Paper:

> Defendants should be entitled to invoke the passing-on defence against a claim for compensation of the overcharge. The standard of proof for this defence

56 *Ibid.*, p. 6, para. 2.3.
57 *Ibid.*, p. 7, para. 2.5.
58 *Ibid.*, para. 2.6.

should be not lower than the standard imposed on the claimant to prove the damage.[59]

Interesting in this respect is a rule relating to the burden of proof, especially when customers (indirect purchasers) bring an action because they are the ones who have suffered from the overcharges passed on to them by the direct purchasers. The question arises to what extent the notion of sufficient causality applies within the same supply chain. In practice it seems that courts tend to interpret the concept of sufficient causality rather strictly, which makes it very hard for indirect purchasers at the end of the supply chain, to prove the harm they suffered as a result of an infringement at the beginning of the supply chain. In order to avoid evasion by infringers of claims for damages by indirect victims, the Commission proposes that "indirect purchasers should be able to rely on the rebuttable presumption that the illegal overcharge was passed on to them in its entirety".[60]

3.3 Implementation of White Paper Proposals

The Commission aimed to provide for (possible and theoretical) solutions for issues concerning claims for damages in competition law that national courts are currently struggling with. The White Paper aimed to set out accessible, clear and efficient solutions for some of the major issues, like those at issue in *Courage*[61] and *Manfredi*.[62] The White Paper is a soft-law document and does not have any direct legal consequences: it is not legally binding.[63] Therefore, the question is whether and when it can be expected that the proposals in the White Paper are implemented into a legislative measure. Previous formal proposals that intended to provide for legislative measures on a European level were not successful. In 2009, a draft directive on infringements of competition law was withdrawn, as a result of remaining resistance from members of the European Parliament.[64] On 26 March 2009, however, the European Parliament embraced the Commission's White Paper proposals in a formal resolution.[65] In summary, the European Parliament agreed with the Commission's general statement that the effectiveness of claims for damages in competition law relies upon the possibility for any individual to actually start a damages procedure, without being impeded by the legal uncertainties currently surrounding these procedures. Moreover, the European Parliament stated that the Commission's proposals are to be complementary to the existing legal system of competition law. Therefore, the realisation of the Commission's proposals on claims for damages in competition law, should be incorporated in the broader reinforcement of competition law on the European level.

59 *Ibid.*, p. 8, para. 2.6.
60 *Ibid.*
61 Case C-453/99, *Courage and Crehan*, [2001] ECR I-6297.
62 Joined Cases C-295-298/04, *Manfredi*, [2006] ECR I-6619.
63 As appears from European Parliament Resolution of 26 March 2009 on the White Paper on damages actions for breach of the EC antitrust rules (2008/2154(INI).
64 <www.cdr-news.com/collective-redress/115-articles/486-which-way-now-for-the-commissions-damages-directive>.
65 European Parliament Resolution of 26 March 2009 on the White Paper on damages actions for breach of the EC antitrust rules (2008/2154(INI).

In line with the Monti Report published in May 2010,[66] the current Competition Commissioner, Joaquín Almunia, announced a meeting[67] organised by three European Union Commissioners: John Dalli (EU Commissioner for Consumer Policy) and Viviane Reding (EU Commissioner for Justice) and Joaquín Almunia (EU Commissioner for Competition) himself. The purpose of this meeting was to specifically discuss the introduction of coherent collective redress mechanisms at the EU-level, being one of the White Paper proposals discussed above.[68] This meeting has resulted in a public consultation "*Towards a more coherent European approach to collective redress*"[69], launched on 4 February 2011[70]. Through this public consultation the Commission intends "to identify common legal principles, should a future Commission initiative be presented on collective redress and how these principles could fit into the EU legal system and into the legal orders of the 27 EU Member States."[71] The broader purpose of the Commission's consultation is to achieve "a coherent approach towards collective redress in the European Union."[72] Thus, collective redress and the lack of a European common legal framework does not solely concern antitrust damages, but applies to more European policy areas, such as environmental protection and consumer protection. According to the Commission, breaches of European law affect a large and varied range of businesses. Meanwhile these businesses currently cannot rely on a European legal framework which provides for collective relief of those breaches and the harm they cause. The public consultation is the most recent legislative proposal of the Commission to provide these businesses with effective instruments of collective redress.

4. Comparative Research on Claims for Damages within the European Union

In order to gain a deeper insight in issues that play a role in procedures concerning claims for damages in competition law, I will now provide for a brief, comparative overview of differences in national legal procedures and competition laws on actions for damages between several EU Member States. More specifically, and for the benefit of the 2011 Conference relating to the enforcement of competition law in new EU Member States, to be held at Utrecht University in fall 2011, I will

66 "A new strategy for the Single Market, at the service of Europe's Economy and Society", Report to the President of the Commission José Manuel Barroso by Mario Monti, 9 May 2010.

67 Joaquín Almunia, Vice President of the Commission, responsible for Competition policy Common standards for group claims across the EU, University of Valladolid, School of Law Valladolid, 15 October 2010, SPEECH/10/554.

68 The Commission was expected to launch a public consultation in November 2010, followed by possible legislative proposals in the second half of 2011.

69 Commission Staff Working Document, Public Consultation: *Towards a Coherent European Approach to Collective Redress*, Brussels, 4 February 2011, SEC(2011)173 final.

70 Contributions can be submitted no later than the 30 April 2011.

71 <http://ec.europa.eu/dgs/health_consumer/dgs_consultations/ca/collective_redress_consultation_en.htm>.

72 <http://europa.eu/rapid/pressReleasesAction.do?reference=IP/11/132&format=HTML&aged=0&language=EN&guiLanguage=en>.

compare the legal framework of the relatively new Member State Hungary with the legal framework of two Member States with more experience in the enforcement of competition law, Portugal and the Netherlands. In doing so I will focus on some of the important bottle neck issues that also the White Paper deals with. I will discuss collective claims and representative actions for damages, the causality between infringement and harm, the passing-on defence and the legal position of indirect purchasers.

In 2004, a comparative "Study on the conditions of claims for damages in case of infringement of EC competition rules",[73] also known as the Ashurst Report, executed on behalf of the Commission, was published. This report comparatively addressed all issues concerning claims for damages in competition law that Member States faced at that moment. Although I have specifically chosen to systematically compare the legal framework on this topic in the different EU Member States mentioned before, the following comment in the Ashurst Report should be taken into consideration. The report recognised that the "diversity in this area means that any attempt at categorization looks very much like shoehorning and is moreover often inadequate due to the non-equivalence of terms in the different Community languages".[74] It is therefore of the utmost importance to keep in mind that the systematic and specific comparison I will make in this paper, is not representative for all EU Member States. Rather, it attempts to give an overview of the great legal divergence concerning claims for damages in competition law that currently still exists within the European Union. It may also focus the discussion between the participants of the meeting of judges within the project 'Removing Obstacles'.

4.1 Collective Claims and Representative Actions for Damages within Individual EU Member States

One of the issues that currently still remains unsolved in most Member States relates to collective redress. In the Commission's White Paper this issue is discussed together with the issue of representative actions. As discussed above, the relatively high costs of procedures, delays, legal uncertainties and business risks that are inextricably connected to legal procedures, 'prevent' individual victims at the end of the supply chain from actually starting such a legal procedure by bringing a claim for damages before a national court. Collective claims or 'representative' claims by, for example, public representatives or consumer organisations could lower the legal and financial thresholds for these individuals to actually start a legal procedure. Obviously, this will contribute to the accessibility and effectiveness of procedures concerning claims for damages in competition law in general. Below, I will schematically set out the possibilities of bringing collective and representative claims in the example Member States.

73 Comparative Report, *Study on the conditions of claims for damages in case of infringement of EC competition rules*, prepared by Denis Waelbroeck, Donald Slater and Gil Even-Shoshan, Ashurst LLP, Brussels, 31 August 2004.

74 *Ibid.*, p. 2.

Table 1

	Portugal[75]	The Netherlands[76]	Hungary[77]
Possible to bring collective claims?	Yes, "Article 26A of the Code of Civil Procedure confers on any person or any associations the right to claim the discontinuation or the prevention of infractions against *inter alia* public health, consumers rights, quality of life, environment or the public domain. Such right encompasses the right, for the claiming parties, to obtain compensation for the damages they have suffered as a result of the violation of the above mentioned interests"	Yes. "According to Article 3:305a Civil Code collective claims and representative actions are possible, provided they are instigated by special-purpose foundations or associations who have a clearly defined and actually pursued interest."	No, actions are not available for collectively claiming damages
Limitations/ Exceptions	n.a.[78]	A very important limitation is that monetary compensation is explicitly excluded in the final sentence of Article 3:305a(3) Civil Code	n.a.
Remarks	"Although Law 83/95 does not mention competition law, the list provided for in Article 52 of the Portuguese Constitution is not exhaustive; therefore, it may be possible to refer to the protection of other interests such as the preservation of competition."	"To avoid the abovementioned limitations, it is common to institute joint actions either by instructing the same lawyer or by assignment of individual claims to a particular (legal) person. The result is a bundle of claims brought to Court by one authorized (legal) person. These actions may be joined procedurally."	n.a.

*All the information used in this scheme is (in)directly extracted from the National Reports provided to the Commission by the EU Member States.[79]
*Information regarding three of the Eastern European Member States participating in the Removing Obstacles conference is included in Annex I.

75 National Report provided by: José Luís da Cruz Vilaça, Pedro Metello de Nápoles, Dorothée Choussy A.M Pereira, Sáragga Leal, Oliveira Martins, Júdice & Associados Edificio Eurolex, Lisboa (p. 4).
76 National Report Provided by: Weyer VerLoren van Themaat and Johannes Hettema, Houthoff Buruma, Brussels (p. 3).
77 National Report Provided by: Tamás Éless, Freshfields Bruckhaus Deringer formerly Réti Szegheõ & Partners, Ágnes Németh, Kovács Réti Szegheõ (p. 5).
78 "Not available".
79 Available on: <http://ec.europa.eu/competition/antitrust/actionsdamages/study.html>.

In the Ashurst Report it was concluded that "nearly all Member States provide for some collective or representative actions of some type".[80] As an analogous development in the majority of Member States, a rise of litigation by representative associations was found. However, as also appears from the scheme set out above, the possibility and effectiveness of bringing collective or representative claims differs between Member States. In some Member States, such as Portugal, this bottle neck issue falls within the scope of the constitution, which allows individuals to bring their claims on the ground of rather general principles of public interest. In other Member States, such as the Netherlands, collective and representative claims for damages in competition law are more restricted and thresholds for individuals to eventually bring these claims might therefore be higher. As opposed to Portugal and other Member States where collective and representative actions are possible, there are still Member States where either one of those or both actions are not possible. As the Ashurst Report concluded, Hungary is only one of the EU Member States where these actions do not belong to the legal possibilities of victims of infringements of competition law.

4.2 Causality between Infringement and Harm

A second bottle neck issue is the requirement of causality between the infringement of competition law and the alleged harm suffered by victims of this infringement. In order to provide a broad and consistent overview of bottle neck issues, I will once again systematically set out the differences between the three example Member States used above.

In addition, it may be noted that, apart from seven EU Member States (Austria, Ireland, Italy, Luxembourg, Malta, Sweden, UK) none of the Member States require direct causation. More importantly, comparing all national reports on this issue, we can conclude that there is no such strict distinction between direct or indirect causation to be made. This is due to the different national interpretations of the notion of causat ion and the way these interpretations influence the burden of proof. Once again this emphasises the great dissimilarities that exist between the national laws of Member States. However, there are also two major similarities, concerning causality that can be found to exist in most Member

80 Comparative Report, *Study on the conditions of claims for damages in case of infringement of EC competition rules*, prepared by Denis Waelbroeck, Donald Slater and Gil Even-Shoshan, Ashurst LLP, Brussels, 31 August 2004.

Table 2

	Portugal[81]	The Netherlands[82]	Hungary[83]
Level of causation to prove	"Article 563 of the Civil Code; the obligation to indemnify only arises in relation to damages that would probably not have occurred, had the illegal conduct not taken place. According to the legal doctrine, the theory of adequate causality applies."	"According to Article 6:98 Civil Code, the complainant has to prove that the infri ngement of antitrust rules is a "*conditio sine qua non*". Further, he has to prove that the damage is *still attributable* to the person infringing antitrust rules."	Both direct and indirect causation can be proved. The causality shall be adequate.
Limitations/ Exceptions	"Causation is established if the occurrence of the damage was objectively and reasonably predictable at the time of the infringement (foreseeability test). A simple indirect causation will not be considered sufficient."	"The Court may decide to mitigate the burden of proof if this is reasonable, especially when a risk of damage has been created by tort and has subsequently resulted in actual damage."	n.a.
Remarks	"The theories of equivalent conditions or of the *sine qua non* condition (whose application could lead to indirect causation being recognised) are not followed under Portuguese law."	"Proving causation and attributability may be very difficult, especially in cases where the complainant is a third party."	"Adequacy of the causation is judged upon by the Court in every and each case."

*All the information used in this scheme is (in)directly extracted from the National Reports provided to the Commission by the EU Member States.[84]

*Information regarding three of the Eastern European Member States participating in the Removing Obstacles conference is included in Annex II.

81 National Report provided by: José Luís da Cruz Vilaça, Pedro Metello de Nápoles, Dorothée Choussy, A.M. Pereira, Sáragga Leal, Oliveira Martins, Júdice & Associados Edificio Eurolex, Lisboa (p. 14).

82 National Report provided by: Weyer Verloren van Themaat and Johannes Hettema, Houthoff Buruma, Brussels (p. 9).

83 National Report provided by: Tamás Éless, Freshfields Bruckhaus Deringer formerly Réti Szegheõ & Partners, Ágnes Németh, Kovács Réti Szegheő (p. 10).

84 Available on: <http://ec.europa.eu/competition/antitrust/actionsdamages/study.html>.

States:[85] (1) Courts are likely to judge these issues using a very practical, case specific approach; (2) The burden of proof of causality often appears to be extremely heavy to fulfil.

4.3 Passing-On Defence and Legal Position of Indirect Purchasers

Directly related to the issue of causality is the question whether indirect purchasers, mostly at the end of the supply chain, can effectively seek redress for the harm they suffered as a result of infringements of competition law at the top of that supply chain. Moreover, the position of indirect purchasers might be negatively affected when overcharges, initially imposed on the first purchasers by the infringer, are passed on by these first purchasers to indirect purchasers further down the supply chain. The question is what legal safeguards Member States provide indirect purchasers with and what the consequences for the effectiveness of claims are when overcharges are passed on to them.

Table 3

	Portugal[86]	**The Netherlands**[87]	**Hungary**[88]
Passing-on defence accepted?	"A passing-on defence or indirect purchaser issue may be taken into account in the calculation and awarding of damages, as both defences aim at diminishing the scope and extent of the injury suffered by the claimant."	"The passing-on defence is not explicitly provided for in the law, nor is the indirect purchaser issue. Such a defence may be taken into account by the judge in assessing the level of damages however. The judge may see reasons to mitigate the damages."	"There is no Court practice published on this issue."

85 Comparative Report, *"Study on the conditions of claims for damages in case of infringement of EC competition rules"*, prepared by Denis Waelbroeck, Donald Slater and Gil Even-Shoshan, Ashurst LLP, Brussels, 31 August 2004, p. 72.

86 National Report provided by: José Luís da Cruz Vilaça, Pedro Metello de Nápoles, Dorothée Choussy, A.M. Pereira, Sáragga Leal, Oliveira Martins, Júdice & Associados Edificio Eurolex, Lisboa (p. 14).

87 National Report provided by: Weyer Verloren van Themaat and Johannes Hettema, Houthoff Buruma, Brussels (p. 9).

88 National Report provided by: Tamás Éless, Freshfields Bruckhaus Deringer, formerly Réti Szegheő & Partners, Ágnes Németh, Kovács Réti Szegheő (p. 10).

Possible redress for indirect purchasers?	Yes	n.a.	"The issue of the indirect purchaser can be considered as a question of indirect causation. If the causality is adequate, even an indirect purchaser can be successful in claiming damages. Further, if the indirect purchaser was able to prove liability in damages of all or more of those upstream in the marketing/production chain, the liability of such persons would be joint."
Limitations / Exceptions	n.a.	n.a.	"If the complainant is not able to prove that he suffered damages (in case of successful passing-on defence) the Court will not order compensation."
Remarks	n.a.	n.a.	n.a.

*All the information used in this scheme is (in)directly extracted from the National Reports provided to the Commission by the EU Member States.[89]

*Information regarding three of the Eastern European Member States participating in the Removing Obstacles conference is included in Annex III.

On the legal position of indirect purchasers the most important general remark to be made concerns causality. The fact is that the lack of a direct causality, as a result of the intervention of the direct purchaser, might hinder these indirect purchasers in finding effective redress for the harm they suffered. The further down the supply chain an indirect purchaser is positioned, the less likely it is that he will be successful in proving that the harm he suffered is the actual result of the initial infringement made at the top of the supply chain. As a result of the case-by-case application of the theory of causality great legal uncertainty exists within and between Member States on this issue.

89 Available on: <http://ec.europa.eu/competition/antitrust/actionsdamages/study.html>.

Legal uncertainty also plays a big role when it comes to passing on overcharges down the supply chain. Being exceptions, Italy, Denmark and Germany are the only Member States where case law on this subject has been developed. Taking Germany as an example; passing on of overcharges has been explicitly accepted at regional level by some courts, while the German government initially intended to explicitly exclude this controversial ground of defence. This example shows the amount of legal uncertainty which exists concerning the passing-on defence, even within Member States where this concept has been accepted. In theory, in Member States where this concept has not been explicitly accepted this ground of defence might be relied upon. Once again, it remains uncertain for both claimants and defendants whether this defence will effectively lead to the exclusion of damages for indirect purchasers.

4.4 Conclusions

As a result of this comparative research on the bottleneck issues concerning claims for damages in competition law, that are to be dealt with in EU Member States a couple of general conclusions can be drawn. First of all it should once more be emphasised that the differences in national laws on claims for damages in competition law make it very hard to compare the legal frameworks of the Member States on this issue. Whereas some Member States only partially regulate the issues concerning claims for damages in competition law, other Member States aim to regulate exhaustively. Irrespective of these similarities and differences between Member States, and most important in respect of the Commission's proposals on claims for damages in competition law, is the existing legal uncertainty. This legal uncertainty manifests itself within nearly all EU Member States. It results in high thresholds for potential claimants who often refrain from actually bringing a claim for damages because of this legal uncertainty. Furthermore, a lot of claims brought before national courts do not appear to be successful. Finally, national civil proceedings tend to yield preliminary questions posed to the ECJ. As a result of the lack of European rules on these issues it is extremely difficult and practically impossible for the Court of Justice to provide more legal certainty within EU Member States. This impossibility also results from the fact that claims for damages procedures generally are very much dependent on national laws and very case and fact specific.

The most important conclusion that can be drawn from the above, is that legal certainty within and between EU Member States can possibly only be provided by harmonising measures of European law. However, this remains a point of debate.

5. Conclusions

The most important conclusion resulting from the above is that the major similarity between EU Member States concerning claims for damages in competition law is legal uncertainty.

The European Union lacks a legal framework on claims for damages in competition law. EU Member States often do provide for such a legal framework. However, these legal frameworks often do not exhaustively regulate this issue, and leave (too) much space for interpretation by national courts. As a result of the case-by-case approach of the national courts, and as a result of the complexity and information-dependency of individual cases, no consistent trend in national case law can be found. As appears from several cases, legal uncertainty therefore surrounds these civil proceedings in which victims of infringements of competition law seek redress of the harm they suffered. Unfortunately, this legal uncertainty does not only affect the (legal) position of the claimants and defendants involved in claims for damages procedures but also raises thresholds for potential claimants to actually start such procedures. Effective redress therefore may exist in theory; whether this effectiveness applies in practice is very questionable.

In order to provide for more legal certainty, initiatives are taken on the European level. These initiatives were provided in the Commission's 2008 White Paper on damages actions for breach of the EC antitrust rules. In this White Paper, the Commission set out that: "Any citizen or business who suffers harm as a result of a breach of EC antitrust rules (Arts. 101 and 102 TFEU) must be able to claim reparation from the party who caused the damage."[90] In order to achieve this goal, multiple legislative proposals were presented in the White Paper. In doing so, the Commission has recognised that the legal issue of claims for damages in competition law should not be regulated solely on the basis of highly differing national legal frameworks that leave room for the amount of legal uncertainty and the negative consequences mentioned before. Although these instruments have not yet come into being, a harmonised legal framework on the European level may be realised in the near future.[91] Even then, the major concern remains: does this harmonisation contribute to the possibility for victims of infringements of European and national competition law to *effectively* find redress for the harm they suffered? Whether or not this question can be answered in the affirmative, the future enforcement of the upcoming European legal framework will have to prove. However, a positive answer to this question is most likely to be legitimate while the major similarity between EU Member States concerning claims for damages in competition law is legal uncertainty.

---

90 *White Paper on damages actions for breach of the EC antitrust rules*, Commission of the European Communities, Brussels, 2.4.2008, COM(2008) 165 final.

91 Joaquín Almunia, Vice President of the Commission, responsible for Competition policy Common standards for group claims across the EU, University of Valladolid, School of Law Valladolid, 15 October 2010, SPEECH/10/554.

Annex I Collective Claims and Representative Actions for Damages in Three of the Eastern European Member States Participating in the Removing Obstacles Conference

	Czech Republic[92]	**Slovak Republic**[93]	**Slovenia**[94]
Possible to bring collective claims?	"Czech law does not recognise collective claims or class actions."	"Section 42 of the Competition Act stipulates the right of consumers to require a person violating competition rules to refrain from such conduct and to rectify the illegal state, however not to compensate any damage." "This right may also be exercised by a legal entity (e.g. consumer assoc.) entitled to protect interests of consumers." "Similar provision may be found in the Commercial Code (ObchZ, § 54)." "Actions by representative bodies for damages are not recognised in the Commercial Code."	"There is no possibility of collective claims, class actions, representative actions or public interest litigation."

92 National report provided by: Pavel Dejl/ Andrea Löfflerová/Filip Kubík Kocián.olc Bala.tík, advokátní kancelář, Prague (p. 4).

93 National report provided by: Tomá. Maretta & Tomá. Rybár, Čechová Rakovský, Bratislava (p. 3).

94 National report provided by: Nina Selih/ Natasa Pipan Nahtigal Selih, Selih, Janezic & Jarkovic, Ljubljana (p. 4).

Annex I continued

Limitations/ Exceptions	"Under Section 91 (1) of the Civil Procedure Code it is possible for several plaintiffs to bring an action jointly. Under Section 92 (1) of the Civil Procedure Code, the court may, upon application of the plaintiff, admit further plaintiffs to pending proceedings." "In addition, Section 93 of the Civil Procedure Code enables a person who has a legal interest in the outcome of the dispute to join the plaintiff as a "supporting participant"."	"In connection with the above, certain principles of class action are applied in this type of public interest litigation, as stipulated in the Commercial Code (ObchZ, §54(2))."	"Joint actions are permissible. Namely, it is possible for several plaintiffs to file a complaint jointly or for a plaintiff (or more) to file a complaint against several defendants. Claims may also be joined by the judge."
Remarks	n.a.	"Nor the public prosecutor, neither the public defender of rights is neither entitled to bring damages claims." "Unlike the legal entity, the affected person may, in addition, claim appropriate relief, compensation of damages and forfeit of the unjust enrichment."	n.a.

*All the information used in this scheme is (in)directly extracted from the National Reports provided to the Commission by the EU Member States.[95]

95 Available on: http://ec.europa.eu/competition/antitrust/actionsdamages/study.html.

Annex II Causality between Infringement and Harm in Three of the Eastern European Member States Participating in the Removing Obstacles Conference

	Czech Republic[96]	**Slovak Republic**[97]	**Slovenia**[98]
Level of causation to prove	"Neither procedural laws nor legal theory in the Czech Republic distinguish clearly between direct and indirect level of causation." "Consequently Czech courts do not deal directly with this issue in their decisions."	"Slovak legal theory does not make a distinction between direct or indirect causation."	"Indirect causation is sufficient."

96 National report provided by: Pavel Dejl/ Andrea Löfflerová/Filip Kubík Kocián.olc Bala.tík, advokátní kancelář, Prague (p. 10).

97 National report provided by: Tomá. Maretta & Tomá. Rybár, Čechová Rakovský, Bratislava (p. 9).

98 National report provided by: Nina Selih/ Natasa Pipan Nahtigal Selih, Selih, Janezic & Jarkovic, Ljubljana (p. 11).

Annex II continued

Limitations/Exceptions	"The Supreme Court ("*Nejvy í soud*") clarifies this topic in its decision no. 5 Cz 39/1965 and in its decision no. 2 Cz 36/1976: "No causal link between the defendant's conduct and the damage can be presumed simply because the defendant has been held liable for that conduct on other legal grounds." This conclusion was reached by the Supreme Court, for example	"A causal link between unlawful conduct of the defendant and damage incurred must be clearly established, probability alone is not sufficient." "The causal link includes indirect causation, if such causation is deemed by the court to be relevant."	n.a.
Remarks	n.a.	"Some case law indicates the court may require the plaintiff to prove the existence of a direct causal link between the infringement and the damage incurred."	"The Civil Code does not contain any rules on causation, so the courts decide on a case-by-case basis, considering the tort system, the theoretical knowledge, and factual circumstances."

*All the information used in this scheme is (in)directly extracted from the National Reports provided to the Commission by the EU Member States.[99]

99 Available on: http://ec.europa.eu/competition/antitrust/actionsdamages/study.html.

Annex III Passing-On Defence and Legal Position of Indirect Purchasers in Three of the Eastern European Member States Participating in the Removing Obstacles Conference

	Czech Republic[100]	**Slovak Republic**[101]	**Slovenia**[102]
Passing-on defence accepted?	"Czech law does not recognize "passing-on" issues." "At the theoretical level, the "passing-on" defence should be successful, the reason being that where a direct purchaser has fully passed on an excessive charge, he will not be able to prove occurrence of damage on his side."	"The passing-on and indirect purchaser issues are not recognised under Slovak law nor have been addressed in the recent case law." "The passing-on defence appears to be possible in case of damages that were claimed by a person positioned downstream to the violator, if such claimant has not suffered any damages due to passing the increased costs arising from the infringement on to its customers."	"The passing-on defence could be used by the defendant as a way of reducing the amount of damages (possibly even to zero)." "There is no presumption that higher prices have been passed on." "However the amount of damages needs to be proven by the plaintiff. The compensation awarded may never exceed the damages suffered."

100 National report provided by: Pavel Dejl/ Andrea Löfflerová/Filip Kubík Kocián.olc Bala.tík, advokátní kancelář, Prague (p. 11).

101 National report provided by: Tomá. Maretta & Tomá. Rybár, Čechová Rakovský, Bratislava (p. 9).

102 National report provided by: Nina Selih/ Natasa Pipan Nahtigal Selih, Selih, Janezic & Jarkovic, Ljubljana (p. 12).

Annex III continued

Possible redress for indirect purchasers?	"Czech law does not recognize "indirect purchaser" issues. An indirect purchaser should be able to recover damage if he can persuade the court that there is a causal link between the unlawful conduct (breach of competition law) and the damage."	"Concerning the indirect purchaser defence, there is no direct link between the damaged entity and the violator required and therefore it makes no difference to the damages claim."	"Indirect purchasers may theoretically claim damages. However, in practice it will be difficult for them to prove causality. Also, in such a case, there exists no presumption that the higher prices have been passed on and the indirect purchasers would therefore have to prove *inter alia* that the higher prices had been passed on to them by the direct purchaser."
Limitations/ Exceptions	n.a.	"The Slovak law does not explicitly address the issue of whether the indirect purchaser does not need to prove the passing on of the higher price." "However, as the plaintiff must prove the causal link between the infringement and damage incurred, it is likely this would involve the need to prove the passing on of the higher price as a result of infringement."	n.a.
Remarks	n.a.	n.a.	n.a.

*All the information used in this scheme is (in)directly extracted from the National Reports provided to the Commission by the EU Member States.[103]

103 Available on: <http://ec.europa.eu/competition/antitrust/actionsdamages/study.html>.

Cartel Damages Claims in the Netherlands: Exploring Obstacles

*N.T. Dempsey**

1. Introduction

After increasing attention by the legislature, legal scholars and legal practitioners in the past decade, the last year or two have shown a significant rise in Dutch private competition law enforcement cases and connected damages claims. In the past two years alone, follow-on damages claims have been brought before the Dutch courts with regard to the gas insulated switch gear,[1] bitumen,[2] air cargo[3] and sodium chlorate cartels.[4] The legal practitioners involved in these and similar cases are faced with various new questions regarding both procedural and material law that are now for the first time being debated and – in the future, barring settlements – decided in court.

2. Legal Framework

The legal framework for cartel damages claims is formed by the general rules regarding liability for wrongful conduct – Article 6:162 Civil Code (CC) –, the specific competition legislation set out in the Competition Act (CA) and the Treaty on the Functioning of the European Union (TFEU), and the Code of Civil Procedure (CCP). For a cartel damages claim to succeed, the claimant will have to establish that the defendant (1) has acted in a wrongful manner (2) that can be attributed to him, and (3) that the claimant has suffered damages (4) which were caused by the defendant's wrongful conduct.

3. Jurisdiction

Dutch courts have jurisdiction to hear cartel damages claims that are instigated against (legal) persons having their domicile in the Netherlands[5] or when the basis

* This chapter was presented by N.T. Dempsey on 20 October 2011 and is an abbreviated and revised version of an article written for the *Private Competition Enforcement Review* 2011 edition. N.T. Dempsey is a senior-associate with Houthoff Buruma, specialising in supreme court litigation, employment law and private enforcement of competition law.

1 Commission Decision 24 January 2007, Case COMP/38899.

2 Commission Decision 13 September 2006, Case COMP/38456.

3 Commission Decision 9 November 2010, Case COMP/39258.

4 Commission Decision 11 June 2008, Case COMP/38695.

5 Art. 2 CCP and Art. 2 Council Regulation (EC) 44/2001.

of the claim is a wrongful act and the harmful event occurred in the Netherlands.[6] In light of Article 7(1) CCP – the Dutch equivalent of Article 6(1) Council Regulation (EC) 44/2001 – a claim for cartel damages against persons who do not have their domicile in the Netherlands and whereby the cartel had no influence in the Netherlands may still be brought before the Dutch courts, but only if this is done together with a claim against a cartelist that is domiciled in the Netherlands *and* both claims are so closely connected that it is expedient to hear and determine them together. Whether this is always the case when suing various members of an alleged cartel before the competent court of one of the cartelists, remains to be seen.

4. Follow-Up Litigation and the Relationship between National Courts and (European) Competition Authorities

So far, cartel damages claims in the Netherlands have mainly been done on the basis of litigation following a decision (and fine) by the European Commission (EC) or Netherlands competition authority (NCA). Pursuant to Article 16 Council Regulation (EC) 1/2003, EC decisions on agreements, decisions or practices under Article 101 TFEU that are no longer open for appeal bind the national courts, effectively meaning that in a claim for cartel damages following such a decision by the EC, the Dutch courts will have to take and apply the breach of Article 101 TFEU found by the EC as a given fact.

As regards the status of NCA decisions in follow-up civil litigation, there is no provision similar to Article 16 Council Regulation (EC) 1/2003. The Dutch courts are free in the weight they attach to such a decision. Possibly the Dutch Courts may be bound to accept the outcome/decision of the NCA to which no further appeal is open as correct on the basis of the rule that administrative decisions that have not been successfully contested through administrative proceedings have legal force.[7] This is, however, a matter of debate in Dutch legal literature and has not yet been decided in case-law. In any case, according to the doctrine of administrative legal force, findings of facts by the NCA are *not* binding upon the Dutch civil courts.[8] Should therefore the defendant to a claim for cartel damages/addressee of an NCA decision contest the facts as found by the NCA in a sufficiently convincing manner, they should at least be allowed the opportunity to disprove the presumption that the facts found by the NCA are correct.

In 2011, in a claim for damages in connection with the bitumen cartel, the Rotterdam District Court decided – for the first time in the Netherlands – on a request for stay of the civil claim proceedings pending an appeal by the defendants against the EC's decision.[9] According to the Rotterdam District Court, the

6 Art. 6(e) CCP and Art. 5(3) Council Regulation (EC) 44/2001.

7 Supreme Court 22 December 2007, *NJ* 2007, 218 (*Van Rattingen Grondverzet/Loenen*).

8 Supreme Court 2 June 1995, *NJ* 1997, 164 (*Aharachi/Bedrijfsvereniging*).

9 Rotterdam District Court 9 February 2011, LJN BP7518.

decision whether or not to grant an (immediate and full) stay hinges upon the demands of fair proceedings, whereby unnecessary and unreasonable delays should be avoided. The Rotterdam District Court took a nuanced view. Because one of the defendants had not appealed the EC Decision, the court decided that as regards that defendant, at the very least questions involving the legitimacy of assignments and statute of limitations could be dealt with already and without delay. These issues would, according to the Rotterdam District Court, have to be decided according to Dutch law and their decision would not depend on the validity of the contested EC Decision thereby not necessitating a (full) stay of the proceedings, at least not yet at this time.

5. Limitation

Claims for damages become time barred in the Netherlands five years after the claimant has become aware of the damages and the person liable for those damages, but in any case after twenty years have passed since the damage causing event.[10] For the short limitation period to start running it is necessary that the claimant is subjectively aware of the damages and liable person. An "ought to have been aware" is insufficient. Depending on the circumstances of the case, it is therefore possible that the limitation period will have started (and run out) before the NCA or the EC has decided that there has been a breach of Article 6 CA or 101 TFEU. An example of this can be found in a 2007 judgment by the Rotterdam District Court in which a claim for damages by CEF, a wholesale distributor of electrotechnical fittings against the individual directors of FEG, a Dutch association in the electrotechnical fittings sector, was dismissed as time barred.[11] The Rotterdam District Court judged that it was irrelevant that the EC had only given its decision that FEG had breached Article 101 TFEU in 1999.[12] CEF was held to have already been aware of the damages and liable person in 1991 when it submitted a complaint to the EC on FEG's conduct. Having failed to interrupt the limitation period until 2000, CEF's claim for damages was dismissed.

6. Settlement Procedures

There are no particular mechanisms that a Dutch court will adopt or impose for settlements. Aside from some specific rules on settlement agreements, the general rules of contract law apply. Settlement negotiations between lawyers enjoy legal privilege, meaning that to disclose the contents of such negotiations in proceedings may result in a disciplinary complaint.

Only rarely are settlement agreements embodied in a court order. One of the (most) noteworthy exceptions to this rule is the possibility for parties to have a

10 Art. 3:310 CC.
11 Rotterdam District Court 7 March 2007, LJN BA0926.
12 Commission Decision 26 October 1999, Case IV/33.884.

settlement agreement declared generally binding. This option was introduced in 2005 by way of the Collective Settlement of Mass Claims Act (CSMCA). Under this act it is possible for one or more associations who, according to their articles of association, protect and promote the interests of persons who have suffered damages due to the acts of another party and who have reached a settlement agreement with one or more other parties who have agreed to compensate those damages to submit, together with the other party/parties to the settlement agreement, a request to the Amsterdam Court of Appeal to have that settlement agreement declared generally binding. The Court must judge the settlement reached on a number of points, among which *e.g.* whether the compensation is not unreasonable and whether the associations that agreed to the settlement can be deemed sufficiently representative for the interests of those on whose behalf the settlement was reached. Part of the settlement may be that any claims for damages under the agreement will be forfeited if they are not submitted within one year of a claimant becoming aware of his claim under the settlement.[13]

If the Court grants the request for the settlement to be declared generally binding, then individuals who would fall within the scope of the settlement have the right to "opt-out" within a period of no less than three months. Individuals who opt-out remain free to start their own proceedings against the tortfeasor and claim more than they would have received under the generally binding settlement.[14]

According to two separate decisions of the Amsterdam Court of Appeal, it has jurisdiction to hear requests for declaring a settlement generally binding that regulates damages (mostly) suffered by individuals outside the Netherlands. In the so-called Shell-settlement the Court decided that Dutch interest associations can be deemed sufficiently representative for foreign claimants and that – as long as a number of the claimants are domiciled in the Netherlands – it also has jurisdiction regarding foreign claimants.[15] This was confirmed more than a year later in an interim judgment regarding the so-called Converium-settlement in which only some 200 of the approximately 12,000 claimants were domiciled in the Netherlands.[16] Both settlements had regard to shareholder claims for damages. However, there are no legal objections to this same regime at some point being used for antitrust settlements, particularly given that a decision by the Court to declare a settlement generally binding (unless they opt out in time) should in principle also have effect against foreign claimants, at least insofar as they are domiciled in the European Union and the European Free Trade Association.[17] Therefore, although not yet applied in practice, the CSMCA provides a potentially interesting instrument for mass settlement of cartel claims within – at least – the European Union and Free Trade Association.

13 Art. 7:907 CC.
14 Art. 7:908 CC.
15 Amsterdam Court of Appeal 29 May 2009, LJN BI5744.
16 Amsterdam Court of Appeal 12 November 2010, LJN BO3908.
17 Art. 33 Council Regulation (EC) 44/2001 and EVEX Convention.

7. Conclusion

Private enforcement of competition law – and particularly cartel damages claims – is proving to be an increasingly hot topic in the Netherlands. Whereas this topic has enjoyed considerable attention by legal scholars over the past decade, case-law has been relatively sparse and mainly limited to claims regarding vertical agreements between distributors and buyers/dealers. In light of the numerous cartel damages claims submitted to the Dutch courts recently, it is to be expected that in the coming years more clarity will be obtained on various legal questions and issues that have up until now only been a matter of debate in legal literature.

Obtaining Evidence in the Private Enforcement of Competition Law

A. Bekkering

1. Introduction

Any business or citizen that suffers harm as a result of a breach of EC antitrust rules has the right to claim compensation, before a national court, from the party that caused the damage. The foundation of this right can be found in European Community law. Despite the possibility to claim damages, in practice victims rarely obtain compensation for the harm they suffered. The Commission underlined this problem and in 2008 published the White Paper on Damages actions for breach of the EC antitrust rules. In this paper the Commission concluded that the reason for this failure of obtaining damages can be found in the various procedures and legal obstacles in the Member States' rules that control actions of antitrust damages before national courts.

One of these obstacles is the difficulty companies or natural persons encounter when they try to obtain evidence to establish an infringement of the competition rules. In civil procedures, the party who alleges the infringement must provide the evidence of the infringing act. A problem that arises is that much of the evidence is held by the defendant or third parties or is concealed if it contains business secrets and may therefore be unknown and/or unattainable for the claimant. The Commission is aware of this problem and suggests in its White Paper a minimum framework to improve the access to relevant evidence *inter partes*. In this framework the Commission takes into account the negative effects that disclosure of information can have for the accused party. The risk of providing access to confidential documents too easily could on the one hand lead to unacceptable disclosure of sensitive corporate information to the public and possible abuse of said information while, on the other hand, disclosure of evidence could certainly enhance the private enforcement of the competition rules which strengthens the working of the Community competition rules.

In addition to the policy options to improve the disclosure of evidence *inter partes*, the Commission also envisages policy options for civil actions following a decision of a competition authority and discusses possibilities to obtain documents that are held by competition authorities, which they have gathered through their own investigations into possible antitrust infringers or through a leniency programme. A lot of information that is held by competition authorities can serve as evidence in a civil procedure in which a victim tries to obtain damages suffered from the antitrust infringer. However, such documents are often confidential and disclosure could therefore be detrimental to the interests of the infringing company.

This contribution examines whether the Dutch legislation is in line with the proposals of the White Paper and if it needs adaptation for this matter. It also takes into account whether corporate sensitive information is safeguarded sufficiently.

2. The Right to Obtain Damages for Loss Suffered

In 2001, the European Court of Justice established in the case *Courage v. Crehan* the right that victims of anti-trust infringers are able to claim reparation for the damages suffered before a civil court from the parties that caused damages by breaching the European competition rules.[1] The judgment established a complement to the public enforcement of the competition rules carried out by the NCAs and the European Commission by enhancing the possibility of private enforcement through domestic courts.[2] The obligation of national courts to safeguard the subjective rights, for example by awarding damages to the victims of an infringement subsequent to the *Courage v. Crehan* case, is established in Council Regulation 1/2003, which came into force on 1 May 2004.[3] The Council made with this Regulation a great effort in enhancing the possibility of the private enforcement of competition rules. Despite the efforts made by the Council in adopting Council Regulation 1/2003 and the express will of the Court in *Courage v. Crehan,* that there should be absolutely no limitation to bring a civil claim before a domestic court to obtain damages. In practice it turned out that it is quite difficult to succeed with such a claim.

The firm Ashurst published in 2004, pursuant to a tender of the Commission, a study on the conditions of claims for damages in case of infringements of EC competition rules in the Union Member States. In this study the researchers concluded that damage actions for breach of competition law in the EU countries were 'totally underdeveloped' and 'astonishingly different'.[4] This had mainly to do with the difficulty to obtain evidence, due to the national rules which are full of barriers and the accompanying high cost of the procedures.[5] As a response to the research, the European Commission published in December 2005 a Green Paper, where the Commission looked at ways to break through the barriers which make victims refrain from bringing a claim before a civil court to obtain damages caused by

1 ECJ EC 20 September 2001, C-453/99, *Courage v. Crehan,* [2001] ECR-I 6297, paras 24 and 25.

2 W. van Gerven, 'Private enforcement of EC Competition Rules in the ECJ', in: J. Basedow, *Private enforcement of EC Competition Law,* Alphen aan den Rijn, Kluwer International 2007, p. 23.

3 Council Regulation (EC) No. 1/2003 of 16 December 2002 on the implementation of the rules on competition laid down in Arts. 81 and 82, OJ 2003 L 1/1, 4 January 2003, para. 7.

4 Ashurst, D. Waelbroek, S. Salter & G. Even-Shoshan, *Study on the conditions of claims for damages in case of infringement of EC competition rules*, 31 August 2004, p. 1.

5 Ashurst *et al.*, 2004, p. 11.

infringements of the competition rules.[6] The Green Paper was open for consultation until April 2006. After the consultation period the Commission published in April 2008 a White Paper, where it further developed policy recommendations to establish a minimum framework to enhance the private enforcement of competition law in the Member States.[7] The White Paper has not yet led to the adoption of binding European legislation. In 2009, a proposal for a council Directive leaked on rules governing damages actions for infringements of Articles 81 and 82 of the Treaty, which followed up broadly in line with the proposals of the White Paper. A lot of criticism was given to the draft Directive by the European Parliament as well as other interested parties and the European Commission decided to postpone further consideration of the draft Directive until after the new Commission took office. It now seems the Commission's plan has come to a halt, because further measures have not been taken yet. It is up to the Commission to take further steps towards binding legislation. Until there are other proposals, the White Paper embodies the Commission's current view on access to evidence in enhancing the private enforcement of competition law.

3. Difficulties to Obtain Evidence

One of the major obstacles in the private enforcement of competition law is the difficulty for the claimant to obtain evidence of the alleged antitrust infringements and (quantification of) the damages suffered.[8] According to Article 2 of Council Regulation 1/2003, the burden of proof rests on thc party that alleges the infringement. The claimant has to prove the infringement, the casual connection between the infringement and damages, and the quantum of damages. Especially in 'stand-alone' action the party that alleges the infringements has to overcome a lot of difficulties to prove its claim.[9]

According to the Commission the difficulty to prove the allegations is the result of three factors: *i.e.* (1) the difficulty to establish an infringement, (2) the information asymmetry that exists between parties and (3) the high standard of proof that in many Member States is required to claim damages.[10]

To establish an infringement of competition rules the claimant first has to prove that the alleged party has infringed the competition rules and only then he can

6 *Green Paper on damages actions for breach of EC antitrust rules,* Commission of the European Communities, 19.5.2005, COM(2005), 672 final. Available at: <http://ec.europa.eu/competition/antitrust/actionsdamages/documents.html>.

7 *White Paper on damages actions for breach of the EC antitrust rules*, Commission of the European Communities, 2.4.2088, COM(2008) 165 final. Available at: <http://ec.europa.eu/competition/antitrust/actionsdamages/documents.html>.

8 Ashurst *et al.* 2004, p.11.

9 In a stand-alone action, a victim of antitrust infringements starts on its own initiative a civil procedure to obtain the damages suffered. There is no prior decision of a competition authority.

10 Commission Staff Working Paper accompanying the White Paper on damages actions for breach of the EC antitrust rules , COM (2008) 404 final, paras 87-89. Available at: <http://ec.europa.eu/competition/antitrust/actionsdamages/documents.html>.

start to establish that he suffered damages caused by the infringing act. To prove the infringement of antitrust rules, it is generally necessary to define the relevant market and that the forbidden conduct has (potential) negative impacts on prices, innovations or output in the common market.[11] The claimant must therefore have sufficient knowledge of the defendant's commercial strategy, trading practices, pricing policy, cost structure and his position on the market. It is therefore quite fact-intensive and it contains often information that is not in the possession of the claimant, but in the possession of the accused party or third parties. In addition, undertakings involved in antitrust infringement will often deliberately conceal evidence of their illegal conduct to the outside world, which makes it even harder to prove the allegations, for example notes on the price overcharged agreed secretly between cartel members.[12] The Commission mentions the aforementioned 'information asymmetry' that exists between parties as the second factor of the difficulties that claimants encounter when they try to bring a successful action for antitrust damages.

Even in situations, where claimants are in the position to prove factual elements, for example in follow-on actions, the difficulty still remains that the claimant has to demonstrate in detail the causation and the quantification of the damages.[13] The latter contains in many cases a difficult comparison of the anti-competitive situation to the situation which would have existed in the absence of the infringement. It is an arduous hypothetical assessment where the claimant for example has to determine what the price or the market position of a certain product would have been in absence of the infringement. This information contains, for example, exact information on how and when the price was influenced and what the market position was before the infringement and during the infringement. The claimant often remains dependent on the information that is held by the defendant, or in cartel cases, is held by their co-conspirators.

The third factor that troubles successful claims relates to the high standard of proof that in many Member States is required to claim damages.[14] The complaining party has to assert in detail the relevant facts of its case and has to hand over specified parts of documents to strengthen its assertion. Especially with regard to the information asymmetry it is a difficult, not to say impossible goal to achieve a damage reward. It is partly for these reasons that victims are discouraged from bringing their claim to court.[15]

3.1 Solutions not Retained

According to Article 2 Council Regulation 1/2003, the burden of proof rests on the party that alleges the infringement. The national procedural rules remain

11 Arts. 101 and 102 TFEU.
12 SWP White Paper 2008, para. 89.
13 *Ibid.*, para. 89. Follow-on actions are procedures where private parties bring a civil action to obtain damages after a competition authority found an infringement.
14 *Ibid.*, para. 87.
15 *Ibid.*, para. 90.

applicable in respect to the *standard* of proof.[16] The Commission rejects solutions of alleviating the burden and lowering standard of proof or even (partly) shifting the burden of proof to make it easier for the claimant to prove his claim. In the Commission's view these options will not constitute as effective a general remedy for the consequences of the information asymmetry in competition cases as measures that improve access to evidence.[17] The claimant then still has to prove that the defendant has infringed the competition rules, and thus needs access to evidence that could be held by the infringer. Also in situations where victims can rely on the finding of an infringement in the decision of a competition authority, the Commission points to the fact that the reversal of the burden of proof is not helping to calculate the damage caused. Judges or claimants need to get access to certain information, to define the market in the absence of the infringing act. According to the Commission, generally shifting the burden of proof would produce undesirable results because it would encourage not only meritorious claims, but also unmeritorious claims. This would establish the wrong incentives and would also entail the risks of procedural abuses and incorrect judgments.[18]

3.2 Solution Retained: Improving the Disclosure of Evidence

The Commission suggests, instead of options of alleviating or shifting the burden of proof or lowering the standard of proof, options to improve the disclosure of evidence. Due to the different rules and approaches on disclosure of evidence in the several Member States, the Commission proposes a minimum standard to disclosure *inter partes* that builds on the Directive on Intellectual Property Rights 2004/48/EC, which is already embedded in the Member States' legal orders.[19] According to Article 6 of the IP Directive, in the field of the disclosure of evidence the central role lies with the judge, *i.e.* obligations to disclose arise only once a court has adopted a disclosure order and are subject to a strict control by the court.[20] With this proposed central role in the disclosure measures, the Commission follows the legal tradition of various Member States and the Draft European Code of Civil Procedure and the ALI/ UNIDROIT Principles of Transnational Civil Procedure.[21] The Commission deliberately avoids establishing a framework that enables the so called 'fishing expeditions' which are not unknown in the United States. This concerns situations where parties are able to collect information from their opponents or third parties based on very general suspicions of an infringement.[22]

16 Commission Staff Working Paper accompanying the Green Paper on damages actions for breach of the EC antitrust rules, COM (2005) 672 final, para. 79. Available at: <http://ec.europa.eu/competition/antitrust/actionsdamages/documents.html>.

17 SWP White Paper 2008, para. 91.

18 *Ibid.*, para. 92.

19 Directive 2004/48/EC on the Enforcement of Intellectual Property Rights, OJ 2004 L 157/45.

20 R. Becker, N. Bessot and E. de Smijter, 'The White Paper on damage actions for breach of the EC antitrust rules', *Competition policy newsletter* 2008, Nr. 2, p. 9.

21 ALI/UNIDROIT, *Principles of transnational civil procedure,* New York: Cambridge University Press 2006, <www.unidroit.org/english/principles/civilprocedure/main.htm>.

22 N. Kroes, 'Opening speech at the European Parliament workshop on damages actions for breach of the EC antitrust rules', Brussels, 6 June 2006, p. 5. See <http://ec.europa.eu/competition/antitrust/actionsdamages/documents.html#linkl>.

According to the White Paper judges are able to order the disclosure of evidence if four conditions are met. (1) The claimant has asserted all the facts and offered all those means of evidence that are reasonably available to him, provided that these are sufficient to make his claim a plausible one. (2) The claimant has shown to the satisfaction of the court that he is unable, applying all reasonable efforts that may expected from him, to produce the means of evidence for which disclosure is envisaged. (3) The claimant has specified sufficiently categories of information or evidence to be disclosed. (4) The court is satisfied that the requested disclosure measure is relevant to the case as well as necessary and proportionate in scope. With these requirements, the Commission tries to prevent that a disclosure order is given too easily, which can be harmful for the alleged party or even third parties if the documents contain confidential information.[23]

3.2.1 Corporate Sensitive Information

A lot of the information and evidence that the claimant needs to prove his case, is under the supervision of the alleged party or third parties. It contains often commercial sensitive information,[24] that is harmful for the defendant or third parties when it is obtainable to the public or to the claimant, which is often a competitor of the alleged party.[25] In general, confidential information is protected under Community law, but may be made public in certain circumstances.[26] The Commission suggests that when Member States apply the rules and principles existing in their jurisdictions on the protection of confidential information and/or business secrets, they also have to ensure the victim's right of obtaining damages for loss suffered. This should be done in an assessment based on proportionality.[27] The Commission underlines that the mere fact that the disclosure of certain information entails unfavourable consequences, cannot constitute a reason for a judge not to order a disclosure. Only an exclusion or limitation of disclosure is justified, when the interest of the protection of certain information clearly outweighs the interest of the claimant. To seek a balance between the two interests, the Commission suggests the possibility that courts can order that the disclosure only will take place in private or between parties. Hearings must be held in private and the parties have to agree that the information is not used for other purpose than in the ongoing proceedings. Courts could also order that the information is only accessible to the parties' lawyers or to designated experts, who can suffice with a summary of the information of a non-confidential form.[28] This will prevent that certain information is obtainable by the public.

---

23 SWP White Paper 2008, paras 100-109.

24 For example data on market position, cost structure, pricing data and strategies of the defendant or third parties.

25 Art. 6 ECHR embodies the right of parties to have access to all the relevant evidence that is brought into the procedure.

26 See for example Art. 27(2), recital 16 and 32 of Council Regulation 1/2003 and Art. 4 of Regulation 1049/2001.

27 SWP White Paper, para. 116.

28 *Ibid.*, para. 117.

3.2.2 Refusal to Produce Evidence

When a party refuses to produce evidence while there is a disclosure order, the White Paper gives the judge an amount of space in the choice which sanction is proportionate in a certain situation. The judge is able to draw adverse inferences, or orders a personal penalty or financial penalty.[29] Also it should be possible to preserve evidence in case there is a real risk that the evidence will be destroyed.[30]

3.2.3 Follow-On Actions

In follow-on actions, private parties bring a civil action to obtain damages, after a competition authority found an infringement. If the European Commission finds a breach of the Articles 101 or 102 TFEU, victims are able to rely on this decision as binding proof in civil procedures for damages before national courts.[31] According to the Commission the same should apply for decisions of national competition authorities (NCAs). If an NCA finds a breach of the competition rules, then this should lead to binding proof in the civil proceedings for damages.[32]

However, several conditions must be fulfilled before victims are able to rely on a decision as binding proof in a national proceeding. (1) Articles 101 or 102 TFEU were at stake and not only domestic rules. (2) The claimant is only able to invoke NCA decisions where it concerns the same infringers that were subject of the NCA proceedings. (3) Only final decisions can be invoked.[33] When claimants are able to rely on prior decisions of NCAs in follow-on cases, they are relieved from the obligation to prove once again that the defendant has infringed the competition rules. This leads to cost and time savings. However, the problem remains that victims still have to establish the damage suffered. It would be an easier task if they could obtain the documents held by the Commission or NCAs.

3.2.4 Access to Documents Held by the Commission

Because the European Commission obtains a lot of documents through an investigation on their own initiative or via a leniency programme, it could be useful for victims of competitions infringements to get access to those documents. Citizens

29 *Ibid.*, paras 11 and 130.
30 *Ibid.*, paras 11 and 133.
31 This follows from Art. 16(1) of Regulation 1/2003 which provides that when national courts rule on agreements, decisions or practices under Arts. 101 and 102 TFEU which are already subject of a Commission's decision, they cannot take decisions running counter to that decision. Commission decisions can only be removed by a judgment of the Community courts under Arts. 263 and 267 TFEU. This is the case, where a Commission decision is challenged before the Community courts (Art. 263 TFEU) or a national court has doubts about the application or legality of the Commission decision. The national court is then able to ask the European Court of Justice for a preliminary ruling (Art. 267 TFEU) and must postpone its decision until the Court has given its final decision.
32 SWP White Paper, para. 141.
33 *Ibid.*, paras 152-155.

of the European Union are able to access documents of the Union institutions. There are some restrictions on the right to obtain documents, because once the documents are released, they enter the public domain.[34] When the documents contain commercially sensitive information, access will be denied.[35] This could lead to a burden in establishing the damage in the private enforcement of competition rules. It is therefore advisable that the information that is submitted to a competition authority could be requested during litigation under the general rules of the disclosure of evidence *inter partes,* because the opponent party or third parties are often in the possession of (copies of) documents which are gathered by the competition authority through an investigation or a leniency programme.[36]

3.2.5 Access by National Courts

National courts are able to request documents that are held by the Commission.[37] However, the Commission is then still, pursuant to Article 339 TFEU, under an obligation of professional secrecy about the revealing of information, especially when it concerns undertakings, their business relations or their cost components. This is also repeated in Article 28(2) Regulation 1/2003. Once the information from the administrative procedure is produced in national legal proceedings, national courts must also guarantee the protection of confidential information, in particular business secrets.[38] When a national court requests information that is held by the Commission, it is then still uncertain whether the documents could be used in the proceedings and a disclosure request *inter partes* would then presumably be a better remedy.

3.2.6 Leniency Programme

Despite the possibility that a company is able to obtain immunity or the reduction of fines through a leniency programme, it is not relieved from the possibility that victims of the cartel can obtain their damages through a civil claim.[39] The incentive

34 Art. 15 TFEU gives to any citizen, natural or legal person of the Union the right to access documents of the Union institutions. This rule has been put into more detail in Regulation 1049/2001, which sets out the principles, conditions and limitations of public access to documents held by the Community institutions.

35 Art. 4(2) Council Regulation 1049/2001 regarding the public access to European Parliament, Council and Commission Documents OJ L 145, pp. 43-48, 31 May 2001.

36 SWP Green Paper, para. 74. See also R. Stürner, 'Duties of Disclosure and Burden of proof', *in* Basedow 2007, p. 178.

37 This follows from Art. 15(1) Regulation 1/2003 which gives national courts the opportunity to ask the Commission to transmit certain information that is in its possession, during proceedings for the application of Arts. 101 and 102 TFEU.

38 ECJ EC 18 September 1996, Case T-353/94 *Postbank NV v. Commission of the European Communities,* [1994], ECR-II 921.

39 The Leniency Notice enshrines: *The fact that immunity or reduction in respects of fines is granted cannot protect an undertaking from the civil law consequences of its participation of an infringement of art. 81 EC (now art. 101 TFEU).* See Commission Notice on Immunity from fines and reduction of fines in cartel cases (2006/C 298/11) para. 39.

of leniency programmes could be considerably reduced when leniency applicants are confronted with private follow-on claims on compensation of damages.[40]

There exists thus a certain tension between the objectives of the leniency programme and the objectives of the private enforcement of the competition law. The Commission therefore seeks a balance that does justice to both objectives. The Commission suggests that leniency applicants should be protected for court orders requesting production or disclosure of information which they submitted to the competition authorities. Only the immunity recipient is still liable for a damage claim, but the Commission suggests that the recipient should only be liable towards direct and indirect contractual purchasers.[41] Other applicants than immunity recipients must be protected. The Commission underlines that this policy option should be examined further.

On 14 June 2011, the ECJ came up with an interesting judgment in the case *Pfleiderer AG v. Bundeskartellamt*. This case was about the accessibility of documents and evidence gathered in antitrust investigations by national competition authorities. The judgment allowed third parties to access information and evidence gathered in antitrust investigations by national competition authorities, but only if national liability rules allow such disclosure and the access must be permitted or refused by weighing the interests protected by European law.[42] With '*the interests that are protected by European Union law*' the court referred to two interests which are embedded in European legislation. This contains on the one hand the usefulness of the leniency programme and on the other hand the right of individuals to obtain damages for loss caused by the competition infringer.[43]

It is questionable, however, if the judgment will have a major impact on future applications. The judgment will not have any consequences for Member States with national liability rules which do not provide a proper legal basis for the disclosure. In addition, the Commission is not a great supporter of the possibility that private parties will grant access to documents that are held by national authorities relating to leniency programmes. This also follows from a speech of Commissioner Almunia at the IBA annual competition conference: *I want to assure you that the Commission is determined to defend its leniency programme and the programmes of the ECN partners.*[44] A week later he announced to the European Parliament that the European Commission is planning to regulate the access to evidence held by competition authorities.[45] According to the Commissioner, this is necessary to

40 Report of the International Competition Network, *Interaction of public and private enforcement in cartel cases*, Moscow, May 2007, p. 41.

41 White Paper, para. 305.

42 ECJ EC 14 June 2011, C-360/09, *Pfleiderer AG v. Bundeskartellamt*, [2011], n.y.r., para. 32.

43 *Ibid.*, paras 25-29.

44 J. Almunia, 'New Challenges in Merger and Antitrust', speech on the IBA annual competition conference, 16 September 2011, (SPEECH 11/581) p. 2.

45 J. Almunia, 'Public enforcement and private damages actions in antitrust', Speech at the European Parliament, 22 September 2011, SPEECH/11/598.

preserve the leniency programmes, which are crucial for the effectiveness of the fight against companies that are infringing the competition rules. The Commission thus attaches greater importance to the leniency programme than to the rights of individuals seeking damages.

4. Obtaining Evidence in the Netherlands

In 2005, the law firm Houthoff Buruma published a report on "The opportunities of private enforcement of competition rules in the Netherlands; an inventory".[46] The main conclusions of the report did not differ much from the conclusions of the Ashurst study. A big obstacle to the private enforcement of competition law in the Netherlands was the difficulty for private parties to provide evidence about the alleged cartel or about an abuse of a company's dominant position. Also, the long duration of the procedures, which entails high financial costs, were considered a burden to effective enforcement, especially when there are no sufficient available means of recovery against the infringer.

4.1 Burden of Proof

The burden of proof in private enforcement of the competition rules is not regulated in the Dutch Competition Act (Mw) but in the Code of Civil Procedure (Rv).[47] Article 150 Rv states the main rule: the party that alleges the infringement must provide the evidence. Different from European legislation, according to Dutch legislation, in exceptional cases, the distribution of the burden of proof can be changed or shifted, when a *specific rule* or *reasons of reasonableness and fairness* demand so.[48] The question whether those exceptions are also applicable in the private enforcement of competition law, will be discussed below.

In the Netherlands parties are normally not obliged to provide certain documents to each other. Often information that is crucial to prove an infringement is under the control of the alleged party or third parties. A judge is able to request these documents *ex officio,* but parties are also able to request the disclosure of documents from the opposite party or, as some authors advocate, third parties during the pre-trial or trial phase using an Article 843a Rv request. With regard to the proposals of the White Paper saying that a party should be able to obtain evidence from the opposite party or a third party, this Article is the most obvious basis.

46 Houthoff Buruma, M.F.J. Haak & I.W. Verloren van Themaat, *De mogelijkheden voor civielrechtelijke handhaving van de mededingingsregels in Nederland. Een inventarisatie in opdracht van het Minister van Economische Zaken,* Amsterdam, 3 November 2005. Full research in Dutch available on: <www.reedbusinessevents.nl/121759/mogelijkheden-voor-civielrechtelijke-handhaving-van-de-mededingingsregels-in-Nederland.pdf>, on <http://rechtennieuws.nl/5092/ez-meer-civiele-handhaving-van-mededingingsregels-wenselijk.html> you will find the report's main conclusion.

47 The burden of proof is regulated in Art. 6(3). This contains cases where a party refers to the legal exception of Art. 6(3) Mw, which is copied word for word from the European legislation of Art. 101 (3) TFEU.

48 Art. 150 Rv.

According to Article 843a Rv, which is referred as the 'exhibitieplicht', a judge can give an order for disclosure, on a party's request, if four conditions are met. (1) The claimant must have a *legitimate interest*, (2) It must concern *specific documents,* (3) It must concern a *legal relationship* and (4) the addressee of the disclosure request must have the documents *under its control*. There are two exceptions when the judge is able to refuse the disclosure request; *i.e.* when the disclosure is *detrimental to the vital interest* of the addressee and when it is *reasonable to assume that a proper legal administration is also safeguarded without providing the requested information*.

4.2 Legitimate Interest

A party must have a legitimate interest in the requested documents. The Dutch Supreme Court has not ruled yet how a 'legitimate interest' can be determined and unfortunately, the parliamentary history does not mention the exact determination of the term; the subject is only briefly mentioned.[49] A sole interest in a certain part of the document is not enough.[50] According to Wesselink-Van Gent the aim of the disclosure request may not lie in obtaining evidence if the applicant is not certain that it will indeed support his claim.[51] In order to decide if the document is necessary for the dispute, the judge makes a preliminary assessment of the dispute. If the judge is of the opinion that the claim of the applicant of the underlying dispute is unlikely to succeed, he often denies the request. In that case the holder of the documents will then not be unnecessarily harassed.[52]

Especially in competition cases the aforementioned example could lead to a burden to establish a claim, for a victim often relies on suspicions that the suspected company infringed the competition rules, and needs the information to ascertain his claim. The second development indicates an improvement of the disadvantaged position of claimants that have insufficient evidence to strengthen their claims. Especially for the private enforcement of competition cases, the judgment *X e.a./Y e.a.* is an interesting case. The court of Amsterdam responded to the disadvantaged position of the claimant in the following way. It stated that "For the establishment of the legitimate interest and the legal relationship, within the meaning of Article 843a Rv, it is not necessary that the legal relationship is initially determined. For it is not possible to initially preclude the establishment of an unlawful act of the suspected party, and thus of a legal relationship within the meaning of Article 843a Rv. Since the request met with the other conditions of the Article, the request is applicable with regard to the disclosure of three e-mails".[53] The case made clear that it is not necessary for the judge to hear both parties about the underlying case before granting the request.

49 J. Ekelmans, *De Exhibitieplicht*, Deventer: Kluwer 2010, p. 89.

50 Bosch-Boesjes 2008, (T&C Rv), Art. 843a, aant. 3.

51 E.M. Wesseling-Van Gent, 'To fish or not to fish, that's the question', *in* P.J. van der Korst, *Het verzamelen van feiten en bewijs: begrenzing versus verruiming, een kruisbestuiving tussen civiel procesrecht en ondernemingsprocesrecht,* Den Haag, Boom Juridische Uitgevers 2006, p. 105.

52 Rb. Arnhem 19 April 2006, LJN *AX7332* and Rb. Rotterdam 17 May 2006, LJN AX6815 and J. Ekelmans, *De exhibitieplicht in kort bestek,* Zutphen: Paris 2007, pp. 31 and 32.

53 Rb. Amsterdam 12 July 2006, HA ZA 05-3636 consideration 4.6.

4.3 Specific Documents

The term 'legitimate interest' is closely connected with the second requirement of the Article, which states that the claimant must specify the documents clearly in his request. The requested documents must have a certain relevance to the claim; *i.e.* documents that have to do with the legal relationship but do not contribute to the underlying procedure should not be disclosed. To prevent 'fishing' in a company's administration, the claimant should give a concrete description of the document to make clear which document should be revealed. This also gives the judge a proper basis to assess whether the claimant has a legitimate interest.[54] But what is 'concrete'? The interpretation varies in both the parliamentary history and the case law. In the parliamentary history of 1988, the Minister explains that the 'exhibitieplicht' is applicable to the situation in which the claimant is aware of the content of the requested document, but is not actually in possession of the document.[55] The reason of the narrow interpretation is the consequence of the limited scope of the Article before the amendment of 2002.[56] Such a narrow interpretation of the article is no longer the case. Several judgments indicate that for a successful request it is no longer necessary that the exact content of the document is known to the applicant and it is not necessary to establish beforehand that a certain document supports a procedural point of view.[57] For if only documents could be requested of which the contents was already known to the applicant, the duty to disclose does not make any sense.

This is also in line with the requirements for granting the hearing of a witness, which can be brought into the procedure as evidence. In case of a request to hear a witness, it is not necessary that the applicant gives an indication in advance of what the witness might reveal.[58] However, the request should be still sufficiently specified. Often requests which are too general and not sufficiently detailed will be rejected. Requests aiming to get access to a document of which the applicant only suspects that it underpins his claim, or of which the claimant only suspects that it exists, will be rejected.[59]

4.4 Legal Relationship

The requested documents should be documents concerning a legal relationship where the applicant or his predecessors takes part in and the request should be directed to the person that has the specific documents under his control. It is not really clear whether the term 'legal relationship' refers to the relation of the

54 Bosch-Boesjes 2008, (T&C Rv), Art. 843a, aant. 3.

55 Parlementaire Geschiedenis nieuw bewijsrecht, p. 417.

56 Until the amendment of Art. 843a Rv in 2002, a party was only able to demand inspection, a copy or an extract of private deeds concerning a legal relationship in which the applicant or its predecessor took place. Even before 1988 the article demanded that the applicant of the document was the (co-)owner of the deed. See Parlementaire Geschiedenis nieuw bewijsrecht, p. 417.

57 Ekelmans 2007, p. 24 and Hof Den Haag 20 May 2003, *SES* 2004, 59. (*X./Gemeente P).*

58 Ekelmans 2007, p. 25.

59 Rb. Den Haag 27 July 2005, LJN AU5178 consideration 12.

documents concerned, or refers to the legal relationship of the underlying claim. In some cases the court supports the first interpretation.[60] This would mean that the requested documents will only concern correspondence and agreements between the two parties.[61] In some cases a judge rejected the request because the applicant requested documents that concerned a legal relation with a third party and not with the applicant.[62] In later case law parties could not request documents to which they were not a party either.[63]

However, according to parliamentary history, the requirement of a legal relationship is also satisfied when the underlying claim is based on an unlawful act.[64] This means that the term 'legal relationship' refers to the underlying claim and not to the legal relationship with the documents. In the obtaining of damages in the private enforcement of competition law, the claim will be based on this legal relationship and it is important for obtaining evidence in those cases that this broader interpretation will be applied, for the opposite party is often a competitor and has no other legal relationship with the applicant than the underlying claim. Some courts are also in favour of the even broader interpretation that documents should be exposed if they are relevant to the case.[65] Case law shows that giving a wider interpretation becomes more regular practice,[66] but it remains inconsistent.[67]

Is it also possible to obtain documents from third parties with this wider interpretation? If the term 'legal relationship' refers to the legal relationship underlying the request and the text of the Article would be interpreted literally, then presumably the answer would be positive. According to the literal text of the article it is only required that a request is made for documents concerning a legal relationship to which the applicant is a party. It is not required that the requested party

60 Pres. Rb. Amsterdam 22 May 2000, KG 2000, 129 consideration 7. (*Bakker e.a./ World Online e.a.)*, see also for more examples Rb. Amsterdam 4 September 2002, *JOR* 2002, 176 consideration 6 (*Walmaro BV/Uni-Invest NV)* and Hof Arnhem 29 August 2006, LJN AY9096 consideration 3.20 (*X./Gemeente Steenwijkerland).*

61 Ekelmans 2007, p. 15.

62 See HR 18 February 2000, *NJ 2001*, 259 consideration 4.1.3 (*News International/ABN Amro)*, see also for more examples Pres. Rb. Amsterdam 22 May 2000, KG 2000, 129 consideration 7 (*Bakker e.a./ World Online e.a.)*, see also for more examples Rb. Amsterdam 4 September 2002, *JOR* 2002, 176 consideration 6 (*Walmaro BV/Uni-Invest NV)* and Hof Arnhem 29 August 2006, LJN AY9096 consideration 3.20 (*X./Gemeente Steenwijkerland).*

63 Rb. Dordrecht 2 July 2003, *SES* 2006, 116 consideration 8 and Rb. Arnhem 29 September 2004, LJN AR3532 consideration 6 *(Koopovereenkomst woonhuis)* and Rb. Amsterdam 31 August 2004, KG 04/1539 consideration 7 and Rb. Groningen 22 November 2002, *NJ* 2003, 102, consideration 6 (*Dekker Aannemingsbedrijf B.V./B. & R.. Roelfina Jonkman-Schuiling).*

64 Parl. Gesch. Burg. Procesrecht, Van Mierlo/Bart, p. 554 and Bosch-Boesjes 2008, (T&C Rv), Art. 843a, aant. 4.

65 Ekelmans 2007, p. 19 and see Rb. Breda 14 January 2004, *JOR* 2004, 70 (*NV Holding BVR-Groep/ Ho-Cla Beheer BV.)* and in appeal Hof 's-Hertogenbosch 28 September 2004, *JOR* 2005, 23 consideration 4.4.1.

66 Ekelmans 2007, p. 19 and see Ktg. Rotterdam 26 September 2003, *SES* 2004, 127 and Rb Amsterdam 24 August 2005, LJN AU4935.

67 Rb. Dordrecht 2 July 2003, *SES* 2006, 116 consideration 8 and Rb. Arnhem 29 September 2004, LJN AR3532 consideration 6 and Rb. Amsterdam 31 August 2004, *KG* 04/1539 consideration 7 and Rb. Groningen 22 November 2002, *NJ* 2003, 102, consideration 6.

is a party to the legal relationship. It would be logical to give the article a broader meaning, for in the case of a request to hear a witness, it is not necessary for the witness to be a party to the legal relationship either.[68] One judgment affirmed the possibility to obtain evidence from third parties, but unfortunately it was not a case that was decided by the Dutch Supreme Court, but by a lower court,[69] so it is still unclear how the term 'legal relationship' should be interpreted and whether it is possible to obtain evidence from third parties. Especially with regard to the different outcomes of the various interpretations, it must be recommended that a clear interpretation of the article is given. Especially with regard to the other channels of providing evidence, like the evidence that could be presented by a witness or the insertion of a preliminary analyses of an expert, which are admissible in court. This contains also evidence from third parties. The evidence that is collected by those channels is also admissible.

4.5 Control of Documents

When the addressee of the request does not have control of the requested documents, he is not obliged to present these documents. A question that arises is whether the documents have to be physically present at the addressee's premises. For example, a company gives its accountant the requested documents for preparing the annual financial statement. Would it be possible to demand from the accountant the return of the documents? According to case law, this should be possible.[70] However, if the addressee has no right to request the documents from a third party, then it should be concluded that he has no control of the documents.

4.6 Exception: Detrimental to the Vital Interests

A party or addressee to a disclosure order can refuse the request if revealing of the documents is detrimental to the vital interests. The parliamentary history leaves it to the discretion of the court to define the exact meaning of the term vital interests.[71] If a party refuses to provide the requested evidence, as doing so is detrimental to the vital interests, the court should balance the interests of the applicant against those of the addressee. The disclosure must not present an unfair benefit for the applicant and the addressee must not suffer an unfair disadvantage. It is a kind of proportionality test.[72] In the field of the private enforcement of

68 P.J.M. von Schmidt auf Altenstadt, 'Opening van Zaken', *TCR* 2002, pp. 12-13. See also J.R. Sijmonsma, *Het inzagerecht. Artikel 843a van het Wetboek van Burgerlijke Rechtsvordering*, Deventer, Kluwer 2010, p. 149.

69 Vrz. Rb. Rotterdam 25 November 2004, *NJF* 2005, 2 consideration 3.3 (*ICS/Ocean en Staat*); see also Ekelmans 2007, p. 22.

70 Ekelmans 2007 p. 13, see the judgments Rb. Rotterdam 2 November 2005, *SES* 2006, 55 consideration 81 (*Lesli/Sinotrans*) and Rb. Middelburg 26 April 2006, LJN AZ5129 consideration 4.1 (*Bouwbedrijf Terpstra/Bouwbedrijf De Delta*).

71 The parliamentary history gives some examples when a disclose order is detrimental to the vital interests. It is the case when information contains one's sexual orientation, medical status or financial position or business secrets. See Parl. Gesch. Burgerlijk Procesrecht, Van Mierlo/Bart, p. 157; see also Kamerstukken II 1995/1996, 24651, A, p. 16.

72 Parl. Gesch. Burgerlijk Procesrecht, Van Mierlo/Bart, p. 157.

competition cases, a company will often try to obstruct the disclosure by claiming that the desired information contains business secrets. The focus should be on the issue when an addressee of a disclosure order refuses the request because the documents contain corporate sensitive information. Case law shows that a judge rarely allows such a refusal. The sole statement that the document's contents contains confidential business information or contains information that is competition sensitive, does not justify the non-disclosure of documents.[73]

The fact that the judge does not grant a refusal solely on the statement that the documents contain confidential business information or contain information that is competition sensitive, is a good development, especially since the negative consequences of the disclosure of confidential information could be safeguarded by other means. Such other means could be the hearing of the parties behind closed doors and that the judge is able to order the parties to exercise confidentiality about facts that were brought into the procedure towards third parties.[74] However, this will not prevent certain business information from being revealed to the opposite party, which often has a detrimental effect. Especially in competition cases, it will usually be a competitor who starts a procedure and a party will not appreciate corporate sensitive information being exposed to its competitor. To prevent that corporate sensitive information is exposed to the opposite party that is also a competitor, Vranken claims that it is also permissible that certain sections of documents, such as names and addresses, are hidden or that only key elements of a document are highlighted, leaving the corporate sensitive information under wraps.[75] Another solution is that only the attorney of the applicant is permitted to take notice of the corporate sensitive information. He is then under the restriction that he may not disclose the information to its client.[76] Also it could be possible that by approval of parties only the judge can take notice of the documents. This right is established in the judgment *Lightning Casino/ Nederlandse Antillen*, which was decided in an administrative matter in the Netherlands Antilles.[77] Vranken and Van Mierlo suggest that this verdict could also have consequences in civil litigation cases, where a judge orders the disclosure of documents *ex officio*.[78]

4.7 Exception: *Ultimum Remedium?*

The second limitation concerns the rejection of granting a request when it is reasonable to assume that a proper legal administration can be safeguarded without

73 J. Ekelmans 2007, p. 39 and Rb. Rotterdam 25 January 2006, *NJF* 2006, 230, consideration 7.4 (*Van D/Van Schoenen v.o.f.*) and Hof 's Gravenhage 20 May 2003, *S&S* 2004, 59 consideration 2.9 (*Church & General/Gebr. Sluyter*), Rb. Groningen 29 March 2006, LJN AV7614 consideration 4.2 (*Heineken/Hooites q.q*).

74 These rights are embedded in Arts. 27 and 29 Rv.

75 J.B.M. Vranken in his annotation under point 8, HR 20 December 2002, *NJ 2004, 4 (Lightning casino/Antillen)*.

76 This solution occurred in industrial property matters. See also J.B.M. Vranken in his annotation under point 8, HR 20 December 2002, *NJ 2004, 4 (Lightning casino/Antillen)*.

77 HR 20 december 2002, *NJ* 2004, 4 *(Lightning casino/Antillen)*.

78 This according to V.C.A. Lindijer, *De goede procesorde. Een onderzoek naar de betekenis van de goede procesorde als normatief begrip in het burgerlijk procesrecht*, Deventer, Kluwer, 2006, p. 254.

providing the requested data. According to the parliamentary history, if evidence could be obtained by another channel, like the hearing of a witness or through an expert analyses, then these channels are preferred above that of the disclosure of documents.[79] The obtaining of evidence through other channels is in line with the legislator's wish that the 'exhibitieplicht' is not used too lightly.

It would seem that Article 843a Rv is a kind of *ultimum remedium* and it is questionable whether that is a practical remedy, seeing that if something can be proven by documents, it may be unnecessary and time consuming to hear a witness or to ask an expert. In most cases the judge is not in favour of this exception, but there are still verdicts in which judges deny a request to documents, because another channel should be used instead.[80]

Another interpretation of this exception was given in a case before the Court of Rotterdam in 2009.[81] The dispute concerned the question whether KPN and Vodafone had made agreements that would have discriminatory effects for other network providers. In the assessment whether *a proper legal administration can be safeguarded without revealing the information concerned,* the judge did not ask himself whether there were other possible channels to obtain the evidence, but asked the question whether the applicant would be put in a (more) disadvantaged position if he could not obtain the requested information. According to this judgment, the aforementioned restriction of Article 843a Rv refers not only to the question whether there are other channels to obtain evidence, like a hearing of a witness or an expert report, but also to the question whether there is other evidence available to ascertain one's claim. Therefore a kind of subsidiarity test is built into Article 843a Rv.

5. Is It Necessary to Change the Legislation with Regard to the White Paper Proposals?

The application of Article 843a Rv is very inconsistent according to the case law. In some cases the requirements are interpreted in a very strict way and in others they are interpreted broadly. If the requirements set in the article are interpreted widely, it could be in line with the proposals in the White Paper.

In the White Paper, the Commission sets as a first condition prior to the disclosure order, that the claimant has asserted all the facts and offered all those means of evidence that are reasonably available to him, provided that these are sufficient to make his claim a plausible one. According to the Commission, the judge should also take into account the difficulties that claimants may have to present detailed

79 Parl. Gesch. Burg. Procesrecht, Van Mierlo/Bart, p. 553.

80 See for example: Vrz. Rb. Amsterdam 4 July 2002, *JOR* 2002, 142 consideration 6 (*Ten Doesschate q.q./AFM*) and Vrz. Rb. Breda 25 October 2006, *NJF* 2006, 596 consideration 4.4 (*SLC/Stakenburg*).

81 Rb. Rotterdam 10 June 2009, 322279/HA ZA 09-131, paras 3.8-3.12. (*KPN/ Colt, Tele2, BT*).

facts to support their claims. This proposal could comply with the requirement of the 'legitimate interest' to which Article 843a Rv refers, but only if the judge's interpretation of 'legitimate interest' is done in a way that does not make it necessary that the legal relationship between the parties and the presumable outcome of the case is established in advance. If the 'legal relationship' refers to the legal relationship underlying the request, which in competition cases should mean the unlawful act and not the legal relationship underlying the requested documents, as is still done in some cases, Article 843a Rv could be used in the obtaining of evidence in competition cases.

The second condition of the Commission states that the claimant must show to the satisfaction of the court that he is unable, applying all reasonable efforts that may be expected from him, to produce the means of evidence for which disclosure is requested. The Commission mentions that in some cases this requirement could be alleviated if there is a real risk that a victim will lose his case just because the relevant evidence is in the possession of the suspected person or third parties and therefore inaccessible to the claimant. This condition includes a subsidiarity test, which can also be found in Article 843a(4) Rv. Article 843a(4) Rv says that if a claimant could use other methods to collect his evidence rather than request documents from the opposite party or a third party, this should be preferred. As the KPN case showed, the subsidiarity test could also be interpreted in a way that lets the judge decide whether the claimant's position becomes disadvantaged if he does not obtain the requested documents.[82] If the last sub of the Article is explained in that way, it could meet also the second condition of the White Paper.

The third condition in the White Paper points out that the court must be satisfied that the requested disclosure measure is relevant to the case as well as necessary and proportionate in scope. According to this condition the court should consider what kind of harm the revealing of certain documents could constitute for the defendant or possible third parties, in matters of revealing commercial sensitive information. This proportionality test can also be found in Article 843a(4) Rv, where a party can refuse the disclosure request if it is detrimental to the vital interests. The judge should weigh the interest of the applicant against the interest of the addressee. As the Commission in the White Paper envisages, it will be less detrimental to the vital interests of the addressee if commercial sensitive information could be sealed or the procedure could take place behind closed doors or is only attended by the parties' lawyers or designated experts. According to what is said by some authors with regard to the possibilities in case of Article 22 Rv, which should also be applicable in case of Article 843a Rv, it should also be possible to meet this proposal of the White Paper. A slight difference between the proportionality and subsidiarity test in the White Paper and the test in Article 843a Rv is that the White Paper demands that the applicant shows to the satisfaction of the court that he complies with those principles, but that in Article 843a Rv it is up to the addressee to invoke the exceptions. This should not make a big difference for eventually the judge decides whether the disclosure request is granted by balancing the interests.

82 Rb. Rotterdam 10 June 2009, 322279/HA ZA 09-131, considerations 3.8-3.12.

The fourth condition set in the White Paper is that the claimant has sufficiently specified categories of information or evidence to be disclosed. This condition of the White Paper seems to be broader than the '*specific documents*' to which Article 843a(1) Rv refers. The Commission adds that the request should be specified as precise and narrow as possible, but must not conflict with the objects set in the framework. It is questionable if Article 843a(1) Rv allows such a wider margin of appreciation. Case law showed that in some cases it is not necessary anymore for the applicant to know the exact content of the documents, but this does not mean that the applicant can request 'categories' of information. The applicant must be certain that the requested documents exist. 'Categories of information' refers to a far wider applicability than 'specific documents'. This could be a slight difference between Article 843a Rv and the White Paper.

Furthermore, the White Paper advocates the possibility for documents to be obtained from third parties, but only if the requested documents could not be obtained from the opposite party in the procedure. According to the foregoing, it is possible that documents could be obtained from a third party, but this also depends on how the term 'legal relationship' is interpreted. This still differs from case to case.

5.1 Answer: No... If

If the requirements in Article 843a Rv are interpreted broadly, it could be in line with the proposals in the White Paper. However, this conclusion is made in a rather premature stage, because the exact content and scope of Article 843a Rv is still very undefined. Recent case law still shows inconsistency about the interpretation of the article, which can lead to totally different outcomes. If the article is interpreted in a strict way, it does not meet the Commission's proposals at all; *i.e.* it should, for example, not be possible to obtain documents from the opposite party if the only 'legal relationship' between the parties is the 'unlawful act' and therefore it should not be possible to obtain documents from third parties. It ought to be up to the legislator and not the judges or legal authors to make clear once and for all what the exact content of the article is, in compliance with the principle of legal certainty. Victims of competition infringers need more certainty to assess whether their request will be granted or not and this ought not to depend on whether the judge is in favour of a broad or strict interpretation of the article.

5.1.1 Amendment of Article 843a Rv

Fortunately the legislator is currently planning to amend Article 843a Rv, which will be referred to in the new legislation as Article 162a-162c Rv.[83] Not only will the new article remove all uncertainties that exist on the article, it will also adopt

83 Wetsvoorstel houdende aanpassing van het wetboek van burgerlijke rechtsvordering in verband met de wijziging van het recht op inzage, afschrift of uittreksel van bescheiden 2011 (*Proposal to the amendment of Article 843a Rv).*

the wide interpretation which was already advocated by authors and some courts. It is also a big advantage that the disclosure of evidence will be brought in line with the other channels to obtain evidence, like the hearing of a witness or the analysis of an expert. Article 843a Rv will then not function as an *ultimum remedium* anymore. Hopefully, the new rules will soon be adopted in the Code of Civil Procedure. Not only will the articles be in line with the White Paper's proposals, victims of antitrust infringements will better able to examine beforehand whether their request will be meritorious. In addition, the broad interpretation of the requirements will give victims more possibilities to obtain evidence from the opposite party or third parties.

5.1.2 Amendment Meritorious?

The question remains, however, if the proposals of the White Paper and of the amendment of Article 843a Rv will indeed enhance the obtaining of evidence in competition cases. It is almost impossible to obtain damages when the crucial evidence has to come from the infringing company. The Dutch procedural rules function as a kind of catalyst.[84] The more plausible the infringing act is, the more the judge is willing to grant a request. If a victim is not able to ascertain his claim with sufficient facts, because the crucial information is under the control of the infringing company, the judge will not grant the request easily.[85]

6. Possible Solution

A solution to this problem could be that the interpretations of the exceptions of Article 150 Rv, which have been developed over the years by the Dutch Supreme Court, become also applicable in competition cases.[86] It would be easier for the victim if it were possible that the burden of proof is shifted or alleviated. An exception that is developed over the years is the aggravation of the obligation to furnish facts on the side of the defendant. This doctrine is especially applied in doctor vs. patient and employer vs. employee cases. In these cases the judge responded to the difficulty those parties encountered in proving their cases, by demanding that the

84 Adviescommissie voor het burgerlijk procesrecht, betreft: Advies over gegevensverstrekking in burgerrechtelijke zaken 2008, p. 11.

85 Two good examples of the difficulties that victims encounter in establishing the infringement of the competition rules and the crucial information is under the supervision of the alleged infringers are Hof Amsterdam 23 December 2009, LJN BG8028 (*British American Tabacco Nederland BV/ Chipknip CV*) and Hof Den Haag 1 June 2010, LJN BM 6398 (*Havenbedrijf/Rotterdam*). In these two cases the claimants accused the opposite party of abusing its dominant position by charging excessive prices. The two cases make clear that when parties have to prove that its counterparty makes an abuse of its dominant position, it is practically impossible to establish the necessary facts.

86 E.J. Zippro, 'Privaatrechtelijke handhaving van het verbod om misbruik te maken van een economische machtspositie: excessieve prijsvoering in de Rotterdamse haven?', *MvV* 10, 2010, p. 267, HR 20 november 1987, *NJ* 1988, 500 (*Antje Timmer/Deutman*) and HR 13 januari 1995, *NJ* 1997, 175 (*De Heel/Korver*).

burden of defence should be higher without shifting the burden of proof. This rule may be applied if certain facts have occurred in the defendant's sphere, to which the victim does not have access. It may be expected from the defendant that he is concerned about the procedural interests of the opposite party and that he is able to present the facts more easily.[87] He has to present sufficient facts to justify the statements of the claimant, to the end that the defendant provides sufficient leads for the providing of evidence.[88] According to Krans, the aggravation to furnish facts by the defendant could also be possible, according to the Dutch procedure rules, by the private enforcement of competition rules.[89] In competition cases a similar information asymmetry exists. This exception of Article 150 Rv has never been applied in the private enforcement of competition rules. The reason for this presumably lies in the fact that when applying competition rules, judges are in favour of staying close to the rules on the European level; a result of the European principle of equivalence. Article 2 Council Regulation 1/2003 demands that the party or authority that alleges an infringement must therefore provide the proof and does not refers to any exceptions. For this reason, it is uncertain whether the exception of Article 150 Rv will be applied in the future by national courts.

Another possibility that exists in Article 150 Rv is the doctrine of *the legal presumption.*[90] On the basis of the *legal presumption* it is possible for the judge to derive from a known fact an unknown fact, in which case the burden of proof is alleviated. The ECJ held in 2004 that the application of the legal presumption is permissible in case the European Commission provides evidence.[91] It would be logical if this is also possible in the private enforcement of competition rules, as the burden of proof of the Commission is captured in the same Article 2 of Regulation 1/2003. Because the Commission in its White Paper rejected all possibilities of shifting or alleviating the burden of proof, this solution runs counter to the White Paper, but will not conflict with the goals of the White Paper. The White Paper's main goal is that victims should encounter fewer obstacles in obtaining evidence.

6.1 Follow-On

The White Paper proposed that the decision of a national competition authority should lead to binding proof in following civil proceedings for damages. In the Netherlands such a rule does not exist. The judge could derive from the decision a presumption that the alleged behaviour has been committed, but the decision is still open to refutable proof.[92] The claimant has to provide once again proof that the opposite party infringed the competition rules, which is very time consuming and fact-intensive. It is therefore recommended that the legislator points out in a specific section of legislation that victims are able to rely on NCA decisions as

87 Zippro 2010, p. 267.

88 *Ibid.*, p. 267.

89 H.B. Krans, *Nederlands burgerlijk procesrecht en materieel EU-recht,* Deventer, Kluwer 2010, p. 63.

90 A.R. Rueb, *Compendium. Burgerlijk procesrecht,* Deventer, Kluwer 2009, p. 142.

91 C-204/00 *Aalborg c.s./Commissie,* paras 55-57. And see Krans 2010, p. 64.

92 According to Art. 152(2) Rv, the weight of the evidence is left to the discretion of the judge.

binding proof in civil procedures. The implementation of the regulation should be bound to the limitations set in the White Paper: *i.e.* that it will concern a final decision, where the defendant has exploited all possible appeals to the NCA decision or that all relevant time limits for appeal have expired.

Until this rule is implemented, it is recommended that claimants should have access to the evidence that is collected by the NCA. Some authors advocate that this could be by the application of Article 843a Rv, by requesting the reports of the NMa that are in the possession of the opposite party or, as one author advocated, from the NMa itself.[93]

6.2 Access to Documents Held by Public Authorities

It is also possible to request documents from the national competition authority (NMa) by way of the *Wob* (Government Information (Public Access) Act), in which it is established that every citizen is able to request documents that are held by public authorities, which is comparable with the possibility at European level.[94] The access is not unlimited, but is subject to certain limitations and the NMa has a wide margin of appreciation in deciding whether a request should be granted. The NMa will not disclose information when the information concerns *inter alia* (1) business or manufacture data, (2) data concerning the privacy, (3) when the disclosure gives a disproportionate disadvantage to persons that are subject of the documents, (4) if the NMa is still busy with an investigation, and (5) in case documents contain information that has been given by a leniency applicant.[95]

The number of grounds to refuse a request based on the *Wob* makes it rather unclear whether a request to the NMa will indeed be meritorious. One of the grounds to refuse an application is when the requested documents contain corporate sensitive information. The rule for exclusion is only applicable if the data concerns technical management or a production process or gives information about the marketing of products or a group of customers and suppliers.[96] This is an absolute ground for a refusal to disclose certain parts of the report that the NMa made. The NMa is able to erase or adjust certain parts of the file when it contains confidential information.[97] In this way, the competition authority can be clear about the grounds of the decision without revealing corporate sensitive information. However, it is often this kind of information that the victim needs to establish the infringement and especially to calculate its damages.

93 L. Haasbeek, 'De Wob en de Eurowob in het mededingingsrecht', *M&M* november 2009, nr. 5, p. 145 and E.J. Zippro, *Privaatrechtelijke handhaving van mededingingsrecht,* Deventer, Kluwer 2009, p. 552.

94 The right is embedded in Art. 3(1) Wob. The Wob is also applicable to a request that seeks access to documents held by the Dutch competition authority. This possibility is affirmed in the case ABRvS 7 February 2007, LJN AZ 7951, para. 2.3.1 (*Koninklijke Gazelle/Raad van Bestuur NMa).*

95 Limitations are embedded in Art. 10 Wob. See also Zippro 2009, p. 647.

96 See case law ARRvS 30 September 1985, *AB* 1987, 43 and ABRvS 3 March 1998 *AB* 1998, 435.

97 See also NMa, Spelregels bij concentratiezaken, 21 January 2009, paras 52- 56. Published on: <www.nma.nl>. Search for: 'Spelregels voor concentratiezaken' and see for an example NMa 21 September 2010, Case 7017, *Wob verzoek zaak 6990/KPN-T for Telecom.*

If the desired information is not obtainable by way of a *Wob* request, a request through Article 843a Rv could work instead. The documents that the victim received from the NMa through a *Wob* request, even if some information is blacked out, gives to the victim a point of reference that the information exists and where it is located. This will enhance his request to the disclosure of documents through an action of Article 843a Rv. It is still uncertain whether the judge will grant the request in the light of the fact that the information is confidential, but according to the case law, this fact in itself does not justify the non-disclosure of documents. Besides, confidential information can be safeguarded in other ways, like hearing the case behind closed doors, blacking out certain areas in the verdict or giving only the attorney of the applicant permission to take notice of the corporate sensitive information.

6.3 Obtaining Evidence from Leniency Applicants

Another ground to refuse a disclosure request through the *Wob* is when the request is aimed at obtaining information that the NMa gathered through a leniency programme. This exception is embedded in Article 10(2)(d), which says that no information is given if the interest in providing such information does not outweigh the importance of inspection, control and supervision by the public authority. It is conceivable that the disclosure of information obtained through a leniency programme does not outweigh the interest of the competition authority in its investigating and enforcement role in competition law. The obligation to reveal certain information to a third party that is planning to bring a civil claim is contrary to the larger public interest at stake. It is important for the NMa to be able to carry out its task to investigate and enforce the competition rules. If an investigation is closed, third parties cannot benefit from the documents that leniency applicants presented to the competition authority by using them in a procedure before the civil court, for example. There may be the risk that future leniency applicants refrain from going to the competition authority with a leniency application. Therefore the disclosure of information could be detrimental to the role of the NMa.[98]

To get access to the documents that a company provided to the NMa as part of a leniency programme, a party could bring an action through 843a Rv before a civil court. In the White Paper, the Commission suggests that a leniency applicant, except when it is an immunity recipient, should be protected against court orders requesting the production of information which was submitted to the competition authority. This kind of protection of leniency applicants in civil proceedings does not exist in Dutch legislation.[99] If a victim requests a document through Article 843a Rv the judge cannot refuse the request solely on the ground that the document contains information that is submitted to a NCA as part of a leniency

98 Zippro 2009, p. 647.

99 Studiekring "Eurogroep" van de Nederlandse Raad voor de rechtspraak, Commentaar op het Witboek betreffende de schadevergoedingsacties wegens schending van de communautaire mededingingsregels, 2008, p. 5.

programme. In the application of Article 843a Rv, there is no room for balancing the interests of the leniency programme against the interests of the applicant. There is only room for balancing personal interests rather than public interests, like the interests of the leniency programme. Now that the leniency applicant is not protected under Article 843a Rv, it is unclear, however, whether the court is willing to grant the request with regard to the other limitations in Article 843a Rv and the risk of *fishing expeditions*.

6.3.1 *Does the Judgment* Pfleiderer AG/Bundeskartellamt *Have Any Consequences for the Netherlands?*

The question arising in this context is whether the Dutch legislation has the means to grant access to documents gathered through a leniency programme that are held by the competition authority. The *Wob* does not provide room for a Dutch court or the NMa to balance the aforementioned interests. As the previous paragraph shows, the NMa can refuse the request if the interests of providing such information do not outweigh the importance of inspection, control and supervision by the public authority. Only when there is a larger public interest at stake, the access could be granted. It seems that there is no room for balancing the interests if it concerns a personal interest, *i.e.* the interest to collect evidence in the preparation of a civil procedure to obtain damages, and the judgment *Pfleiderer AG/Bundeskartellamt* makes no difference in this matter.

What remains, as Haasberg advocates, is the possibility to request the documents through an action based on Article 843a Rv.[100] It is not unthinkable, however, that the request will be rejected because of the limitations set in Article 843a Rv, which are designed to prevent a *fishing expedition*. Presumably, there is also no room for a balancing of interests as called for in the case *Pfleiderer AG/Bundeskartellamt* on the basis of this article.[101] Under Article 843a Rv there is only room for a balancing of the personal interests at stake. A disclosure request could be refused when the disclosure of the documents is *detrimental to the vital interests* of the addressee, in this case the leniency applicant. The protection of a leniency programme is a larger public interest and not a personal interest of the addressee, as provided by Article 843a(4).

Pfleiderer AG/Bundeskartellamt will probably not have any consequences for the Dutch rules on the accessibility of documents the Dutch competition authorities gathered through a leniency programme.[102]

6.3.2 *Obtaining Documents from the NMa. Meritorious?*

It is unclear whether the documents that parties can obtain from the NMa are sufficiently meritorious to make their claim feasible in a civil proceeding against

---

100 Haasbeek 2009, p. 145.

101 M. Kuijper, 'Pfleiderer AG/ Bundeskartellamt', *M&M* 2011-5, p. 5.

102 See para. 2.6.3.1 for a full description of the judgment.

an alleged infringer. According to the number of requests that have been filed with the NMa since 2007, companies use the possibility widely.[103] However, it is difficult to determine how many of these requests are made with the intention to start a civil procedure against an alleged infringer of the competition rules to obtain damages. According to the previous paragraphs the NMa has a wide margin of discretion in deciding whether a request will be granted or not. Corporate sensitive information is severely protected from disclosure but it could be precisely this kind of information that would be helpful in establishing the infringing act or the exact amount of damages derived from the infringement. If the necessary information is not obtainable through a *Wob* request, the documents which are held by the competition authority could enhance the disclosure request through an action under Article 843a Rv. The inspection of the documents of the NMa, even if some crucial information is blacked out, enables a party to determine where possibly crucial information from the potential opposite party is kept. This can be used to make his request stronger, especially with regard to the fact that requests sometimes run into a blind wall because parties often are not aware where the requested documents are held or if they even exist. This will presumably increase the chances of an Article 843a Rv request. However, the risk remains that a request will be rejected if it does not satisfy the other requirements of Article 843a Rv and especially if the disclosure could be detrimental to vital interests when the documents contain corporate sensitive information. If a requested document contains confidential business information or contains information that is competition sensitive, this fact is not enough to justify the non-disclosure of the documents, especially because the judge may be able to protect corporate sensitive information in some other way, for example by giving a third party or an independent expert access to the information concerned. Other possibilities for the judge are revealing the relevant information without the parties being present, or the other previous discussed possibilities that are aimed to safeguard the protection of confidential information.

7. Conclusion

As set out above, there are still a lot of uncertainties with regard to the question whether a victim of antitrust infringements is indeed able to obtain evidence from the opposite party or a third party. It could be very enlightening if in the near future many victims of anti-trust infringers were to go to court to collect damages from the infringers. Not only will this rightfully punish the infringing companies and give victims reparation for the losses suffered, it will also give a good insight into the question whether the legislation examined in this article is sufficient to enhance the private enforcement of the competition rules.

103 See <www.nma.nl/search.aspx> search word: "Wob".

An Exchange of Information under Slovenian Competition Law

P. Kotnik and M. Kovač

1. Introduction

Efficient regulatory mechanisms that induce innovation, co-operation and deter competition law infringements have recently been the subject of growing attention and intense scholarly debate. The prospect of future economic growth and increased social welfare requires innovation and technological progress. To bring them about, undertakings must invest in new products and processes. In doing so, they face substantial costs associated with R&D that they often cannot bear individually. They confront technical risk and uncertainties (costs) related to market acceptance and, due to the increasing complexity of new applications, they come up against the limits of their internal capabilities. To overcome this challenge, firms have responded with mergers and by co-operating (information sharing) with each other, where they share costs, pool risks and complement or enhance individual capabilities through joint R&D or technology development.[1] This emphasis on the speed of innovation is part of the European Union's endeavour to increase its world competitiveness. Yet, the uncertainty surrounding technological change in a highly dynamic sector implies it is difficult to evaluate the likely effect of inter-firm collaborations that are the principle target of the EU's anti-competitive practices (subject to EU competition rules: self-assessment, information sharing as an infringement of EU competition rules etc.).[2] The last few decades have witnessed the unprecedented success of European competition policy which has resulted in significant efficiency gains, benefiting European consumers and consequently substantially increasing European social welfare. This traditional EU competition policy aims at providing level playing fields for firms where perfect price competition and static efficiency are at the core of focus (*i.e.* consumer surplus). Deviations, like for example an exchange of information between undertakings, from such a benchmark are perceived as infringements of EU competition law.

1 J. Lorentzen & P. Mollgaard, 'Competition Policy and Innovation', *in* P. Bianchi & S. Labory (eds.), *International Handbook on Industrial Policy*, Edward Elgar 2006.

2 For a discussion on whether those are indeed the most proper and efficient goals see R. van den Bergh & P.D. Camesasca, *European Competition Law and Economics: A Comparative Perspective* (2nd ed.), Thomson Sweet & Maxwell 2006.

However, the sharing of knowledge (information), enhancement of information flows between undertakings, and co-operation in R&D activities appear to be fundamental for creating the dynamic evolution of markets, improving cost-efficient processes and enhancing social welfare. Moreover, the economic literature identifies entrepreneurship as a crucial development and initiating factor which actually spurs the process of the discovery, evaluation and exploitation of opportunities, combines new things or innovates, introduces new products or new quality in products, introduces new methods of production, a new organisation within an industry etc. The notions of entrepreneurship and innovation are thus clearly interrelated and obviously, without the role and function of the entrepreneur, the amount of innovation would be substantially lower.

Understanding the effects of the current EU and Slovenian competition law enforcement mechanisms on undertakings, entrepreneurs and their innovative activities is, therefore, essential. Whereas it is generally accepted that entrepreneurship and innovation are an instrument of economic progress, their relationship with the current competition law enforcement remains controversial. The analysed EU competition law provisions on information exchange and R&D horizontal agreements (in addition to the inefficient 25% market share criterion) through the self-assessment procedures and vague evaluation criteria for when an information exchange amounts to an infringement of those EU rules may deter the optimal amount of entrepreneurial activity. Consequently, also current Slovenian competition law enforcement deters the utilisation of deliberately acquired productive information and thus hinders innovation and entrepreneurial activity. This may consequently also deter innovative activity, reduce competitiveness and eventually diminish social welfare. Such a reverse incentive mechanism, we argue, presents the identified EU competition law deterrence paradox. Namely, we argue that the identified expected benefits from certain entrepreneurial activity may well, under the current EU (and Slovenian) enforcement regime, be outweighed by the inefficient risk shifting and increased transaction costs (self-assessment and vague rules on information exchange are a costly and uncertain process) assigned to the entrepreneur. In other words, the re-stating of competition policies and evaluating criteria as to when a certain exchange of information amounts to an infringement of competition law may be necessary to induce more important innovations. The current Slovenian competition law enforcement regime may thus in this respect deter innovation, entrepreneurship and technological progress. Furthermore, the implementation and application of the relevant Slovenian competition law provision (Art. 6 ZPOmK-1) is not coherent and is not consistent with Article 101 of the Treaty on the Functioning of the European Union (hereinafter: TFEU) and the related European case law.

The first part of this contribution (section 2) starts with a survey of the relevant substantive EU law provisions and then offers a set of economic criteria to establish when and in which conditions an exchange of information should not be regarded as an infringement of current EU competition law. In addition, the relationship between entrepreneurship, innovation and competition law enforcement (the deterrence paradox) is also thoroughly discussed. The second part (based on the provided set of economic criteria) critically comments on Slovenian competition law enforcement and related, currently applied, standards, provisions and decisions where the need for statutory reform appears obvious (section 3). A conclusion is provided in section 4.

2. Information Flow, Entrepreneurship, Innovation and Competition Law Enforcement

It is commonly contended that competition is essential for both the innovation process and for entrepreneurship activity, which is regarded as one of the most important driving forces enabling innovation and competitiveness.[3] But so too is the co-operation between firms which requires an exchange of information (even outside of specific R&D agreements) and which might possibly lead to inefficient collusive behaviour. This collusive behaviour then, according to the literature, actually distorts competition.[4] Obviously, we are describing here a circular paradox whereby the mechanisms supposed to protect and enforce competition (that aim to enhance competitiveness, innovation, entrepreneurship, allocative efficiency and finally social welfare) may in fact partly impair entrepreneurship and innovative activity, thereby causing a decrease in such wealth-increasing activities. Hence, providing incentives for technological innovation (spurring the generation and utilisation of productive information), entrepreneurship and co-operation, and deterring opportunism are essential for economic growth and the maximisation of social welfare. Yet, as pointed out, the related optimal trade-off between the provision of stable and optimal entrepreneurial incentives (which generate innovation and competitiveness) and the related EU competition law infringements has largely been exempted from the current scholarly debate. Below, after surveying the general features of current EU competition law,[5] the exact framework for such an optimal trade-off and of the EU competition law deterrence paradox will be discussed and compressed into a single principle.

2.1 The Substantive EU Law

Competition law has always played an important part in Community law where the enhancement of efficiency, protection of consumers and creation of a single

---

3 EU competition law is currently aimed at encouraging market competition and discouraging activities that could in any way prevent, distort or restrict it.

4 For an excellent synthesis of antitrust economics, see P. Buccirossi, *Handbook of Antitrust Economics*, MIT Press 2008. Also see M. Motta, *Competition Policy: Theory and Practice*, Cambridge University Press 2004; R.D. Blair & D.L. Kaserman, *Antitrust Economics*, Richard D. Irwin Inc. 1985; H. Hovenkamp, *Economics and Federal Antitrust Law* (Hornbook Series), West Publishing Co. 1985; R.A. Posner, *Antitrust Law* (2nd ed.), Chicago University Press 2001.

5 In relation to information exchange and R&D agreements. For a synthesis on US antitrust law, see *e.g.* P. Areeda & L. Kaplow, *Antitrust Analysis: Problems, Text, Cases* (5th ed.), Little Brown and Company, 2004; C.J. Goetz & F.S. McChesney, *Antitrust Law: Interpretation and Implementation*, Lexis Law Publishing 2008.

European market have been advanced as some of the most relevant objectives and priorities.[6] A competitive economic system is also regarded in the EU as necessary for a prosperous, free and equitable society. The last few decades have thus witnessed the unprecedented success of such a policy, resulting in significant efficiency gains. Moreover, substantial benefits for European consumers and the related improved overall social welfare have been marked as some of the most remarkable achievements of European integration. In this context one should also note that the economic analysis of competition law provisions has recently become central to the assessment of competition cases throughout all fields of EC competition rules.[7] The EC competition rules were set out in the Treaty establishing the European Community where, among other provisions,[8] Article 81 (now Art. 101 TFEU, OJ C115/47, 9.5.2008) prohibiting anticompetitive agreements appears as the principal remedy to deter anti-competitive behaviour. Namely, Article 101 prohibits all agreements, decisions or concerted practices which could in any way prevent, distort or restrict competition and automatically voids all such prohibited agreements.[9] Obviously, the rationale for the broad, wide meaning of Article 101 TFEU, encompassing agreements, decisions or concerted practices, lies in the fact that if the competition rules were to operate only when an explicit, formal agreement has been made then they would have little practical use since undertakings would try to achieve their anti-competitive goals in less formal ways.[10] Moreover, even if there is no agreement at all, undertakings might be caught by the provisions of Article 101 if there is concerted practice (collusion).[11]

6 Its precise role is, however, contestable and a number of differing objectives can be pursued by competition policy, not all of which are mutually compatible; P. Craig & G. De Búrca, *EU Law: Text, Cases and Materials* (4th ed.), Oxford University Press 2008, at p. 950 *et seq*. Also see L. Ritter, D.W. Braun & F. Rawlinson, *European Competition Law: A Practitioner's Guide*, (2nd ed.), Kluwer Law International 2000, p. 46 *et seq*.

7 See H.W. Friederiszick, 'Economic Analysis in EU Competition Cases', *in* J. Drexl, L. Idot & J. Monéger (eds.), *Economic Theory and Competition Law*, Edward Elgar 2009.

8 This also includes the key Art. 102 (ex Art. 82) of the TFEU prohibiting the abuse of a dominant position.

9 The following shall be prohibited as incompatible with the common market; all agreements between undertakings, decisions by associations of undertakings an concerted practices which may affect trade between Member States and which have as their object or effect the prevention, restriction or distortion of competition within the common market, and in particular those which: (a) directly or indirectly fix purchase or selling prices or any other trading conditions; (b) limit or control production, markets, technical development, or investment; (c) share markets or sources of supply; (d) apply dissimilar conditions to equivalent transactions with other trading parties, thereby placing them at the competitive disadvantage; (e) make the conclusion of contracts subject to acceptance by the other parties of supplementary obligations which, by their nature or according to commercial usage, have no connection with the subject of such contracts. 2. Any agreements or decisions pursuant to this Article shall be automatically void;" Art. 101(1), (2), Treaty Establishing the European Community.

10 Craig & De Búrca 2008, at p. 954. Also see *ACF Chemiefarma NV v. Commission,* C-41, 44, and 45/69 (1970), ECR 661; Dec. 86/398 (1986), OJ L230/1, (1988) 4 *CMLR* 347; Dec. 89/190 PVC (1989) OJ L74/1, (1990) 4 *CMLR* 345; *Commission v. BASF AG*, C-137/92 (1994) ECR I-2555; *Italian Flat Glass* (1989) *OJ* L33/44, (1990) 4 *CMLR* 535.

11 On the problems of concerted practices and on the theory of oligopolistic interdependence, see R. Whish, *Competition Law* (6th ed.), Oxford University Press 2009, at p. 510 *et seq*.

Yet, if price uniformity is really the result of rational action in an oligopoly,[12] and there is no actual collusion, then such uniformity is exempted from the scope of Article 101.[13] Further, Article 101(1) also requires that the agreement, decision or concerted practice has the object or effect of preventing, restricting or distorting competition in the Common Market. The interpretation of those conditions has invoked intense scholarly debate in which a consensus has not yet been reached.[14] Yet, as commentators argue, a case law analysis shows that the European Court of Justice condemns certain types of agreements on the basis of their object or purpose without any extensive market analysis; in this sense, it effectively proscribes these agreements as *per se* illegal.[15]

However, an agreement, decision or concerted practice is not necessarily unlawful since Article 101(3) provides a legal exception to the prohibition contained in Article 101(1).[16] This exemption applies provided that four conditions are satisfied. To satisfy Article 101(3) an agreement: a) must contribute to improving the production or distribution of goods or to promoting technical or economic progress; b) consumers must receive a fair share of the resulting benefit; c) the agreement must not impose restrictions on the undertakings concerned which are not indispensable to the attainment of these objectives; and d) it cannot lead to the elimination of competition in respect of a substantial part of the products in question. As commentators note, these four conditions are cumulative: they must all be fulfilled before any exemption can be granted.[17]

The Commission had until recently the exclusive right to grant so-called "individual exemptions" to agreements notified to it and subject to review by the Court.[18] However, the previous system of the ex ante notification of agreements to the Commission and the possible grant of an individual exemption was abolished by

---

12 Then the problem is actually structural since such a type of market will naturally generate this type of response. See *e.g. ICI v. Commission,* C-48/69 (1972) ECR 619; *Hüls AG v. Commission,* C-199/92 (1999) ECR I-4287.

13 For an economic discussion of the uniformity of prices in an oligopoly, see G. Stigler, 'The Kinked Oligopoly Demand Curve', 55 *J. Pol. Econ.* pp. 431, 1947.

14 See *e.g.* V. Korah, 'The Rise and Fall of Provisional Validity – The Need for a Rule of Reason in EEC Antitrust', 3 *NW J. Int. L. and Bus.* 320, 1981; R. Whish & B. Sufrin, 'Article 85 and the Rule of Reason', 7 *YBEL* 12, 1987.

15 The Court has also engaged in economic analysis within Art. 101(1), while it has not employed the language of the rule of reason; Craig & De Búrca 2008, at p. 974. Also see P. Roth & V. Rose, *European Community Law of Competition* (6th ed.), Oxford University Press 2008; R.J. Barry & A. MacCulloch, *Competition Law and Policy in the European Community and United Kingdom,* Cavendish Publishing Limited 1999, p. 157 *et seq.*; Whish 2009, p.122, *et seq.*; V. Korah, 'The Judgment in Delimitis A Milestone Towards a Realistic Assessment of the Effects of the Agreement – or a Damp Squib', 14 *E.I.P.R.* 167, 1992.

16 Whish 2009, p. 148 *et seq.* Also see generally Craig & De Búrca 2008, at 976, and G.D. Goyder, *EC Competition Law*, Oxford University Press 2003, p. 112 *et seq.* For a detailed discussion of Art. 81(3), see J. Faull & A. Nikpay (eds.), *The EC Law of Competition* (2nd ed.), Oxford University Press 2007, and P. Roth & V. Rose (eds.), *Bellamy & Child: European Community Law of Competition* (6th ed.), Sweet & Maxwell 2008.

17 Faull & Nikpay 2007, p. 300 *et seq.*; Roth & Rose 2008, p. 189 *et seq.*; Craig & De Búrca 2008, p. 977; Barry & MacCulloch 1999, p. 131 *et seq.*

18 Whish 2009, p. 149.

Council Regulation No. 1/2003[19] on the implementation of the rules of competition laid down in Articles 101 and 102 of the TFEU. The new Council Regulation, which came into effect on 1 May 2004, replaces Council Regulation No. 17 which had been in force for over forty years and had been the key to the enforcement of Community competition law.[20] New Regulation No. 1/2003 thus replaces the centralised notification and authorisation system with an enforcement system based on the direct application of Articles 101 and 102.[21] Since then, Article 101(3) has been directly applicable and national courts and national competition authorities can apply it in its entirety.[22] Regulation No. 1/2003 aims at establishing a new system which ensures that competition in the common market is not distorted (more effective enforcement) and it is designed to meet the challenges of an integrated market and any future enlargement of the Community.[23] The European Commission also adopted a series of documents which complete the landmark modernisation of the European Union's antitrust enforcement rules and procedures and which should provide guidance to national courts and national competition authorities. The "Guidelines on application of Article 101(3) of the Treaty"[24] in this respect provide a useful framework and should be applied reasonably and flexibly rather than in a purely mechanical manner.[25] As pointed out by Whish,[26] additional guidance concerning the application of Article 101(1) and (3) to agreements can be found in the Commission's guidelines on vertical agreements,[27] horizontal co-operation agreements,[28] and technology transfer agreements.[29] In addition, Whish also stresses that an alternative way of satisfying Article 101(3) is to draft an agreement to satisfy one of the so-called block exemptions issued by the Council of the European Union.[30] It should also be noted that the system of block exemptions is unaffected by Regulation No. 1/2003, also known as the "Modernisation Regulation".[31]

---

19 The so called 'Modernisation Regulation', *OJ* (2003) L 1/1, (2003) 4 *CMLR* 551.

20 For a synthesis see F. Müller, 'The New Council Regulation (EC) No. 1/2003 on the Implementation of the Rules on Competition', 5 *German Law Journal* 6, 2004.

21 For an elaborated discussion of a new enforcement system, see Faull & Nikpay 2007, p. 88 *et seq.*

22 The Commission actually shares the competence to apply Art. 101(3) with national competition authorities; Whish 2009, p. 149.

23 Müller 2004; Faull and Nikpay 2007, p. 89.

24 *OJ* (2004) C 101/97.

25 L. Kjolbye, 'The New Commission Guidelines on the Application of Article 101(3): An Economic Approach to Article 81', 9 *E.C.L.R.* 566, 2004.

26 Whish 2009, p. 149 *et seq.*

27 Guidelines on Vertical Restraints, OJ (2000) C 291/1.

28 Guidelines on the applicability of Article 81 to horizontal co-operation agreements, OJ (2001) C 3/2.

29 Guidelines on the applicability of Article 81 to technology transfer agreements, OJ (2004) C 101/2.

30 "...or by the Commission under powers conferred on it by the Council"; Whish 2009, p. 149. Also see Goyder 2003, p. 112 *et seq.*; Roth & Rose 2008, at p. 226 *et seq.*

31 *E.g.* Council Regulation 19/65, JO (1965) p 533, as amended by Regulation 1215/99, OJ (1999) L 148/1 on vertical agreements and on bilateral licenses of intellectual property rights; Council Regulation 2821/71, JO (1971) L 285/46 on a block exemption in respect of standardisation agreements, research and development agreements and specialisation agreements; Council Regulation 3967/87, OJ (1986) L 378/1 on block exemptions for certain agreements in the air transport sector etc.

However, before proceeding with an economic assessment, several substantive preliminary features should be briefly addressed. First, one should tackle the question of the burden of proving that the conditions of Article 101(3) are satisfied. The "Modernisation Regulation" confirms that the burden of proof is on the Commission, on the national competition authorities or on the person opposing an agreement in a national court to show that it infringes Article 101(1). Yet, it is on the undertaking or undertakings seeking to defend an agreement to demonstrate that it satisfies the four conditions in Article 101(3).[32] Second, the abolition of the individual exemption notification system means that lawyers can no longer notify agreements to the Commission (and await an administrative stamp of approval) but must now be self-reliant and conduct their own "self-assessment of the application of that provision".[33]

Further, this brief survey shall also address the particular issue of the application of Article 101(1) and (3) to R&D agreements. The Commission generally considers that, unless there is a possibility of a foreclosure effect, R&D agreements at a rather theoretical level, far removed from the exploitation of results, fall outside Article 101(1).[34] As emphasised, co-operation between undertakings in research and technological development represents an essential tool for making EU industry internationally competitive.[35] Agreements whose true object is not R&D but the creation of a disguised cartel almost always fall within Article 101(1), whereas agreements that may have the effect of restricting competition must be analysed in their economic context (invoking the self-assessment procedures on the market player's side) where the co-operation is close to the market launch and is between competitors in an existing product or technology market or innovation markets.[36] Council Regulation 2821/71[37] introduces a block exemption for R&D agreements (expiring on 31 December 2010) where the parties' market share is below 25 percent. This block exemption shall apply for the duration of the R&D agreement and, where the results are jointly exploited, for seven years from the time the contract products are first put on the market within the common market.[38] However, this block exemption is not applicable where agreements contain severe anti-competitive restraints which directly or indirectly, in isolation or in combination with other factors under the control of the parties, infringe one of the related provisions.[39]

32 Moreover, the Commission must examine the arguments and evidence put forward by the undertakings relying on Art. 101(3); if it is unable to refute them it may be that undertakings will be taken to have discharged the burden of proof upon them; Whish 2009, p. 149. Also see Case T-168/01 *GlaxoSmithKline Services Ltd v. Commission* (2006) ECR II-2969, (2006) 5 *CMLR* 29.

33 Faull & Nikpay 2007, p. 91; Whish 2009, p. 149; Ritter, Braun & Rawlinson 2000, p. 132 *et seq.*

34 *Supra* note 22.

35 Roth and Rose, *supra* note 15, p. 587.

36 Paras 60 to 67, 'Guidelines on the applicability of Article 81 to horizontal co-operation agreements', OJ (2001) C 3/2.

37 OJ (1971), L 285/64.

38 *Ibid.*

39 Art. 5(1), OJ (1971), L 285/64.

Last but not the least, one should also address the question of whether undertakings run the risk of infringing Article 101 when they exchange information with one another. In general, whether the exchange of information between competitors infringes Article 101(1) depends on whether or not that information would normally be regarded as a business secret.[40] Commentators also note that the assessment of an information exchange depends mainly on three distinctive factors: a) the market structure; b) the type of information exchanged;[41] and c) the frequency of the information exchange.[42] In many cases the Commission has held that the exchange of information was unlawful where it was part of a mechanism for monitoring and/or enforcing compliance with some other agreement that was itself unlawful.[43] Moreover, any exchange of information about their current and future prices is likely to be regarded as giving rise to an anti-competitive price-fixing agreement.[44]

Yet, would a mere exchange of information (without an explicit information exchange agreement), which is not ancillary to some other anti-competitive practice, also amount to an infringement of Article 101? In fact, the question of whether an exchange of information could have an adverse effect on competition by providing a platform for undertakings to co-ordinate their behaviour and to act in a parallel manner without explicitly entering into agreement or concerted practice (collusive behaviour) has been addressed in several recent decisions. The European Court of Justice in *Thyssen Stahl AG v. Commission*[45] stated that ". . .it does, however, strictly preclude any direct or indirect contact between such traders, the object or effect of which is to create conditions of competition which do not correspond to the normal condition of the market in question. . ."[46] Moreover, in the *Asnef-Equifax v. Ausbanc* case the European Court of Justice explicitly stated that ". . .according to the case-law on agreements on the exchange of information, such agreements are incompatible with the rules on competition if they reduce or remove the degree of uncertainty as to the operation of the market in question with the result that competition between undertakings is restricted."[47] An effect analysis is then required as an assessment of the relevant agreements and actions, whereby a full review of the context in which the exchange of information is taking place is required.[48] In other words, any type of information that is directly or indirectly capable of being seen as collusive behaviour cannot be exchanged without causing EU competition authorities' concerns. To summarise, a survey of relevant cases shows that the assessment criteria for whether an exchange of information infringes the EU competition provisions (except in cases of business

40 Roth & Rose 2008, p. 354.

41 Here two main components arise: a) the level of detail; and b) whether the information constitutes historical information or recent data; Faull and Nikpay 2007, p. 734.

42 Faull and Nikpay 2007, p. 732.

43 Whish 2009, p. 523.

44 *Ibid.*, p. 524.

45 Case C-194/99 (2003), ECR I-10821.

46 *Ibid.*

47 Case C-238/05 (2006) ECR I-11125, (2007) 4 *CMLR* 224.

48 *Ibid.* Also see Whish 2009, p. 527; Roth & Rose 2008, p. 354.

secrets) remains unsettled, vague and is open to a judicial assessment of the relevant facts in a disputed case.[49]

2.2 *The Optimal Exchange of Information – A Synthesis of Law and Economics Scholarship*

This section identifies several principles which should provide the courts with an assessment tool for establishing whether the exchange of information could have an adverse affect on competition, and tries to compress them into a general principle. Information is a key factor in strategic decision-making and the main reason competition authorities are concerned with the exchange of information among competitors (the horizontal level) is that this practice can help firms monitor each other's behaviour. Monitoring is an essential element of collusion and allows firms to better and more promptly detect deviations facilitating the emergence of a collusive outcome.[50] In addition, one of the most important findings of economic scholarship is the notion that to tell nothing is always to say something. What that something is depends on the type of market. In some markets, parties (entrepreneurs, undertakings, competitors) who receive no information on the quality of a product will for example presume it is average in quality.[51] Thus, any type of information exchanged between undertakings may raise expectations of the other party and may induce certain behaviour of competitors to whom this information has been transmitted.

Yet, would this then imply that the simple rule of banning all information exchanges between undertakings should be introduced and enforced? This may indeed be a straightforward argument, yet the economic literature identifies several arguments supporting a more prudent approach.[52]

Analytically, it may be argued that all of the problems discussed so far are essentially problems of information – the asymmetric information problem.[53] Information is the essential ingredient of choice, and choice among scarce resources is also the central question of economics.[54] A lack of information impairs one's ability to make decisions of the fully rational kind postulated in economic discourse and

49 Roth & Rose point out that the exchange of information on prices and markets if it is intended to help co-ordinate the participants' commercial strategies generally constitutes an infringement, whereas dissemination by a trade association of anonymised, historical data may be unobjectionable. Between those two extremes, difficult issues arise and the decision on whether an information exchange amounts to an infringement rests on the specific facts of the case: Roth & Rose 2008, p. 354.

50 P. Buccirossi, 'Facilitating Practices', *in* P. Buccirossi (ed.), *Handbook of Antitrust Economics*, The MIT Press 2008, p. 318.

51 A.G. Akerlof, 'The Market for Lemons: Qualitative Uncertainty and the Market Mechanism', 84 *Quarterly Journal of Economics* 488, 1970.

52 The administration costs of such a rule may well be prohibitive.

53 The term information is used here in a very broad, general sense, encompassing "data," "knowledge" and "information".

54 For an excellent treatise on the economics of information, see J. Hirschleifer & J.G. Riley, *The Analytics of Uncertainty and Information*, Cambridge University Press (3rd reprint) 1995.

thus they must be made in the presence of uncertainty.[55] This uncertainty causes parties to make decisions different from what they would have in conditions of abundant information. Such decisions may then entail a loss or failure to obtain a gain that could have been avoided with better information.[56] Uncertainty is thus generally a source of disutility, and information is the antidote to it.[57] Hence, also almost all legal problems are, in one way or another, a direct consequence of an imperfect information problem. Shaping laws that give parties an incentive to act in a way that leaves everyone better off is a straightforward matter as long as all the parties and those who craft and enforce legal rules possess enough information. A complication arises when the necessary information is not known, or is known but not to all parties, or not to the court – information asymmetries.[58]

De Geest and Kovač identify thirteen principles which could be applied as a guiding framework for establishing the essential features of an information exchange in the light of a possible competition law infringement.[59] The first major distinction should be, as Shavel argues,[60] made between productive and redistributive information.[61] Information is productive and has a social value when it can be used to increase the value of the good for the party that possesses it – innovation.[62] The transaction costs of resource allocation would be reduced by more than the information costs, or directly affect the final resource allocation. The effects of productive information are, for example, improvements in production functions, interpreted in the widest sense to include the possible production of new commodities, the discovery of new resources (innovation) etc.[63] Since productive information can be used to produce more wealth, efficiency demands that strong incentives are given to generate and utilize such information. Note that the effort to acquire this productive information is socially desirable as long as the cost of generating it is lower than its expected value ($C^p < p\ V$). Thus, obviously a

55 E. Mackaay, *Economics of Information and Law*, Kluwer Nijhof Publishing 1982, p.107.

56 *Ibid.*, p. 108.

57 In most instances, efficiency will be enhanced by moves that improve the flow of information in society.

58 D.G. Baird, R.H. Gertner & R.C. Picker, *Game Theory and the Law* (6th ed.), Harvard University Press 2003.

59 G. de Geest & M. Kovač, 'The Formation of Contracts in the Draft Common Frame of Reference – A Law and Economics Perspective', 17 *European Private Law Review* 2, 2009.

60 S. Shavel, 'Acquisition and Disclosure of Information Prior to Sale', 25 *RAND Journal of Economics* 20, 1994. For a synthesis see M. Kovač, *Comparative Contract Law and Economics*, Edward Elgar Publishing 2011, p. 20 *et seq*.

61 This distinction originates in Hirschleifer's canonical article 'The private and social value of information and the reward to inventive activity', where Hirschleifer initially developed the distinction between *social* and *private* information and between *technological* and *pecuniary* effects of invention. The social-private information distinction is thus actually a productive-redistributive one. See J. Hirschleifer, 'The private and social value of information and the reward to inventive activity', 61 *Am. Econ. Rev.* 561, 1971.

62 Since it allows people to alter their plans accordingly, thus effecting a person's allocation decisions: *e.g.* if a war has in fact come to an end, it may now be worth planting hops again; while if there are valuable minerals under a plot of land, it may not be worth planting hops on it.

63 *E.g.* the productive value of inventing a new fertilizer is its contribution to overall production by, for example, the ability to grow better potatoes at a cheaper cost.

voluntary exchange of productive information between competing undertakings (the horizontal level) should be allowed, and should not be regarded as a competition law infringement.

Conversely, mere redistributive information has no social value and does not lead to any improvement in productive arrangements. It merely shifts wealth due to the price revaluations that take place upon utilisation of the information.[64] Despite this, individuals would have the incentive to use resources in a socially wasteful way in the generation of such information since they have effects on the distribution of the surplus.[65] Investments in discovering purely redistributive information wastes resources directly and indirectly[66] and should be discouraged.[67] Moreover, one should also deter any deliberate exchange of redistributive information between undertakings. Such an exchange should be regarded as an infringement of competition law.

De Geest introduces also the notion of *entrepreneurial information*[68] whereby the deliberate exchange of such information between undertakings should be allowed and not be regarded as a competition law infringement, yet any non-intentional one should be seen as such an infringement and be deterred.[69] Such *entrepreneurial information* should be perceived in line with Schumpeter and other members of the *Austrian School of Economics,* who emphasised the importance of individuals who add information to the market. Entrepreneurial information is information that is costly to produce, impossible to protect via intellectual property rights, and valuable to other market players so that without a right to keep that information secret, free-rider problems would discourage the production of the information.[70] This distinction also implies that the deliberate exchange of such productive information will occur only in cases where the exchange aims at innovative activity. Otherwise, undertakings would rarely voluntary reveal such productive information since a free-rider problem would impair previous relationship-specific investments and the related comparative advantage. Moreover, game theoretical models also show that the dominant strategy in this respect is not to reveal productive information, even though complete information sharing would be profitable.[71] Hence, a voluntary exchange of such productive information between horizontal competitors might be an indicator

64 *E.g.* in the case of new fertilizer for potatoes, redistributive information increases the value of shares held by the inventor.

65 Hirschleifer 1995.

66 By inducing defensive expenditures by people trying not to lose their wealth, which then just prevent redistribution rather than produce something innovative.

67 See S. Shavell, 'Acquisition and Disclosure of Information Prior to Sale', 25 *RAND Journal of Economics* 1, 1994.

68 Information which is costly to produce, either directly or indirectly, in the sense that it takes several years to obtain the expertise; G. de Geest, *Economische Analyse van het Contracten en Quasicontractenrecht*, MAKLU 1994.

69 De Geest & Kovač 2009.

70 The only way to give incentives to produce entrepreneurial information is to give a right-to-lie-and-conceal with respect to such information; De Geest and Kovač 2009.

71 See *e.g.* M. Raith, 'A General Model of Information Sharing in Oligopoly', 71 *Journal of Economic Theory* 1, 1996.

of their entrepreneurial and innovative activity where the expected benefits from such an exchange/activity exceed the individual ones.

Obviously, by exchanging information, undertakings may pursue goals other than the restriction of competition – collusion.[72] Therefore, the above listed arguments in essence call for a welfare-enhancing exchange (productive information) of information as criteria for the optimal competition law enforcement. If the information in question is productive in nature (social-welfare enhancing), then its exchange should not be regarded as a competition law infringement. Otherwise, such a *per se* illegality rule may deter undertakings from innovative activity, entrepreneurship and consequently prevent them from improving competitiveness and market efficiency.[73] Hence, the observed productive information sharing between undertakings (horizontal competitors) should not be regarded as evidence supporting the claim that the undertakings have entered into an explicit agreement. Moreover, the existence of many circumstances in which information sharing is an equilibrium formed by dominant strategies makes the inference of an explicit agreement unfounded.[74]

2.3 Entrepreneurship, Innovation and Competition – The Incentive Stream

Information and the knowledge developed on its basis lie at the heart of innovation activities. To remain competitive, firms must invest in new products and processes. In so doing, they face costs associated with R&D that often they cannot bear individually. They confront technical risk and uncertainties, which are the source of increased transaction costs[75] retarding the movement of scarce resources towards the most efficient uses, related to market acceptance and, due to the increasing complexity of new applications, they come up against the limits of their internal capabilities. To overcome this challenge, firms have responded with mergers and by co-operating (information sharing) with each other, where they share costs, pool risks and complement or enhance individual capabilities through joint R&D or technology development.[76] This emphasis on the speed of innovation is actually also reflected in the European Union's endeavours to boost its world competitiveness.

As Jorde and Teece argue, today's innovation is a simultaneous, continuous interplay between various stages, and innovation often requires lateral or horizontal linkages (very often informal, coincidental or continuous) in addition to vertical

72 Buccirossi 2008, p. 318.

73 *Vice versa,* if information that has been exchanged is redistributive in nature (it does not enhance welfare, but is just redistributive), then a prohibition does not have any of the adverse affects the policymaker would like to avoid; Buccirossi 2008, p. 318.

74 *Ibid.*, at 328.

75 From an economic point of view the risk and uncertainty of successful utilisation of an innovative activity represents a cost. It is a cost for society as whole since the resources needed for the process of allocating goods to their highest-valuing users are increased – the socially inefficient use of resources; and may lead to excessive relation-specific innovation investment, precaution investments and also represents potential opportunity costs.

76 Lorentzen & Mollgaard 2006.

relations.[77] Moreover, as they argue, for innovations to be commercialised the economic system must somehow assemble all the relevant complementary assets and create an interactive and dynamically efficient system of learning and information exchange.[78] Firms are basing more of their own innovation on knowledge assets lying beyond their boundaries (so-called "open innovation").[79] Innovation theory evidences that networks are important for innovation development and diffusion and therefore firms heavily involved in networking should outperform firms that make limited use of their networks.[80] One of the types of open innovation that has become increasingly popular recently is co-opetition, namely, simultaneous co-operation and competition between firms.[81]

Yet, the uncertainty surrounding technological change implies that it is difficult to evaluate the likely effect of inter-firm collaborations where the costs of activity are borne with certainty, whereas the benefits should be discounted with the probability of an economising failure (expected benefits). These costs of innovative activity (implying an exchange of information) encompass information exchange, research, search and all the other related costs, including the costs of a possible anti-competitive examination (self-assessment, litigation, administrative and other costs associated with self-assessment procedures). If, for example, an information exchange, which leads to entrepreneurial activity and innovation, is open to anti-competitive practices,[82] then the costs of such probable practices should be taken into account as the costs of such an entrepreneurial activity.[83]

When discussing the issues of innovation and the related optimal incentive structure one should also include the notion of entrepreneurship in the current discussion. The economic literature recognises entrepreneurship as a crucial factor in economic development.[84] The focus of the research on entrepreneurship

77 T.M. Jorde, & D.J. Teece, 'Innovation and Cooperation: Implications for Competition and Antitrust', 4 *Journal of Economic Perspectives* 3, 1990. Also see S. Martin, *Advanced Industrial Economics*, Blackwell 2000; S. Martin & P. Valbonesi, 'State Aid in Context', in G. Galli & J. Pelkmans (eds.), *Regulatory Reform and Competitiveness in Europe*, Vol. 1, Edward Elgar 2000; S. Martin & J.T. Scott, 'The Nature of Innovation Market Failure and the Design of Public Support for Private Innovation', 29 *Research Policy* 437, 2000; S. Martin, 'The Evaluation of Strategic Research Partnerships', 15 *Technology Analysis & Strategic Management* 2, 2003; S. Conway & F. Steward, *Managing and Shaping Innovation*, Oxford University Press 2009.

78 They also argue that competition policy should also allow alliances, joint ventures and horizontal agreements in commercialisation as well as exclusive practices and other conduct that is normally taken to signify monopolisation or an abuse of dominance; Jorde & Teece 1990.

79 S. Box, *OECD Work On Innovation – A Stocktaking Of Existing Work*, STI Working Paper, 2009/2.

80 P.A. Havnes & K. Senneth, 'A panel study of firm growth among SMEs in networks', 16 *Small Business Economics* 293-302, 2001.

81 D.R. Gnyawali & B.-J. Park, 'Co-opetition and Technological Innovation in Small and Medium-Sized Enterprises: A Multilevel Conceptual Model', 47 *Journal of Small Business Management* 308-330, 2009.

82 Subject to EU competition rules: self-assessment, information sharing as an infringement of EU competition rules etc.

83 Moreover, these costs are borne with certainty.

84 For a synthesis, see P. Morlacchi, 'Schumpeterian Legacies for Entrepreneurship and Networks', *in* S. Brusoni & F. Malerba (eds.), *Perspectives on Innovation*, Cambridge University Press 2007.

in management and business studies is on the processes of the discovery, evaluation and exploitation of opportunities and their effect on the creation of new undertakings.[85] According to Schumpeter, the entrepreneur's main function is combining new things or innovating, introducing a new product or new quality in a product, a new method of production, a new market, or a new organisation within an industry.[86] The notions of entrepreneurship and innovation are clearly interrelated and obviously the amount of innovation would be substantially lower without the role and function of the entrepreneur.[87]

Antitrust laws were set up to protect the freedom to engage in entrepreneurship and the freedom to innovate.[88] Let us first consider the role of competition policy in government policy that aims to foster entrepreneurial activity. A number of factors have been identified in the research literature as being associated with the level of entrepreneurial activity acting as either promoters or inhibitors. These factors influencing entrepreneurship can be classified in three main areas: a) factors inducing entrepreneurs (focusing on the individual); b) factors influencing enterprises (*i.e.* market-specific determinants of entrepreneurship); and c) factors from the surrounding environment. Another way of looking at the determinants of entrepreneurship is to distinguish between factors shaping the demand for entrepreneurship on the one hand and those influencing the supply of entrepreneurs on the other. Government policy uses instruments to shift either the demand or the supply side. One of the demand-side policies is competition policy, which has an impact on the accessibility of markets (for example, by decreasing the market power of large firms and lowering the barriers to the entry of small businesses). The role of competition policy for entrepreneurship is important. The USA, for example, does not have an entrepreneurship policy – it only has a competition policy in which small businesses play a key role.[89] Based on an empirical study of firm dynamics in ten OECD countries, Bartelsman *et al.* conclude that the entry and exit of firms (the process of "creative destruction" that Schumpeter sees as crucial for innovation and growth) depends on market concentration, among other things, confirming the role of policies fostering market competition.[90]

The competition policy therefore affects the extent to which new firms rather than incumbents fill the market gap and thus the exploitation of business opportunities

85 S. Shane & S. Venkataraman, 'The Promise of Entrepreneurship as a Field of Research', 25 *Academy of Management Review* 1, 2000.

86 J.A. Schumpeter, *The Theory of Economic Development*, Harvard University Press, 1934; J.A. Schumpeter, 'Economic Theory and Entrepreneurial History', *in* R.V. Clemence (ed.), *Essays on Entrepreneurs, Innovations, Business Cycles, and the Evolution of Capitalism*, Transaction Publishers 1949.

87 See *e.g.* M. Brouwer, 'Entrepreneurship and Uncertainty: Innovation and Competition among the Many', 15 *Small Business Economics* 149, 2000.

88 M.A. Golodner, 'Antitrust, Innovation, Entrepreneurship and Small Business', 16 *Small Business Economics* 31, 2001.

89 D. Storey, 'Entrepreneurship, Small and Medium Sized Enterprises and Public Policies', *in* Z.J. Acs & D.B. Audretsch (eds.), *Handbook of Entrepreneurship Research*, New York: Springer 2005.

90 E. Bartelsman, S. Scarpetta & F. Schivardi, *Comparative Analysis of Firm Demographics and Survival: Micro-Level Evidence for the OECD Countries*, OECD 2003.

and entrepreneurial activity.[91] Entrepreneurial small firms are also increasingly viewed as making a crucial contribution to innovative activity and technological change.[92] A new set of interventions within entrepreneurship policy was designed to promote the viability of such firms, encompassing various support mechanisms, incubators, science and technology parks, subsidies for R&D, the support of linkages between universities and the private sector, fostering industrial clusters, technology transfers and so on,[93] and for some of them the exchange of information is crucial.

When it comes to determining the effect of competition on innovation and growth, neither theory nor empirical evidence offers an unequivocal answer. The common view that is reflected in policy initiatives – that competition is necessary since it encourages new entries and keeps incumbents on their toes, forcing them to innovate – is contradicted by the theoretical industrial organisation literature and growth theories, whereas microeconometric empirical studies of the issue in the 1990s only added to the confusion.[94] Aghion and Griffith proposed an extended theoretical model, confirmed by empirical testing, that integrated some of the key insights from the various theories, taking into account that competition affects both pre- and post-innovation rents. They conclude that product market competition will have opposite effects on frontier and laggard sectors; innovation in sectors in which firms are close to the technological frontier will react positively to an increase in competition where innovation reacts less positively or even negatively in sectors in which firms are further below the technological frontier.[95] However, even when competition policy will benefit innovation in frontier sectors it needs to be taken into account that the greater uncertainty connected to the information exchange will have an adverse effect on the level of innovation and entrepreneurship.

A previous survey on substantive EU law shows that the traditional EU competition policy aims at providing level playing fields for undertakings where perfect price competition and static efficiency lie at the core of the policy focus (*i.e.* consumer surplus).[96] However, this focus on the consumer surplus might be doubtful

91 D.B. Audretsch, I. Grilo & R. Thurik, 'Explaining Entrepreneurship and the Role of Policy: A Framework', *in* D.B. Audretsch, I. Grilo, & R. Thurik (eds.), *Handbook of Research on Entrepreneurship Policy*, Edward Elgar 2007.

92 Z.J. Acs & D.B. Audretsch, 'Entrepreneurship, Innovation and Technological Change', 1 *Foundations and Trends in Entrepreneurship* 4, 2005.

93 M. Minniti, 'The Role of Government Policy on Entrepreneurial Activity: Productive, Unproductive, or Destructive', *Entrepreneurship Theory & Practice*, September 2008.

94 P. Aghion & R. Griffith, *Competition and Growth – Reconciling Theory and Evidence*, MIT Press 2005.

95 *Ibid.*

96 Just as a remark, deviations from such a benchmark are perceived as lowering welfare and are therefore the target of EU competition policy. For a thorough discussion on whether EC competition law should promote efficiency at all, see *e.g.* W. Kerber, 'Should Competition Law Promote Efficiency? Some Reflections of an Economist on the Normative Foundations of Competition Law', *in* J. Drexl, L. Idot & J. Monéger (eds.), *Economic Theory and Competition Law,* Edward Elgar 2009. Also see D. Hildebrand, *The Role of Economic Analysis in the EC Competition Rules*, 17 European Monographs, Kluwer Law International 1998.

since society's welfare can also be enhanced if radically new and improved products are introduced to the market. According to Schenk and others, society benefits from innovation by taking advantage from the development of new or improved products or new processes aimed at increasing productive efficiency.[97] A radical innovation in products may result in a significant increase in production and/or in living standards – thereby increasing social welfare.[98]

Economic literature also suggests that sharing knowledge, enhancing information flows between undertakings, and co-operation in R&D activities appear to be fundamental for creating the dynamic evolution of markets, improving cost-efficient processes and enhancing social welfare.[99] In other words, to produce/induce more important innovations it may be necessary to re-state competition policies and evaluate criteria concerning when a certain exchange of information amounts to a competition law infringement. The current EU competition law enforcement regime may thus in this respect deter innovation and technological progress. Yet, one may argue that the needed incentives and rewards for such innovative behaviour may be alternatively provided by intellectual property rights (IPR) and that the benefits of current competition law enforcement would be preserved. This IPR mechanism of "protecting" investments in R&D, however, might work but, as already contended, it is inadequate in instances where "free-rider problems" (imitation or reverse engineering) appear and hinder the operation of such an incentive structure – underinvestment in innovative activities.[100] In addition, in most industries formal IPR do not play an important role in the appropriating of innovation benefits. Studies have shown that not all innovations are patented,[101] patents are not always effective in preventing imitation,[102] and the propensity to patent differs widely across industries.[103]

---

97 Achieving lower costs has, according to them, greater welfare consequences. A price reduction merely represents a transfer of economic benefit from one producer to the consumer, whereas a reduction in costs represents a net economic benefit for society as whole by making resources available that can then be deployed in other economic activities; H. Schenk, E. Cefis, M. Grondsma & A. Sabidussi, *The Role of Innovation in Merger Policy: Europe's Efficiency Defense versus America's Innovation Markets Approach*, Tjalling C. Koopmans Research Institute working paper series no. 07-21, 2007.

98 *Ibid.*

99 For a synthesis, see S. Brusoni & F. Malerba, *Perspectives on Innovation*, Cambridge University Press 2007.

100 See *e.g.* D.B. Audretsch, W.J. Baumol, & A.E. Burke, 'Competition Policy in Dynamic Markets', 19 *International Journal of Industrial Organization* 5, 2001.

101 R. Levin *et al.*, 'Appropriating the returns from industrial research and development, 3 *Brookings Papers on Economic Activity*, 783-820, 1987; W.M. Cohen,, R.R. Nelson & J.P. Walsh, *Protecting Their Intellectual Assets: Appropriability Conditions and Why U.S. Manufacturing Firms Patent (or Not)* 2000, SSRN eLibrary.

102 E. Mansfield, 'R&D and innovation: Some empirical findings', *in* E. Griliches Zvi (ed.), *R&D, Patents and Productivity,* University of Chicago Press 1984, pp. 127-148; E. Mansfield, 'Microeconomics of Technological Innovation', *in* R.N. Landau (ed.), *The Positive Sum Strategy. Harnessing Technology for Economic Growth*, National Academy Press 1986, pp. 307-325.

103 A.K.I. Arundel, 'What percentage of innovations are patented? Empirical estimates for European firms', 27 *Research Policy* 2 1998, 127-141.

2.4 Enforcement of Competition Law and the Deterrence Paradox

After discussing the relationship between competition, entrepreneurship and innovation, where competition appears as one of the pre-conditions for inducing entrepreneurship and innovative activity, our discussion turns to the related notion of actual competition law enforcement and to the, as we argue, identified *deterrence paradox*. The analysed EU competition law provisions on information exchange and R&D horizontal agreements (besides the inefficient 25% market share criterion discussed by Ruble and Versaevel[104]) and the observed self-assessment procedures which have been in force since the introduction of the new "Modernisation Regulation"[105] actually impose needless transaction costs on entrepreneurs while they, *ex ante*, assess the benefits and costs of an entrepreneurial/innovative activity.[106]

As already pointed out, the uncertainty surrounding technological change in a highly dynamic sector implies that it is difficult to evaluate the likely effect of inter-firm collaborations where the costs of activity are borne with certainty, whereas the benefits should be discounted with the probability of an economising failure (expected benefits). These costs of innovative activity (implying an exchange of information) encompass information exchange, research, search and all the other related costs, including the costs of a possible anti-competitive examination (self-assessment, litigation, administrative and other costs associated with self-assessment procedures). If, for example, an information exchange which leads to entrepreneurial activity and innovation is open to the EU's anti-competitive practices,[107] then the costs of such probable practices should be taken into account as the costs of such an entrepreneurial activity.[108]

We argue that this evident uncertainty, along with the increased probability that an entrepreneur will be subjected to anti-trust policies and procedures (risk – increased transaction costs) combined with the vague evaluation criteria concerning when an information exchange amounts to an infringement of those EU rules may deter the optimal amount of entrepreneurial activity, and consequently also

---

104 R. Ruble & B. Versaevel, *Market Share, R&D Cooperation, and EU Competition Policy*, Cahiers de Recherche EMYLON Business School working papers no. 2009/03, 2009.

105 *E.g.* Council Regulation 19/65, JO (1965) p. 533, as amended by Regulation 1215/99, OJ (1999) L 148/1 on vertical agreements and on bilateral licences of intellectual property rights; Council Regulation 2821/71, JO (1971) L 285/46 on block exemption in respect of standardisation agreements, research and development agreements and specialisation agreements; Council Regulation 3967/87, OJ (1986) L 378/1 on block exemptions for certain agreements in the air transport sector etc.

106 The main reason for introducing the self-assessment system was to better use the Commission's resources, since "the notification regime no longer constituted an efficient tool for the protection of competition"; Faull and Nikpay 2007, p. 90.

107 Subject to the EU's competition rules: self-assessment, information sharing as an infringement of EU competition rules etc.

108 Moreover, these costs are borne with certainty.

deter innovative activity, reduce competitiveness and finally diminish social welfare – this is the identified EU competition law deterrence paradox.

Namely, as we argue, the identified expected benefits from certain marginal entrepreneurial activity may well, under the current EU enforcement regime, be outweighed by the inefficient risk shifting and increased transaction costs (self-assessment and vague rules on information exchange are a costly and uncertain process, plus the expected fines) assigned to the entrepreneur. Thus, by applying these arguments, one may establish a version of the Learned Hand Formula[109] where the identified EU *competition law deterrence paradox* may be formulated as one where the decision to start with certain entrepreneurial/innovative activity is deterred since the benefits of such activity (B), which are discounted by the probability (p) of actual commercialisation/economisation (an intrinsically uncertain event), are lower than the ex ante expected costs of such an activity (p Ea). These costs are borne with certainty (a high probability of enforcement, fines, litigation and administration costs, costs of innovative activity, search, etc. – one may call them the costs of competition law deterrence), since the self-assessment procedures must, for example, be duly made. The *deterrence paradox* may be stated as follows:

$$p\,B < p\,Ea$$

This *EU competition law deterrence paradox* then in effect hinders the optimal level of entrepreneurial activity since a certain amount of such welfare-enhancing activities will not take place and hence may be a source of stark inefficiencies (diminishing social welfare).

In other words, although competition is regarded as one of the necessary preconditions for optimal entrepreneurial activity (and consequent innovation) the current application of EU competition law criteria/policy (whose main object is the protection of perfect market competition and hence an improvement in social welfare) actually deters such an optimal level of activity and hence reduces social welfare and is a source of inefficiencies.

3. A Comment on Current Slovenian Competition Law Enforcement

Commentators note that a very important consideration in the assessment of possible infringements of Article 6 of the Slovenian "Zakon o Preprečevanju

109 Judge Learned Hand negligence formula, denoting P as the probability of a loss, L as the magnitude of the loss and B as the cost of precaution. Judge Hand wrote that a potential injurer is negligent if but only if B < PL (see *United States v. Caroll Towing Co.*, 159 F.2d 169, 173 (2d Cir. 1947). Although the Hand Formula is relatively recent, the method it encapsulates has been used to determine negligence ever since negligence was first adopted as the standard to govern accident cases: see R.A. Posner, 'A Theory of Negligence', 1 *J. Leg Stud.* 29, 1972; T.H. Terry, 'Negligence', 29 *Harv. L. Rev.* 40, 1915.

Omejevanja Konkurence" (ZPOmK-1) in cases of pure exchanges of information[110] is the type of information which has been exchanged.[111] According to those commentators, an exchange of information which is already in the public domain, of a historical nature, does not, in accordance with EU enforcement policy, infringe Article 6.[112] Yet, information which is not historical and which relates to matters such as price, capacity and cost is commercially sensitive and therefore its exchange is more likely to infringe than other types of information.[113] An analysis of the only relevant Slovenian case *Festival Ljubljana & Cankarjev Dom v. UVK*[114] shows that practically any type of information that is not publicly available cannot be exchanged without causing concerns for Slovenian competition authorities.

Obviously, the application of such broad, all inclusive and vague criteria concerning when an exchange of information between undertakings may be regarded as an infringement of Article 6 ZPOmK-1 may be a source of uncertainty and a needless increase in transaction costs. The previously described features and sources of inefficiencies clearly materialise in the observed vague and all-inclusive judicial criteria. Particularly, as we argue, such wide open and vague criteria for the enforcement of Slovenian competition law which increase risks and uncertainty may actually amount to what we identify as a *competition law deterrence paradox* which may become a source of inefficiencies, deter the exchange of information and consequently entrepreneurial activity and innovation and may, in the final instance, also reduce competitiveness. Moreover, analysis shows that such a broad implementation and enforcement of the Slovenian provision (Art. 6 ZPOmK-1) is not in accordance with the application and enforcement of Article 101 TFEU and the related case law. Hence, there is need for further improvement, harmonisation (and uniform EU competition law application) of Slovenian competition law enforcement practices as well as from the legal and from the economic viewpoint.

In addition, the proposed efficiency-based criteria would clearly introduce certainty, lower transaction costs and could also prevent the materialisation of the identified competition law deterrence paradox. The application of such economically inspired criteria may thus induce entrepreneurial activity, innovation, competitiveness and increase social wealth, which is also the main goal of competition policy. However, a statement of self-restraint is in place and further research into the related case law is needed in order to offer conclusive results.

4. Conclusion

Efficient regulatory mechanisms that induce innovation, co-operation and deter competition law infringements have recently been the subject of growing attention and intense scholarly debate. Competition is essential to the innovation process

110 Which is not ancillary to some other anti-competitive practice.
111 Repas, Martina, "Konkurenčno Pravo v Teoriji in Praksi," Uradni list, 2010.
112 *Ibid.*
113 See C-199/92 P, ZOdl. 1999, p. I-4287.
114 UVK 3072-4/00, 19.06.2001.

which in general terms enables entrepreneurship. But so too is co-operation between firms which requires the disclosure of information and may lead to inefficient collusive behaviour. Providing incentives for technological innovation (spurring the generation and utilisation of productive information), entrepreneurship and co-operation, and deterring opportunism are vital for economic growth and the maximisation of social welfare. The last few decades have witnessed the unprecedented success of European competition policy (theoretical backgrounds, implications and daily enforcements) which has resulted in related efficiency gains, benefitted European consumers and consequently substantially increased European social welfare. Yet, the related optimal trade-off between the provision of stable and optimal entrepreneurial incentives and the related EU competition law infringements has largely been exempted from the current scholarly debate. Hence, the challenge for the optimal regulation policy is to find the right balance between these seemingly conflicting issues and policies. This contribution offered an economic evaluation of optimal entrepreneurial incentive mechanisms and provides legal and economic arguments for an improved regulatory response.

The main propositions and conclusions are the following: (1) In principle, the least-cost information gatherer should produce and communicate information. (2) There should be no duty to reveal entrepreneurial information. (3) Current Slovenian competition law enforcement deters the utilisation of deliberately acquired productive information and thus hinders innovation and entrepreneurial activity. This in effect hinders the optimal level of entrepreneurial activity and may be a source of stark inefficiencies (thereby ultimately diminishing social welfare). (4) Implementation and enforcement of Slovenian competition law provision (Art. 6 ZPOmK-1) is not in accordance with the application and enforcement of Article 101 TFEU and of the related case law.

Constitutional Right to the Privacy of Correspondence and Other Means of Communication as a Potential Obstacle to Enforcement of EU and National Antitrust Law in Slovenia

J. Cepec and S. Zgaga

1. Introduction

Under Article 3(1) of the Treaty on the Functioning of the European Union (hereinafter: TFEU) the Union shall have exclusive competence in the establishing of the competition rules necessary for the functioning of the internal market. The main competition rules are contained in Chapter 1 of Title VII of Part III of the TFEU (Arts. 101-109). The TFEU contains both substantial and procedural provisions. Article 103 confers a general power on the Council after consulting the European Parliament to adopt secondary legislation (procedural) to give effect to the principles said down in Articles 101 and 102 (substantial). The procedural rules were adopted in Regulation 1/2003.[1]

According to Article 3(1) TFEU the Union has exclusive competence in the competition rules, when the firms' agreements and practices affect trade between Member States. Under one of the general principles of the Union, the principle of subsidiarity, the Member States can regulate on their own all competition rules, when the consequences have an effect only on the territory of a single Member State and the effect does not affect the trade between the Member States. In Slovenia, according to the EU Commission report,[2] about 20% of the Slovenian Competition protection office (hereinafter: UVK) cases are potentially affecting trade between Member States and consequently EU law has to be used.

Whilst Article 3 Regulation 1/2003 requires the application of Articles 101 or 102 TFEU to cases capable of affecting trade between Member States, it does not

1 Council Regulation (EC) No 1/2003 of 16 December 2002 on the implementation of the rules on competition laid down in Articles 81 and 82 of the Treaty Official Journal L 1, 04.01.2003, pp. 1-25.

2 Commission Staff Working Paper, 2009.

impose an obligation to apply EU law in "national" cases.[3] Article 3(3) states, that without prejudice to general principles and other provisions of Community law, paragraphs 1 and 2 do not apply when the competition authorities and the courts of the Member States apply national merger control laws nor do they preclude the application of provisions of national law that predominantly pursue an objective different from that pursued by Articles 81 and 82 of the Treaty.

While Member States significantly harmonised substantive competition rules, a similar convergence of procedural rules or institutional designs has not taken place.[4] Regulation 1/2003 has not provided for any harmonisation of national procedural law with respect to the conduct of inspections by national competition authorities (hereinafter: NCAs). Each NCA exercises its inspection powers in accordance with its own national law.

Under the supremacy principle, the EU law provisions prevail over the national law, even if the national law is the Constitution. Having that in mind, we discuss in this paper the issues of the very extensive investigatory powers in competition cases in EU and Slovenian national law and the possible limitations to those powers under the European Convention on Human Rights and the Slovenian Constitution. The limitations are especially interesting in the "national cases" where national law, which is very similar to the EU law, is used. Unlike EU law, national law is limited by the European Convention on Human Rights (hereinafter: ECHR) and the Slovenian Constitution.

2. Public Enforcement of Antitrust Law in EU Law – Short Review

European competition law is legislated through directly applicable Treaty provisions and regulations and thus European competition rules directly enter national legal systems and represent a higher pressure and form an important incentive to align national law.[5]

The system of enforcing Articles 101 and 102 TFEU is regulated by Regulation 1/2003. The enforcement of the antitrust provisions is decentralised, so that the Commission and the NCAs have parallel competence to apply the rules. The Commission's powers in enforcement of antitrust rules combines investigative, prosecutorial, and adjudicative functions, all in one body. In the context of public enforcement, the conditions of Article 101(3) TFEU are principally being assessed where the provision is invoked as a defence in enforcement cases.[6]

The public enforcement of EU competition law takes place in a multiple layered setting composed of EU and national rules and supervised by the Commission and

3 *Ibid.*

4 K. Cseres, 'Comparing Laws in the Enforcement of EU and National Competition Laws', *European Journal of Legal Studies*, Vol. 3, Issue 1, 2010.

5 Cseres 2010.

6 Report on the functioning of Regulation 1/2003.

27 NCAs. The Commission, NCAs and courts have the power to apply Articles 101 and 102 TFEU in full.

Before modernisation in 2004 the enforcement of European competition law was concentrated in the hands of the Commission and was an important exception to the general enforcement method of Community law by Member States' authorities. This meant, on the one hand, that the relations between Community and national competition law remained mostly unaddressed, in contrast to the judicial supremacy doctrine in other substantive areas of EU law, and, on the other hand, that competition policy was immune from general problems of multi-level governance. Modernisation and more specifically Article 3(1) of Regulation 1/2003 have imposed not only a possibility but also an obligation on the Member States' NCAs to apply Articles 101 and 102 TFEU parallel to their national competition rules when the effect on trade criterion is fulfilled, and introduced a strict supremacy standard. In fact, this meant that national provisions have to comply with the EU interpretations of Articles 101 and 102 TFEU when they are applied parallel to their national rules. In accordance with Article 3(2) and (3) of Regulation 1/2003 the convergence rule does not apply to unilateral conduct, national merger laws and laws pursuing a predominantly different objective such as unfair trade practices.[7]

The Regulation in Article 3(1) obliges NCAs and courts to apply Articles 101 and 102 TFEU to agreements or conduct capable of affecting trade between Member States. The obligation to apply EC competition law is intended to ensure that the EC competition rules are applied to all cases within their scope. Compliance also entails that the cooperation mechanisms involving the Commission and NCAs and courts, as set forth in Articles 11-13 and 15, are fully applicable in such cases and are not avoided by applying only national law.

The convergence rule contained in paragraph 2, seeks to create a level playing field by providing for a single standard of assessment which allows undertakings to design EU-wide business strategies without having to check them against all the relevant national sets of competition rules. In its current wording, the obligation of convergence covers only the application of national competition law to agreements, concerted practices and decisions by associations of undertakings. Member States remain free to enact and maintain stricter national competition laws than Article 102 TFEU to prohibit or sanction unilateral conduct.

2.1 Investigation Powers of the Commission and the Powers of the National Competition Authorities of the Member States

The Commission has under Regulation 1/2003 extensive investigatory powers. The powers are regulated in the Articles 17-22. The Commission's exercise of those powers (respectively the powers under Regulation 17, which were similar) have often been subject to judicial review by the ECJ on the ground that the Commission

7 *Ibid.*

acted in breach of the general principles of law or of fundamental rights. In many cases the Court has sought to reconcile human rights and the protection of those subject to the Commission's investigation and penalties with the task entrusted to the Commission.[8]

Article 18 of Regulation 1/2003 gives the Commission the power to obtain all necessary information from undertakings. This power can be used at any stage in the Commission's procedure and is not limited to the fact-finding stage.[9] When sending a request for information or when demanding information by decision the Commission shall state the legal basis and the purpose of the request/demand, specify what information is required and fix the time-limit within which the information is to be provided and the penalties provided for in Article 23 for supplying incorrect or misleading information. If the Commission only requests the undertaking to provide all necessary information and the undertaking does not comply with the request it can be penalised with a fine to a maximum of 1% of the undertaking's total turnover in the preceding business year. It can demand the information by adopting a decision. Article 11 of Regulation 17 foresaw a two-stage procedure whereby failure to respond to a simple request was a prerequisite to a request by decision which obliges the addressee to reply.

Article 19 empowers the Commission to interview any natural or legal person who consents to be interviewed for the purpose of collecting information relating to the subject-matter of an investigation. Article 3 of Commission Regulation 773/2004 sets out further detail in this regard. The possibility to conduct an interview pursuant to Article 19 has to be distinguished from the right of the Commission to ask oral questions during on-site inspections pursuant to Article 20(2)(e) and to impose sanctions on the undertaking concerned in case of incorrect or misleading answers.[10]

Article 20 (Inspections in business premises) enables the Commission to conduct all necessary inspections of undertakings and on their premises. The Commission can exercise the powers immediately, and does not have to make a prior request for information. To conduct an inspection the officials and other accompanying persons authorised by the Commission are empowered:

a. to enter any premises, land and means of transport of undertakings and associations of undertakings;
b. to examine the books and other records related to the business, irrespective of the medium on which they are stored;
c. to take or obtain in any form copies of or extracts from such books or records;
d. to seal any business premises and books or records for the period and to the extent necessary for the inspection;

8 A. Jones and B. Sufrin, *EC Competition Law, Text, Cases and Materials* (3rd ed.), Oxford University Press, 2008, p. 1147.

9 Commission Staff Working Paper, 2009.

10 *Ibid.*

e. to ask any representative or member of staff of the undertaking or association of undertakings for explanations on facts or documents relating to the subject-matter and purpose of the inspection and to record the answers.

Unannounced inspections in business premises have always been the Commission's most important tool in its fight against cartels and other anticompetitive behaviour. Already provided for by Regulation 17, these powers have been reinforced by Regulation 1/2003 and further enhanced by new provisions which are set out in more detail below.[11]

Article 20(2)(d) confers on Commission inspectors the power to seal premises, books and records insofar as it is necessary for the inspection. It permits a more extensive inspection to be conducted without the risk that documents will be removed.

Article 20(2)(e) empowers the Commission during inspections in business premises to "ask any representative or member of staff of the undertaking or association of undertakings for explanations of facts or documents relating to the subject-matter and purpose of the inspection and to record the answers". Failure to comply can attract fines and/or periodic penalty payments on the company in accordance with Articles 23 and 24.

Undertakings and associations of undertakings are required to submit to inspections ordered by decision of the Commission. The officials may either give advance notice of their arrival or come even without warning, "armed with a decision".[12]

Unannounced investigations are known as "dawn raids" and can be also made as simultaneous surprise arrivals at undertakings across the different EU countries. Simultaneous raids were, for example, conducted during the Polypropylene cartel investigation, where ten raids were done simultaneously.[13]

Where the officials and other accompanying persons authorised by the Commission find that an undertaking opposes an inspection ordered pursuant to this Article, the Member State concerned shall afford them the necessary assistance, requesting where appropriate the assistance of the police or of an equivalent enforcement authority, so as to enable them to conduct their inspection.

Under Article 20(8), the national judicial authority shall control that the Commission decision is authentic and that the coercive measures envisaged are neither arbitrary nor excessive having regard to the subject matter of the inspection. In its control of the proportionality of the coercive measures, the national judicial authority may ask the Commission, directly or through the Member State

11 *Ibid.*

12 Jones and Sufrin 2008, p. 1155.

13 Jones and Sufrin 2008, p. 1555; the "dawn raid" example can be found in the case *Polypropylene Cartel* OJ L230/1, 1988.

competition authority, for detailed explanations in particular on the grounds the Commission has for suspecting infringement of Articles 101 and 102 of the TFEU, as well as on the seriousness of the suspected infringement and on the nature of the involvement of the undertaking concerned.

However, the national judicial authority may not call into question the necessity for the inspection nor demand that it be provided with the information in the Commission's file. The lawfulness of the Commission decision shall be subject to review only by the Court of Justice.

The Community Courts in *Hoechst,*[14] *Roquette Frères,*[15] and more recently in *France Télécom,*[16] have confirmed the powers of investigation conferred on the Commission by Regulation 17 and now by Regulation 1/2003.[17]

In *National Panasonic*[18] an undertaking subjected to the first unannounced investigation (on the basis of Regulation 17, Art. 14(3)) claimed that the procedure infringed its fundamental rights.

It relied in particular on Article 8 ECHR and also claimed that in this case the principle of proportionality was infringed.[19] Under Article 8 ECHR everyone has the right to respect for his private and family life, his home and his correspondence. National Panasonic considered that those guarantees must be provided also to legal persons.

The ECJ pointed out that Article 8(2) of the European Convention on Human rights, in so far as it applies to legal persons, while stating the principle that public authorities should not interfere with the exercise of the rights referred to in Article 8(1), acknowledges that such interference is permissible to the extent to which it is in accordance with the law and is necessary in a democratic society in the interests of national security, public safety or the economic well-being of the country, for the prevention of disorder or crime, for the protection of health or morals, or for the protection of the rights and freedoms of others.[20]

The application of Article 8(1) ECHR was considered again in the *Hoechst* case.[21] The case arose from a dawn raid in the course of the Commission's investigation into the PVC and polyethylene cartels. Hoechst, unusually, simply refused to admit the Commission inspectors when they arrived. In short, because of

14 Joined Cases 46/87 and 227/88, *Hoechst AG* [1989] ECR 2859, para. 26.

15 Case C-94/00, *Roquette Frères SA* [2002] ECR I-9011, para. 42.

16 Cases T- 339/04 and T-340/04, *France Télécom v. Commission* [2007] ECR II-521, paras 49-53.

17 Commission Staff Working Paper Accompanying the Communication from the Commission to the European Parliament and Council, Report on the Functioning of Regulation 1/2003, Brussels 2009.

18 Case 136/79, *National Panasonic v. Commission.*

19 Jones and Sufrin 2008, p. 1155.

20 Case 136/79, *National Panasonic v. Commission*, point 19.

21 Cases 46/87 and 227/88, *Hoechst AG v. Commission.*

the non-compliance the Commission set a periodical penalty in the event of non-compliance.[22] Hoechst brought an action before the ECJ claiming that the European Commission officials had violated their obligations under Article 8 of the European Convention on Human Rights.

The ECJ stated that there was a general principle of Community law that

> any intervention by the public authorities in the sphere of private activities of any person, whether natural or legal, must have a legal basis and be justified on the grounds laid down by law, and, consequently, those systems provide, albeit in different forms, protection against arbitrary or disproportionate intervention.[23]

The court simultaneously stressed, however, that this was not the same as saying that there existed a general fundamental right concerning the inviolability of the business premises of legal persons. The court conceded that individuals had a fundamental right to inviolability of their homes, but an extension of this principle to encompass corporate premises did not necessarily follow from this conclusion.[24] The court, in making this distinction, relied on Article 8 ECHR, whose protective scope, the ECJ considered, "is concerned with the development of man's personal freedom and may not therefore be extended to business premises."[25]

> None the less, in all the legal systems of the Member States, any intervention by the public authorities in the sphere of private activities of any person, whether natural or legal, must have a legal basis and be justified on the grounds laid down by law, and, consequently, those systems provide, albeit in different forms, protection against arbitrary or disproportionate intervention. The need for such protection must be recognized as a general principle of Community law.[26]

The ECJ also stressed that: That right of access would serve no useful purpose if the Commission's officials could do no more than ask for documents or files which they could identify precisely in advance. On the contrary, such a right implies the power to search for various items of information which are not already known or

22 Jones and Sufrin 2008, p. 1159.

23 Case 46/87, point 19.

24 Jones and Sufrin 2008, p. 1157.

25 ECJ: Since the applicant has also relied on the requirements stemming from the fundamental right to the inviolability of the home, it should be observed that, although the existence of such a right must be recognized in the Community legal order as a principle common to the laws of the Member States in regard to the private dwellings of natural persons, the same is not true in regard to undertakings, because there are not inconsiderable divergences between the legal systems of the Member States in regard to the nature and degree of protection afforded to business premises against intervention by the public authorities. No other inference is to be drawn from Article 8(1) of the European Convention on Human Rights which provides that: "Everyone has the right to respect for his private and family life, his home and his correspondence". The protective scope of that article is concerned with the development of man's personal freedom and may not therefore be extended to business premises. Furthermore, it should be noted that there is no case-law of the European Court of Human Rights on that subject.

26 ECJ, point 19.

fully identified. Without such a power, it would be impossible for the Commission to obtain the information necessary to carry out the investigation if the undertakings concerned refused to cooperate or adopted an obstructive attitude.

In the case the ECJ has also pinpointed the Commission powers, stating:

> Article 14 of Regulation No. 17 deals in the first place with investigations carried out with the cooperation of the undertakings concerned, either voluntarily, where there is a written authorization, or by virtue of an obligation arising under a decision ordering an investigation. In the latter case, which is the situation here, the Commission's officials have, inter alia, the power to have shown to them the documents they request, to enter such premises as they choose, and to have shown to them the contents of any piece of furniture which they indicate. On the other hand, they may not obtain access to premises or furniture by force or oblige the staff of the undertaking to give them such access, or carry out searches without the permission of the management of the undertaking.
>
> The situation is completely different if the undertakings concerned oppose the Commission's investigation. In that case, the Commission's officials may, on the basis of Article 14(6) and without the cooperation of the undertakings, search for any information necessary for the investigation with the assistance of the national authorities, which are required to afford them the assistance necessary for the performance of their duties. Although such assistance is required only if the undertaking expresses its opposition, it may also be requested as a precautionary measure, in order to overcome any opposition on the part of the undertaking.

The role of the NCAs and the national courts in Article 20 inspections is determined by Article 20 (5, 6,7) and was also subject to ECJ case law.

The role of national courts becomes important if the undertakings do not submit to the investigation. The ECJ demonstrated the powers of national courts in the case *Hoechst* (see above). The powers of the national courts are regulated in Article 20(7). If the assistance provided by the police or by an equivalent enforcement authority is required for conducting the inspection by the Commissions officials, this requires authorisation from a judicial authority according to the national rules, and such authorisation shall be applied for. Under Article 20(8) The national judicial authority shall control that the Commission decision is authentic and that the coercive measures envisaged are neither arbitrary nor excessive having regard to the subject matter of the inspection. In its control of the proportionality of the coercive measures, the national judicial authority may ask the Commission, directly or through the Member State competition authority, for detailed explanations in particular on the grounds the Commission has for suspecting infringement of Articles 81 and 82 of the Treaty, as well as on the seriousness of the suspected infringement and on the nature of the involvement of the undertaking concerned. However, the national judicial authority may not call into question the necessity for the inspection nor demand that it be provided with the information in the Commission's file. The lawfulness of the Commission decision shall be subject to review only by the Court of Justice.

The most significant extension of the Commission investigation powers was introduced by Article 21 of Regulation 1/2003 in the form of inspections in other than business premises, including for instance the homes of directors, managers and other members of staff of the undertakings and associations of undertakings concerned.[27] This is a new power that was not provided in Regulation 17/62. However, a number of conditions must be met. First, the Commission must order the inspection by decision. Second, such a decision can only be adopted if a "reasonable suspicion" exists that books or other records related to the business and the subject matter of the inspection, which may be relevant to prove a "serious" violation of Article 101 or Article 102 TFEU, are being kept in these places. The decision must specify the subject matter and purpose of the inspection, appoint the date on which it is to begin and indicate the right to have the decision reviewed by the Court of Justice. In particular, it must state the reasons that have led the Commission to conclude that a "reasonable suspicion" exists. The Commission shall take the decision only after consulting the competition authority of the Member State in whose territory the inspection is conducted. Third, the decision ordering the inspection cannot be executed without prior authorization of the national judicial authority of the Member State concerned. The scope of review by the national court is similar to the one provided in case of opposition of companies to inspections. Fourth, the powers of the inspectors are more restricted: they do not have the power to seal the premises nor are they allowed to ask questions.[28]

3. The Restriction of the Slovenian Constitutional Right for Respect of Correspondence and Other Forms of Communication

The Slovenian Prevention of the Restriction of Competition Act (ZPOmK-1) is very similar to the EU Regulation 1/2003 which means that the Slovenian Competition protection office (the Office) has a similarly wide range of powers regarding competition protection as the EU Commission, under Regulation 1/2003.[29] The Office's investigating powers are regulated in the Article 29, where it is stated that a person employed at the Office can *inter alia*:

- review business books and other documentation, regardless of the medium on which it is written or stored;
- seize or obtain copies of or extracts from business books and other documentation in any form using photocopying devices and computer equipment of the undertaking or the agency. If it is impossible to make photocopies with photocopying devices and computer equipment belonging to the undertaking or the agency due to technical reasons, authorized persons may take away

27 Commission Staff Working Paper 2009.

28 Y. Van Gerven, 'Regulation 1/2003: Inspections ("Dawn Raids") and the Rights of Defense', *in* Carl Baudenbacher (ed.), *Neueste Entwicklungen im europäischen und internationalen Kartellrecht*, 13. St. Galler Internationales Kartellrechtsforum, 2006, pp. 327-357.

29 See also for example: *Results of the questionnaire on the reform of Member States' national competition laws after EC Regulation No. 1/2003; International Comparative Legal Guide, Enforcement of Competition Law 2009, Global Legal Group, Cartels & Leniency 2009, Country Reports, 2009.*

the business books and other documentation for the time required to make photocopies. An official note of this shall be made;
- seal all business premises and business books and other documentations pending investigation and in the scope required;
- seize items and business books and other documentation for a period no longer than twenty working days;
- perform other actions in accordance with the purpose of the investigation.

In our view, the broad investigating powers of the Office constitute a breach of the Slovenian Constitution.

According to Article 37 of the Slovenian Constitution, privacy of correspondence and other means of communication shall be guaranteed. Only a law may prescribe that on the basis of a court order the protection of the privacy of correspondence and other means of communication and the inviolability of personal privacy can be suspended for a set time where such is necessary for the institution or course of criminal proceedings or for reasons of national security. Therefore the basic conditions for infringements to this right are the following:
- prescribed by law;
- for a set time;
- court order;
- constitutional reasons; national security and institution/course of criminal proceedings.

The examination of correspondence in question *is* prescribed by law for a set time, more exactly by ZPOmK-1, however, the other two constitutional conditions are controversial.

First, ZPOmK-1 does not demand a court order. Contrary to that, it is the Office itself which issues an order for inspection, that states which investigative acts should be done and which correspondence should be examined.[30] Moreover, it is not necessary to state exactly, which documents (or correspondence) should be examined, since it is supposed to be impossible to know this in advance.[31] Instead of a court order the investigated undertaking is given an order, issued by the Office, which is an independent state body according to the ZPOmK-1, but still a part of the executive branch of government (Ministry of Economy) and certainly not a judicial body.[32]

ZPOmK-1 also states that unless otherwise stipulated by it, the provisions of the act governing the general administrative procedure shall apply to the procedure of decision-making by the Office. However, in our opinion in spite of such clear statement the investigative procedure according to the ZPOmK-1[33] is in fact by its nature a punitive procedure. Namely, the Office may *ex officio* issue an order on the commencement of

31 P. Grilc, T. Bratina, A. Galič, E. Perševan, M. Kocmut, K. Podobnik, V. Klemen, A. Vlahek, B. Zabel, *Zakon o preprečevanju omejevanja konkurence s komentarjem*, Gospodarski vestnik, Ljubljana 2009, p. 328.

32 Art. 55 ZPOmK-1.

33 Official Gazette, 36/2008, last change 26/2011.

this procedure when it learns of circumstances that raise a probability that the provisions on prohibition of restrictive measures, prohibition of abuse of dominant position or relevant provisions of the European Communion Treaty[34] have been infringed.

Also, the European Convention on Human Rights (ECHR) should be taken into consideration.[35] Its Article 6 on a right to fair trial speaks about criminal charges against the defendant. The European Court of Human Rights (ECHR) developed in its case law a term of criminal charges, which content is much broader than criminal acts *stricto sensu,* which are defined as such by law. In this manner some criminal conduct, which is strictly speaking a misdemeanour or an administrative infringement according to the written law, can also be subsumed under the term "criminal charge", if it fulfils certain conditions, which have also been developed by ECHR. In its case law, misdemeanours or other infringements, which fulfilled these conditions, were equalised to criminal acts, regarding the application of ECHR safeguards. These conditions are:
- classification of criminal conduct in the national legal system;[36]
- nature of the breach;
- type and gravity of the prescribed sentence (maximum potential sentence).[37]

The first condition is not fulfilled, since the criminal conduct is according to ZPOmK-1 in Slovenian legal system classified as a misdemeanour and not as a criminal act. However, the second and third conditions are fulfilled. With regard to the nature of the breach the procedure is instituted by a public authority, namely the Office, the procedure and measures can be enforced, the rules of ZPOmK-1 are not addressed exclusively to a specific group, but to all subjects on the market, they have a deterrent, but also punitive purpose (judging on the height of the financial penalty). And regarding the third criterion;[38] the Office has the power to issue a fine of up to 10% of the annual turnover of the undertaking involved in a concentration together with other undertakings in the group in the preceding business year,[39] which represents a grave fine.

According to the nature of many of the ZPOmK-1 misdemeanours they could be subsumed under the term criminal charge according to Article 6 ECHR. *The same findings were also made by ECHR for the EU competition law,*[40] in in the *Société Stenuit* case.[41] The fine imposed under national competition law was in this case

34 More detailed, Arts. 81 and 82 EC Treaty (now Arts. 101 and 102 TFEU).

35 Official Gazette, 33/1994, MP 7-41/1994.

36 This is a formal condition, which is not decisive and is only a starting point for analysis.

37 *Öztürk v. Germany*, Judgment ECHR 8544/79, 21 February 1984, *Engel v. The Netherlands*, Judgment ECHR 5100/71; 5101/71; 5102/71; 5354/72; 5370/72, 8 June 1976, *Lutz v. Germany*, Judgment ECHR 9912/82, 25 August 1987. See also European Court of Human Rights: Key case-law issues: Compatibility Ratione Materiae Article 6 (Notion of "Criminal Charge"), p. 1, Zakon o prekrških 1 z uvodnimi pojasnili, pp. 49-50.

38 See for example 8th part of ZPOmK-1 and its Art. 37.

39 Art. 73 ZPOmK-1.

40 For the purposes of the ECHR, the EU competition procedures and penalties should be regarded as criminal in nature.

41 Case *Société Stenuit v. France*, Judgment ECHR 11598/85, 27 February 1992.

considered of a criminal nature because of the nature of competition law itself and the severity of the fine. The European Court of Human Rights (hereinafter: ECHR) considered that the aim of the French competition law is the protection of free competition within the French market, *i.e.* general interests of society that are normally protected by criminal law. The maximum fine to which those responsible for the infringements make themselves liable namely amounts to substantial sums (in the present case 5% of the annual turnover).[42]

The main intention of the ECHR's case law is to determine basic conditions, under which criminal conduct, which is formally a misdemeanour or other criminal conduct according to national legislation, should be classified as a criminal charge and consequently also be given safeguards, which apply to criminal charges in criminal procedures *stricto sensu*. Basically, its intention is to spread the safeguards of criminal procedures to criminal conduct, which is in its quality and quantity equal to criminal acts, but is not defined as such by the legislation *(Etikettenschwindel)*. The emphasis is on the spreading of safeguards. It could be said that from a qualitative and quantitative point of view we are dealing with *de facto* criminal acts and should consequently apply equal safeguards.

This leads us first to the regulation of such investigative acts in misdemeanour procedure. According to the Act on Misdemeanours (ZP-1)[43] the Office would be a misdemeanour authority, which leads a misdemeanour procedure and issues decisions and orders according to ZP-1, more detailed according to its summary proceeding (instead of regular judicial proceeding).[44]

The more general ZP-1 regulates the possibility to seize and investigate electronic and other devices and mediums of electronic data. According to the relevant provision on this question provisions of ZP-1, which regulate the judicial proceeding, should be used.[45] Therefore, the right for respect of correspondence and other forms of communication should be equally protected in both types of misdemeanour procedure. However, even the relevant provisions of the judicial proceeding do not regulate this question themselves. They refer to *mutatis mutandis* application of relevant provisions of Slovenian Criminal Procedure Act (ZKP).[46]

Last, but not least, ZKP enables the police to get communication data from the operator of the electronic communications network.[47] Upon stricter grounds the

42 C. Wik, *The Interface between Human Rights and Competition Law, Lex Mundi European Regional Conference Antitrust & Competition Practice Group*, May 2002.

43 Official Consolidated Text, Official Gazette, 29/2011.

44 Namely, according to Slovenian ZP-1 (and based on the case law of European Court of Human Rights), grave misdemeanours are tried in judicial proceeding and only minor in summary proceeding, with a right to judicial review.

45 Art. 58, para. 2 of ZP-1.

46 Art. 67(1) ZKP, see Criminal Procedure Act, Unofficial Consolidated Text, <www.dz-rs.si/index.php?id=101&vt=1&cl=K&mandate=-1&unid=UPB|E9AF40467BDF77D9C125770A00243BD7&showdoc=1> (16 June 2011).

47 Art. 149b ZKP.

state prosecutor can also order in writing the monitoring of electronic communications using listening and recording devices and the control and protection of evidence on all forms of communication transmitted over the electronic communications network, control of letters and other parcels, control of the computer systems of banks or other legal entities which perform financial or other commercial activities or listening to and recording of conversations with the permission of at least one person participating in the conversation.[48] This regulation would give misdemeanour authorities, including the Office, wide powers in misdemeanour procedures. However, ZP-1 mentions one important limitation. Seizure and investigation of electronic and other devices and mediums of electronic data is allowed only, as long as it does not represent an infringement of the right to protection of privacy of correspondence and other means of communication. The wording of this right is the same as in the Slovenian Constitution (URS)[49] and the Slovenian Constitutional Court has already delivered many decisions, according to which Articles 149b, 150 and others represent infringement of the right to protection of the privacy of correspondence and other means of communication.[50] Since the mentioned provisions from ZKP represent such an infringement, they cannot be applied in misdemeanour procedures, neither in summary nor in the regular judicial one. In such manner ZP-1 complies with the Constitution.

On the other side the ZPOmK-1 as *lex specialis* also regulates the Office's powers. Especially relevant are those in the investigative procedure, because it strongly resembles the criminal investigative procedure, run by the investigative judge. According to Article 28 the Office issues an order for inspection, which specifies the subject-matter and purpose of the inspection, the date on which the inspection will begin, the authorized person in charge of the inspection, and most important, *the scope of powers with a notice on the penalty that can be imposed for refusal to cooperate or obstruction of an inspection*.[51] On the basis of such an order an authorized person of the Office may, among other things, *examine* the books, contracts, papers, *business correspondence*, business records and other information relating to the business of the undertaking, irrespective of their medium.[52] Only letters, notifications and other means of communication between the undertaking and its attorney, to the extent that such communications pertain to the procedure in question are considered privileged and consequently excluded from examination.[53]

If an undertaking denies access, obstructs or otherwise interferes with the inspection or where this is reasonably expected, the authorized person has the right to enter the premises or access business books and other documentation against the will of the undertaking with the assistance of the police. The Office may also issue

48 Arts. 150 and 152 ZKP.

49 Constitution of the Republic of Slovenia, Unofficial Consolidated Text, <www.us-rs.si/en/about-the-court/legal-basis/constitution/> (16 June 2011).

50 See following decisions of the Slovenian Constitutional court: U-I-25/95 and U-I-18/93.

51 Art. 28(1) ZPOmK-1.

52 Art. 29(2) ZPOmK-1.

53 Art. 32(1) ZPOmK-1.

an order imposing a penalty payment amounting up to 1% of its annual turnover in the preceding business year.[54]

In our opinion such a power of the Office could represent an infringement of human (and constitutional) right of an individual to protection of the privacy of correspondence and other means of communication, especially of the employees. The content of undertaking's correspondence can be business, but it can also be private. In the latter case the author's (employee's) right to protection of the privacy of correspondence and other means of communication would be infringed. According to the Commentary to the Slovenian Constitution, the form and content of the communication are irrelevant for constitution protection.[55] It is also irrelevant, which form of communication is used and who owns it (for example the undertaking).[56] What matters, is the expectation of privacy[57] and the ECHR decided in *Halford v. United Kingdom* that a police officer has a reasonable expectation of privacy also in her working place, even when using work phone.[58] Consequently, the Office's inspection of an undertaking's communication, where the employee has a reasonable expectation of privacy, would represent an infringement of the employee's right to privacy, guaranteed by ECHR and also by the Slovenian Constitution. Such an opinion can also be found in the Commentary to the ZPOmK-1, according to which the investigation should be limited only to business correspondence (as opposite to an employee's private letters).[59] The question is under which conditions this human right can be infringed according to the Slovenian Constitution.

There is another problem with ZPOmK-1. As already mentioned before, the procedure has a punitive nature. Namely, the Office is authorized to issue a decision establishing the existence of an infringement of ZPOmK-1 or the TFEU Treaty, and to require undertakings to bring such an infringement to an end, or even to impose on it the obligation to take reasonable measures to bring an infringement and its consequences to an end, in particular through the disposal of business or part of the undertaking's business, division of an undertaking or disposal of shares in undertakings, transfer of industrial property rights and other rights, conclusion of license and other contracts which may be concluded in the course of operations between undertakings, or ensuring access to infrastructure.[60] Such a breach is a misdemeanour, i.e. a milder type of criminal conduct. Criminal conduct is therefore a general term for any contravention of legal rules, which are defined as criminal conduct. A criminal act is the gravest criminal conduct and

54 Arts. 31(1) and 31(2) ZPOmK-1. This actually refers to the defendant's right to remain silent, which is not discussed here in details, since it is in itself a broad question.
55 L. Šturm (ed.), *Komentar Ustave Republike Slovenije*, Fakulteta za podiplomske državne in evropske študije, Ljubljana, 2002, p. 396.
56 *Ibid.*, p. 398.
57 *Ibid.*, p. 398.
58 *Halford v. United Kingdom*, Judgment ECHR 20605/92, 25 June 1997.
59 Grilc *et al.* 2009, p. 328.
60 *Ibid.*, Art. 37.

must as such be defined by law, as must be its elements and criminal sentence.[61] A misdemeanour is a lesser criminal conduct. There is no more penalty of prison for commission of a misdemeanour; however some financial penalties, especially in commercial law procedures can be even higher than financial penalties according to the Criminal Code 1 (KZ-1).[62] However, also other (legal) consequences, which cause a criminal act to be considered a graver form of criminal conduct, should be taken into consideration.

Also the principle of legality must be considered. No one may be punished for an act which had not been declared a criminal act under law, or for which a penalty had not been prescribed, at the time the act was performed. Its basic elements are therefore:

- principle of written law: any criminal act needs to be defined by written law and not in case law or theory;
- *lex certa:* any law must definite;
- prohibition of *(iuris and legis)* analogy.[63]

There is therefore a major (qualitative and quantitative) difference between a criminal act and a misdemeanour and they cannot be equalised in this manner. This applies also to the powers in procedures of investigating the commission of a criminal act or misdemeanour. Generally, the principle should be applied that the worst infringements of human rights in criminal procedure can only be approved for the (proportionally) worst criminal acts.[64] And also, the worst infringements of human rights in criminal procedure cannot be approved for petty criminal acts.[65] If this principle is transferred into the relationship between criminal acts and misdemeanours, a conclusion must be reached that generally, more infringement of human rights should be allowed in criminal procedures (for criminal acts) than in misdemeanour procedures.

And this principle was obviously applied also by the drafters of the Slovenian Constitution. Namely, the legitimate aims of restrictions of Article 37 are only two: national security or criminal procedure.

The reason of national security is covered by activity of the Slovenian intelligence agency and especially by the Act on Slovenian Intelligence Agency,[66] which regulates that the infringement can be approved by the president of the Supreme Court.[67]

The question, however is, whether the powers of the Office according to ZPOmK-1 can be subsumed under the criminal procedure. A criminal procedure,

61 L. Bavcon, A. Šelih, D. Korošec, M. Ambro & K. Filipčič, *Kazensko pravo splošni del, Uradni list*, Ljubljana, 2009, p. 122. See also Art. 28 of Slovenian Constitution and Art. 2 of Slovenian Criminal Code-1.

62 Criminal Code-1, Official Gazette, 55/2008.

63 Bacon *et al.* 2009, pp. 124-125.

64 See the decision by Slovenian Constitutional Court, U-I-25-95, para. 56-58.

65 See the regulation of special investigative methods in ZKP.

66 Official Consolidated Text, Official Gazette, 81/2006. Nastajanje slovenske ustave, pp. 418-420.

67 Art. 24 Act on Slovenian Intelligence Agency. Even with the intelligence agency this measure has to be approved by the court!

of course, presumes the commission of a criminal act and not the commission of a misdemeanour. However, is there a way to equalise criminal act and misdemeanour to justify the power to examine business correspondence according to the already mentioned ECHR case law on a criminal charge? Namely, any infringement of this right with a different purpose is considered unconstitutional and unlawful.[68]

As already mentioned, according to the nature of many of these misdemeanours they could be subsumed under criminal charges according to Article 6 ECHR. Still, this does not justify the infringement of the right of privacy of private correspondence according to ZPOmK-1. Why?

The main intention of ECHR's case law is to spread the safeguards of criminal procedures to criminal conduct, which is in its quality and quantity equal to criminal acts, but is not defined as such by legislation *(Etikettenschwindel)*. The emphasis is on the *spreading* of safeguards. However, in our case we are dealing with a completely opposite question. The question here is, whether an infringement of a right, which is by the Constitution approved only for criminal acts, can be spread also to other (lesser) criminal conduct. It is an infringement of human rights, an analogy to the detriment of the perpetrator and not to his benefit (as it is in the case law of the ECHR). Such an interpretation would be considered unconstitutional and very much distorted. Basically, one would widen the possibility of investigative acts in the misdemeanour procedure and by that infringement of a certain human right under the pretence of spreading constitutional ECHR safeguards.

From a qualitative and quantitative point of view we are dealing with *de facto* criminal acts and consequently such infringements might be legitimate, but still unconstitutional according to the current Slovenian Constitution. Namely, our Constitution is very strict and narrow regarding infringements to this right, even in comparison to the ECHR.[69] The present regulation of Article 29 ZPOmK-1 is therefore unconstitutional, because it does not follow any constitutionally regulated aim of infringement of this right.

Acting upon Article 29 ZPOmK-1 towards private correspondence currently represents a violation of Article 37 of the Slovenian Constitution due to the lack of a court order and constitutional aim of the infringement of this right. Consequently, the order for inspection according to Article 28 represents legal grounds for the submission of a constitutional complaint of the individual whose right has been violated. Also, any act which represents infringement of this constitutional right outside constitutional limits (therefore also acting upon Art. 29 ZPOmK-1) is unlawful.[70]

---

68 Šturm 2000, pp. 400-401.

69 *Ibid.*, p. 398.

70 *Ibid.*, p. 401.

4. Human Rights Arguments on the EU Competition Procedure Law

There are basically three main issues in the interface between human rights and EU competition law:

1. The nature of competition law procedures and penalties.
2. The privilege against self-incrimination (Article 6 ECHR).
3. The interface between the Commission's power of inspection and Article 8 ECHR.[71]

There is another very important issue concerning the relationship between the ECHR and the EU. States are not only members of the European Union, but as a condition of their membership to the EU, they also have to be parties to the ECHR. The corollary of this position is that the EU, being an International Organization, is not party to the ECHR. Only States can be. This creates a legal vacuum whereby no action can be brought against the EU before the ECHR, nor can one formally rely upon the ECHR and the ECHR's case law before the EU Courts.[72]

Nevertheless human rights arguments have been raised by applicants before the European Court of Justice (ECJ) since the late seventies (*Pioneer* case in 1979) and in almost all cases they have been rejected.[73]

Since we have already discussed the questions of the nature of competition law procedures and penalties in the chapter about Slovenian law, we will focus this chapter on the question of the privacy of correspondence and other means of communication, which is protected by Article 8 ECHR.

4.1 Right to Respect for Private and Family Life (Art. 8 ECHR) – Application to Commercial Premises

According to Article 8 ECHR everyone has the right to respect for his private and family life, home and correspondence. There should be no infringement by a public authority except such as is in accordance with the law and is necessary in a democratic society in the interests of national security, public safety or the economic well-being of the country, for the prevention of disorder or crime, for the protection of health or morals, or for the protection of the rights and freedoms of others. It can be seen on first glance that the ECHR has a wider selection of justifiable aims to infringe this right than the Slovenian Constitution. Consequently, a wider range of infringements is justifiable.

In the cases *Chappell v. United Kingdom*[74] and *Cremieux v. France*[75] the ECHR illustrated the nature of the safeguards required. It stated three conditions

71 *Ibid.*

72 I. Aslam & M. Ramsden, 'EC Dawn Raids: A Human Rights Violation?', *Competition Law Review*, Vol. 5, Issue 1, Art. 2, 2008.

73 Wik, 2002.

74 *Chappell v. United Kingdom* 12 EHRR 1, 30 March 1989.

75 *Cremieux v. France* 16 EHRR 357, 25 February 1993.

namely: a) requirement of a judicial warrant, b) the authorities concerned may not only act at their own discretion and c) proportionality between the interference of the applicant's right and the legitimate aim pursued.[76]

It can be recalled from the *Hoechst* case above, that the ECJ stated that the principle of the inviolability of the home in Article 8(1) ECHR does not apply to commercial premises. However, the ECHR subsequently said in the *Niemitz* case[77] that the words "private life" and "home" in Article 8(1) included certain professional or business activities or premises. The ECHR said that the

> Respect for private life comprised to a certain degree the right to establish and develop relationships with others. There was no reason of principle why the notion of "private life" should be taken to exclude professional or business activities, since it was in the course of their working lives that the majority of people had a significant opportunity of developing such relationships. To deny the protection of Article 8 on the ground that the measure complained of related only to professional activities could lead to an inequality of treatment, in that such protection would remain available to a person whose professional and non-professional activities could not be distinguished.

The ECHR said this interpretation was necessary because otherwise unequal treatment could arise, in that self-employed persons may carry on professional activities at home and private activities at their work place.[78]

The ECHR confirmed that Niemitz also applied to legal persons in *Société Colas Est*.[79] The Court held that the time had come to acknowledge that in certain circumstances the rights guaranteed by Article 8 ECHR could be construed as including the right to respect for a company's head office, branch office or place of business. The Court found that the investigators had entered the applicants' premises without a warrant, which amounted to trespass against their "home". The relevant legislation and practice did not provide adequate or sufficient guarantees against abuse. The Court considered that at the material time the relevant authority had had very wide powers and that it had intervened without a magistrate's warrant and without a senior police officer being present. The Court held unanimously that there had been a violation of Article 8.[80]

The ECHR states in the *Huvig v. France*[81] case that the Regulations must meet a three-part test: a) the measure must have some basis in domestic law, b) it must refer to the quality of the law and c) its consequences must be foreseeable and compatible with the rule of law.[82]

76 Wik 2002.
77 *Niemietz v. Germany*, 72/1991/324/396, Council of Europe: European Court of Human Rights, 16 December 1992, available at: <www.unhcr.org/refworld/docid/3f32560b4.html>.
78 Jones and Sufrin 2008, p. 1170.
79 *Société Colas Est v. France*, Case of European Court of Human Rights, April 16, 2002.
80 See The Netherlands Institute of Human Rights, <http://sim.law.uu.nl/sim/caselaw/Hof.nsf/1d4d0dd240bfee7ec12568490035df05/ffbf026de6ad30da41256b9f00442468?OpenDocument>.
81 *Huvig v. France*, Application No.11105/84, Judgment of 24 April 1990.
82 Aslam & Ramsden 2008.

Nevertheless in the *PVC Cartel II* case[83] the CFI said that the fact that the case law of the ECHR had evolved since *Hoechst* had no direct impact on the merits of the solutions adopted in the *PVC Cartel II* case. On appeal the ECJ did not find it necessary to rule on the matter.[84]

In the light of the conflict between the ECHR and the EU, the ECJ finally decided, in *Roquette Frères*[85] to endorse the ECHR's position. The ECJ reaffirmed that "the need for protection against arbitrary or disproportionate intervention by public authorities in the sphere of the private activities of any person, whether natural or legal, constitutes a general principle of Community law", took into consideration the developments that had occurred in ECHR case law since it established the general right to protection of private activity in 1989 and mentioned the judgment of the ECHR in *Colas Est*.

The ECJ held that:

> For the purposes of determining the scope of that principle in relation to the protection of business premises, regard must be had to the case-law of the European Court of Human Rights subsequent to the judgment in Hoechst. According to that case-law, first, the protection of the home provided for in Article 8 of the ECHR may in certain circumstances be extended to cover such premises (see, in particular, the judgment of 16 April 2002 in Colas Est and Others v. France, No 37971/97 in the Reports of Judgments and Decisions, § 41) and, second, the right of interference established by Article 8(2) of the ECHR 'might well be more far-reaching where professional or business activities or premises were involved than would otherwise be the case'.[86]

However, the triumph was short-lived because Regulation 1/2003 adopted in 2004 superseded the case law on Regulation 17/62.[87] From the above case law it can be seen that a tension exist in the jurisprudence between the ECJ and the ECHR on the legitimacy of the Commission's powers of investigation. The EU decided to adopt Regulation 1/2003 with even broader powers, even though the ECJ case law suggested that the powers are an infringement of basic human rights.

The question remains if the law will have to change after the Lisbon Treaty which introduced its own Charter of fundamental rights of the European Union and general principles and the possibility that the EU can accede to the ECHR.

4.2 Human Rights Issues after the Lisbon Treaty

According to the Lisbon Treaty the EU gives more attention to human rights protection. The legal basis for this is the EU's accession to the ECHR system, the

83 Cases T-305, 313-16, 318 and 335/94, *Limburgse Vinyl Maatschappij NV v. Commission*.

84 P. 1170.

85 ECJ Case C-94/00, *Roquette Frères SA v. Directeur general de la concurrence, de la consommation et de la répression des frauds*.

86 *Ibid*.

87 Aslam & Ramsden 2008.

Charter of Fundamental Rights of the European Union and the general principles defined by the European Court of Justice (ECJ) in a dialogue with national courts.[88] The Lisbon Treaty brings namely the possibility for the EU to accede to the ECHR.[89] This should bring important advantages for human rights protection in the EU, since individuals will be able to petition to the ECHR even against legal act of the EU or against legal acts of Member States, which implement EU legislation.[90]

The Charter of Fundamental Rights of the EU has also become legally binding. This means that the provisions which contain principles from this charter may be implemented by legislative and executive acts taken by institutions, bodies, offices and agencies of the Union, and by acts of Member States when they are implementing EU law, in the exercise of their respective powers. They shall be judicially cognizable only in the interpretation of such acts and in the ruling on their legality.[91] Also, the provisions of this charter are addressed to the institutions, bodies, offices and agencies of the EU with due regard for the principle of subsidiarity and to the Member States only when they are implementing EU law. They shall therefore respect the rights, observe the principles and promote the application thereof in accordance with their respective powers and respecting the limits of the powers of the EU.[92] Basically, EU bodies are obligated to implement it and take it into consideration while drafting EU law, but is there also a judicial protection of these human rights?

There is no new legal basis according to the Lisbon Treaty, which would give individuals a right to petition an EU court, similarly to the petition in the ECHR system or to the constitutional petition in Member States.[93] Namely, the charter does not extend the field of application of EU law beyond the powers of the EU or establish any new power or task for the EU, or modify powers and tasks as defined in the Treaties.[94] All that is left to individuals, whose human right has presumably been violated, is the "old" procedure according to Article 263(4) TFEU, which range has not been widened by the Lisbon Treaty. According to it any natural or legal person may, under the conditions, institute proceedings against an act addressed to that person or which is of direct and individual concern to them, and against a regulatory act which is of direct concern to them and does not entail implementing measures.[95]

The Charter includes also the right to private and family right. According to Article 7 everyone has the right to respect for his or her private and family life, home

88 M. Accetto, K. Vatovec, M. Avbelj, J. Hojnik & M. Smrkolj, *Lizbonska pogodba z uvodnimi pojasnili*, Gospodarski vestnik, Ljubljana, 2010, p. 56.
90 *Ibid.*, p. 61.
89 Art. 281 TFEU and Accetto *et al.* 2010, p. 60.
91 Art. 52(5) Charter of Fundamental Rights of the EU and Accetto *et al.* 2010, p. 58.
92 Art. 51(1) Charter of Fundamental Rights of the EU.
93 Accetto *et al.* 2010, p. 59.
94 Art. 51(2) Charter of Fundamental Rights of the EU.
95 Art. 263(4) TFEU.

and communications. This right (as any other in the Charter) can be infringed must be provided for by law, based on the principle of proportionality, only if it is necessary and genuinely meet objectives of general interest recognised by the EU or the need to protect the rights and freedoms of others in respect the essence of those rights and freedoms.[96] Also, another provision should be taken into consideration; In so far as the charter contains rights which correspond to rights guaranteed by the ECHR, the meaning and scope of those rights shall be the same as those laid down by ECHR. This provision shall not prevent EU law providing more extensive protection.[97] Since the right to private and family life is regulated also in the ECHR, its conditions of infringement must be taken into consideration.[98]

Consequently the level of protection of right to private and family life should be equal in EU and ECHR systems after the Lisbon Treaty. Additionally, if any discrepancy would remain, this could be set right with the ECHR petition system (after ECHR accession, of course).

5. Conclusion

While harmonisation and convergence of substantive competition laws is well-advanced, a similar convergence and harmonisation of the procedural rules and institutional frameworks has not taken place. The Commission has taken an initial step towards further harmonization of substantive rules on unilateral conduct and procedural rules. It has stated that it considers soft harmonisation or the adoption of certain minimum standards through legislative rules[99]

The Commission's intention to further harmonise national procedural rules for the public enforcement of EU competition law exhibits similar legal problems as the Commission's on-going ambitious policy project on private enforcement, where in fact the harmonisation of private law rules and civil procedures is at stake. In both cases, the Commission faces the problem that it lacks competence and a clear legal basis to harmonise procedural rules. The private law consequences of competition law infringements as well as the administrative procedures fall within the competence of the Member States in accordance with the principle of subsidiarity and so-called national procedural autonomy. It is, therefore, for the Member States to provide for remedies to effectuate damages actions and it is for the national courts to hear cases.[100]

With regard to the national competition authority in Slovenia a few conclusions can be drawn. First, examination of correspondence is authorized according to *lex*

96 Art. 52(1) Charter of Fundamental Rights of the EU.

97 *Ibid.*, Art. 52(3).

98 Explanations relating to the Charter of Fundamental Rights to Article 7 and Accetto *et al.* 2010, p. 613. See also M. Smrkolj, 'Pristop EU k Evropski konvenciji o človekovih pravicah', *Pravna praksa*, 34/2011.

99 Cseres 2010.

100 Cseres 2010.

specialis ZPOmK-1, but not according to the more general law on misdemeanours (ZP-1). Second, examination of private correspondence of persons, employed in the undertaking, which is under supervision, in Slovenian competition procedures represents an infringement of the constitutional right to privacy of correspondence and other means of communication. Third, such an infringement according to ZPOmK-1 is not regulated inside the limits of the Slovenian Constitution, thus it is unconstitutional. Consequently any authorized person of the Office, who acts in such manner according to ZPOmK-1, commits a breach of a constitutional right and the act represents grounds for a constitutional complaint.

In this respect the author proposes an amendment to the Slovenian Constitution, which is very narrow and strict regarding the constitutional aim for infringement of this right (also in comparison to the ECHR) in a manner of widening the scope of constitutional aims for infringement of this right according to ECHR, for example for protection of rights of other or for the economic well-being of the country. However, the constitutional conditions of prescription by law for a set time and by court order should remain intact and ZPOmK-1 should also be amended according to the proposed constitutional change.

Human rights arguments are likely to gain more weight in national and EU competition law proceedings in the future as competition law offenses are increasingly criminalised and because the EU is in a process of acceding to the ECHR. According to the latter the ECHR will gain the power to judge acts of the EU and national acts, accepted due to the implementation of the EU legislation, from the viewpoint of breach of human rights, guaranteed by the ECHR, including the right for privacy and family life. As the powers in competition procedures could fall under the “economic well-being of the country” or some other exception to Article 8 ECHR, the ECHR should decide on the adequacy of such an exemption on the basis of principle of proportionality, as established in the ECHR’s case law.

Although the possibility of the infringement of the human rights for privacy is much wider according to the ECHR than according to the Slovenian Constitution, there is still a question, what would happen, if a certain investigative power would be forced by the EU law to guarantee protection of competition in EU, which would represent an infringement of the right to private and family life according to the ECHR. Is this scenario even possible, which law prevails in this case, can a state not enforce the investigative power due to its obligations under the ECHR and what are consequences for the state according to the ECHR? These are only a couple of relevant questions.

The Recovery of Unlawful State Aid

E.M.F de Vette

1. Introduction

Generally speaking, state aid represents an intervention in the market which will generate effects on competition both within the country providing state aid and between the country and foreign economies. State aid is monitored and regulated by the European Commission (hereinafter: Commission) by requiring Member States to notify the Commission in advance. According to Article 108 of the Treaty on the Functioning of the European Union (hereinafter: TFEU), Member States may not implement state aid measures without the prior approval of the Commission. This is called the 'standstill obligation'.[1] Exclusively, the Commission has the task to examine the compatibility of proposed aid measures with the common market based on the criteria laid down in Articles 107(2) and 107(3) TFEU.

There are three exemptions to the standstill obligation. First, the Member State is relieved of its obligation to notify the planned aid measure where a measure meets all the requirements of a Block Exemption Regulation. Originally, the Commission adopted several Block Exemption Regulations on the basis of Regulation No. 994/98.[2] Part of this regulation has now been replaced by Regulation No. 800/2008.[3] Second, existing aid is not subject to the standstill obligation. This includes aid granted under a scheme which existed before a Member State's accession to the European Union or under a scheme previously approved by the Commission.[4] Third, State aid does not have to be notified to the Commission if it qualifies as '*de minimis* aid'.[5]

When state aid is not notified by Member States, or if it is put into effect before the Commission has come to a decision on its compatibility with the TFEU, the Commission may order recovery of the aid.[6] The Commission cannot, however,

1 Commission notice on the enforcement of state aid law by national courts, OJ C 85, 09.04.2009 (hereinafter: Enforcement Notice), para. 14.

2 Council Regulation (EC) No 994/98 of 7 May 1998 on the application of Articles 92 and 93 of the Treaty establishing the European Community to certain categories of horizontal State aid, OJ L 142, 14.5.1998.

3 Commission Regulation (EC) No 800/2008 of 6 August 2008 declaring certain categories of aid compatible with the common market in application of Articles 87 and 88 of the Treaty (General block exemption Regulation), OJ. L 214, 9.8.2008.

4 Enforcement Notice, para. 15.

5 Council Regulation No 1998/2006 of 15 December 2006 on the application of Articles 87 and 88 of the Treaty to *de minimis* aid.

6 Art. 14 Council Regulation (EC) No 659/1999 of 22 March 1999 laying down detailed rules for the application of Article [93] of the EC Treaty [Article 108 TFEU], OJ L 83, 27.3.1999.

order recovery solely on the basis that the aid was not notified to the Commission. This means that the Commission must conduct a full compatibility assessment regardless of whether the standstill obligation has been respected or not.[7] Where a national court is confronted with unlawfully granted aid, it must in principle order the full recovery of unlawful State aid from the beneficiary regardless of its compatibility with the common market.[8] It follows that recovery can be quicker when unlawful State aid has been contested before a national court than when it has been addressed through a complaint with the Commission.[9] Still, in both cases the recovery of the aid must take place on the national level.

This paper focuses on the practice of the recovery of unlawfully granted state aid. Section 2 first analyses the development of the European principle that unlawful state aid must be recovered. Thereafter, section 3 elaborates on the difficulties that may arise in relation to national recovery procedures. Section 4 deals with the validity of the justifications of Member States against the effectuation of recovery. Finally, section 5 scrutinises the problem of insolvency of the recipient of the state aid. In section 6 several conclusions are drawn.

2. Development of the Principle that Unlawfully Granted State Aid Must Be Recovered

2.1 Introduction

Unlawful state aid is to be understood as any new aid put into effect by a Member State in violation of Article 108(3) TFEU. Unlawful state aid includes (i) aid which is not notified; (ii) aid which is notified to the Commission but is put into effect before the Commission has come to a decision on its compatibility with the TFEU; and (iii) aid that exceeds the provisions which have been authorized.[10] As indicated above, it is the task of the Commission to examine the compatibility of proposed aid measures with the common market based on the criteria laid down in Articles 107(2) and 107(3) TFEU. It should be noted that *misused aid* refers to the situation where the aid has been approved by the Commission but where the beneficiary has used this approval in contravention with the Commission's approval decision. Most rules applicable to unlawful aid equally apply to misused aid.[11]

---

7 Case C-301/87 *France v. Commission* [1990] ECR I-307; Case C-142/87 *Belgium v. Commission* [1990] ECR I-959.

8 Case C-71/04, *Xunta de Galicia*, [2005] ECR I-7419, para. 49.

9 Enforcement Notice, para. 31.

10 C. Quigley Q.C., *European State Aid Law and Policy*, 2009, pp. 391-392.

11 T. Jestaedt, J. Derenne & T. Ottervanger (coordinators), *Study on the Enforcement of State Aid Law at National Level*, Luxembourg: Office for Official Publications of the European Communities 2006 (hereinafter: Enforcement Study), p. 513.

2.2 The Recovery Procedure

In the *Kohlegesetz* Judgment of 1973 the European Court of Justice (hereinafter: ECJ) first confirmed the Commission's power, in order for a negative decision 'to be of practical effect', to 'require repayment of aid granted in breach of the Treaty' in addition to requiring the Member State concerned to abolish or modify any aid found to be incompatible with the common market.[12] The right to recover unlawful aid is now laid down in Regulation No. 659/1999[13] (hereinafter: Procedural Regulation). Under these provisions, the Commission is not only empowered but in principle also required to order recovery of the aid.[14]

The Member States are obliged to assist the Commission. This includes ensuring that its decisions are implemented. It is furthermore the responsibility of the Member States which granted the unlawful State aid that recovery is effected without delay and in accordance with the procedures under national law, provided that these allow the immediate and effective execution of the Commission's decision.[15]

Where a national court is confronted with unlawfully granted aid, it must in principle order the full recovery of the aid from the beneficiary regardless of its compatibility with Article 107(2) TFEU or Article 107(3) TFEU.[16] The national court's recovery obligation is, however, not absolute. There may be exceptional circumstances under which the recovery of unlawful State aid is not appropriate.[17] The legal standard to be applied in this respect should be similar to the one applicable under Articles 14 and 15 of the Procedural Regulation.[18] Accordingly, defences put forward by Member States, which would not stand in the way of a recovery order by the Commission, cannot justify a national court to refrain from ordering full recovery either.[19] The Commission stresses that the standard that national courts should apply in this respect is very strict.[20]

2.3 Restoring the Previously Existing Situation

The aim of the recovery is to restore the previous situation by eliminating the distortion of the competition caused by the unlawful aid. This objective is obtained once the aid is repaid by the beneficiary of the aid who thereby forfeits the advantage which it had enjoyed over its competitors on the market.[21] Recovery of aid is not regarded as a penalty, the Commission cannot sanction a particularly

12 Case 70/72 *Commission v. Germany* [1973] ECR 813, para. 13.
13 *Supra* note 6.
14 K. Bacon, *European Community Law of State Aid*, 2009, p. 478; see Art. 14(1) Procedural Regulation.
15 Art. 14(3) Procedural Regulation.
16 Case C-71/04, *Xunta de Galicia*, [2005] ECR I-7419, para. 49.
17 Case C-39/94 *SFEI and Others*, [1996] ECR I-3547, paras 70-71.
18 Enforcement Notice, para. 32.
19 The relevant defences of Member States as to the implementation of recovery orders will be elaborated on in section 4.
20 Enforcement Notice, para. 32.
21 Quigley 2009, pp. 418-419.

serious infringement of the state aid rules by ordering recovery of an amount in excess of the value of the benefit received by the recipient of the aid.[22] As a rule, recovery of aid extends to the whole amount of the unlawful State aid granted, regardless of subsequent events. The Commission does not have a margin of appreciation as to the amount of the aid to be recovered.[23]

Nevertheless, the ECJ has ruled that Community Law does not impose an obligation of full recovery of unlawful aid in the event that the Commission subsequently declares the aid in question compatible with the common market. In the *CELF/SIDE*-case the ECJ made clear that the purpose of the prohibition in Article 108(3) TFEU is to guarantee that only compatible aid will be implemented.[24] According to the ECJ, this purpose has not been frustrated by premature payment when the Commission adopts a positive decision. This judgment has been criticized since a positive decision of the Commission does not take away the fact that there has been a serious breach of Community law in such a situation, namely a breach of the procedural obligations provided for in Article 108(3) TFEU.[25]

3. Difficulties Arising in Relation to National Recovery Procedures

3.1 Introduction

Decisions of the Commission are binding in their entirety upon the addressees (Art. 288 TFEU). According to the case law of the ECJ, this principle extends to all the organs of the relevant Member State, including the domestic courts. Any organ of a Member State to which a recovery decision is addressed is thus obliged to execute the decision. Additionally, national authorities are bound by the principle of loyal cooperation to facilitate the achievement of the Community's tasks and to abstain from any measures which could jeopardize the attainment of the Treaty objectives.[26] Member States might, however, still face difficulties in relation to the effectuation of the recovery of unlawful State aid. The following sections examine some problems and questions that may arise in this respect.

3.2 The Competent National Authority and Legal Basis for the Recovery

3.2.1 The Competent Authority

Community law does not indicate which organ of the Member State should be in charge of the practical implementation of a recovery decision. It is for the

22 Bacon 2009, p. 479.

23 *Ibid.*

24 Case C-199/06 *CELF/SIDE* [2008] ECR I-469.

25 P.C. Adriaanse, 'Appropriate Measures to Remedy the Consequences of Unlawful State Aid: An analysis of the ECJ Judgment of 12 February 2008 in Case C-199/06 (CELF/SIDE)', *Review of European Administrative Law*, Vol. 2, No. 1, pp. 79-81.

26 Case 249/85 *Albako Margarinefabrik Maria von der Linde v. Bundesanstalt für landwirtschaftliche Marktordnung* [1987] ECR 2345, para. 17.

domestic legal system of each Member State to designate the bodies that will be responsible for the implementation of the recovery decision. In most cases recovery is effectuated by the authority that granted the aid.[27] Some Member States have a central body that controls and oversees the recovery process.[28] In other Member States, however, a variety of central, regional and local bodies, as well as public entities may be involved in the recovery process. This may be an obstacle for the efficient implementation of recovery decisions. According to the Enforcement Study, which, amongst others examines the effectiveness of measures taken at the national level to enforce decisions on State aid recovery, the existence of a central body in charge of implementing recovery decisions that has ongoing contact with the Commission is more likely to ensure efficient implementation of recovery decisions.[29]

3.2.2 The Applicable Law

In most cases recovery is effected either on the basis of administrative or civil law or sometimes by a combination of both. The applicable substantive law is determined by the measure underlying the grant of the aid. The authorities have no discretion in determining whether administrative or civil rules should apply.[30] As regards the applicable procedural law, the Member State is free to choose the means of fulfilling the obligation to comply with the Commission's decision, as long as national procedures do not adversely affect the scope and effectiveness of Community law.[31] This means that both administrative and civil procedures can be applied to pursue the recovery of unlawful and incompatible aid. In most Member States, the applicable recovery procedure is determined by the nature of the measure underlying the granting of the aid. In principle, the procedural rules follow the applicable substantive rules.[32] Nevertheless, administrative procedures tend to be more efficient than civil procedures because administrative recovery orders are or can be made immediately enforceable.[33] This is not the case where recovery is sought pursuant to civil law. In civil law proceedings, the national authority seeking repayment will normally be the claimant that must apply for interim relief and support the application with evidence. In particular, this will require the establishment of urgency. According to the Enforcement Study, it could be argued that in such cases Article 14 Procedural Regulation presupposes immediate repayment of the amount of the aid. Nonetheless, given the supremacy of EC law, it must be questioned whether fundamentally reshaping the Member States' law would be appropriate.[34]

27 Enforcement Study, p. 51.
28 In France the Ministère de l'Économie et des Finances and in Germany the Bundesministerium der Finanzen.
29 Enforcement Study, p. 522.
30 *Ibid.*
31 Bacon 2009, p. 480.
32 Enforcement Study, p. 523.
33 Notice from the Commission – Towards an effective implementation of Commission decisions ordering Member States to recover unlawful and incompatible aid, OJ C 272, 15.11.2007 (hereinafter: Recovery Notice), para. 51.
34 Enforcement Study, p. 525.

The Commission notes that Member States should be aware that the choice and application of a national procedure is subject to the condition that such a procedure allows for the immediate and effective execution of the Commission's decision and that they should use fast-track procedures under national law.[35] The ECJ has laid down three conditions which must be satisfied by measures to recover aid: (i) they must be suitable for restoring the conditions of competition distorted by the grant of the aid; (ii) they must be sufficiently transparent to enable the Commission and other interested parties to identify that the first condition is satisfied, and; (iii) they must be unconditional and immediately applicable.[36]

The Dutch State Aid Recovery Bill[37] (hereinafter: legislative proposal) creates a new legal basis for implementing the obligation to recover state aid. The legislative proposal takes into account that various branches of national law may be relevant to the enforcement of European state aid law. State aid may particularly be subject to administrative law, private law and tax law. In the legislative proposal the Dutch Government has opted for an approach which is in line with the general statutory regimes applicable in these main branches of national law, these are the Dutch Civil Code (*Burgerlijk Wetboek*), the General Administrative Law Act (*Algemene Wet Bestuursrecht*) and the State Taxes Act (*Algemene Wet inzake Rijksbelastingen*). Accordingly, the implementation of State aid law is shaped and incorporated into the regular statutory rules. As a consequence, legal protection in the relevant branch will be guaranteed.[38] Alternatively, the Dutch government could have adopted a General State aid act. It is, however, likely that such an act would have conflicted with the specific legal principles that apply in different branches of the national law.

3.3 A Lack of Clarity as to the Identification of the Beneficiary and the Amount of Aid

3.3.1 The Identification of the Beneficiary of the Aid

The aid must be recovered from the undertaking that actually benefited from it.[39] Difficult questions may arise where the assets of the aid recipient have been transferred to another undertaking or where the aid has indirectly benefited undertakings other than the direct recipient of the aid. In such cases it is necessary to examine which entity should bear the obligation to repay the aid.

Where the assets have been sold at a price lower than the market value, especially to a successor company set up to circumvent the recovery order, the recovery

35 Recovery Notice, para 52.

36 Case C-209/00, *Commission v. Germany* ECR I-11695.

37 Parliamentary Papers II 2007-2008, 31 418, no. 2.

38 P.C. Adriaanse & W. Den Ouden, 'Enforcement of State Aid Law in the Netherlands: Legislative Initiative for Effective Recovery Procedures in Dutch Law', *European State Aid Law Quarterly*, 1, 2009, p. 21.

39 Case C-303/88 *Italy v.* Commission [1991] ECR I-1433, para. 57; Case C-277/00 *Germany v. Commission* [2004] ECR-I-3925, para. 75.

obligation can be extended to the third party.[40] If the sale, however, took place under non-discriminatory competitive conditions and at a market price, the purchaser cannot be regarded as having benefited from the state aid. In these cases, the previous situation is restored through repayment by the third party[41] or by repayment of the beneficiary itself where it has retained its own legal personality notwithstanding the sale.[42]

Where the true beneficiary of the aid is not the direct recipient of the financial subsidy the repayment must be ordered against the undertaking that actually benefited from it.[43] The Commission may not impose an obligation to repay part of the unlawful aid where the transfer of state resources, from which the undertaking benefited, is only hypothetical.[44] A difficulty that may arise on the national level is the lack of a legal basis to recover the aid.[45] For example, according to Dutch administrative law, the recovery of subsidies may only be ordered against direct recipients.[46] In order to solve this problem the Dutch legislative proposal allows addressing a recovery decision to third party beneficiaries who were not the addressees of the original aid decision.[47]

The identification of the beneficiary may be inherent in the recovery decision of the Commission. Still, when the Commission adopts a recovery decision regarding aid schemes, the Commission is normally not in a position to identify all the undertakings which have received unlawful and incompatible aid. This will have to be done at the start of the implementation process by the Member State concerned.[48]

If the Member State has any serious doubts as to the identity of the persons and/or entities from which it should claim recovery, it should consult the Commission for clarification.[49] In this way the problem can be solved in accordance with the principle of loyal cooperation. According to Sinnaeve this solution is not satisfactory. On the one hand it may be inappropriate to leave such important aspects of the recovery decision to the Member State, whilst, on the other hand, this practice is likely to lead to protracted discussions between the Commission and the Member State after adoption of the recovery decision, thereby delaying its implementation.[50]

---

40 Case C-277/00 *Germany v. Commission* [2004] ECR-I-3925, para. 72.

41 *Ibid.*, paras 80-81.

42 Case C-305/89 *Italy v. Commission* [1991] ECR I-1603, para. 40.

43 Case C-457/00 *Belgium v. Commission* [2003] ECR I-6931, paras 55-62.

44 Quigley 2009, p. 431.

45 P.C. Adriaanse, 'Terugvordering van onrechtmatige staatssteun: Knelpunten', *in* T. Barkhuysen *et al.* (eds.), *Europees recht effectueren, Algemeen bestuursrecht als instrument voor de effectieve uitvoering van EG-recht* 2007, pp. 223-224.

46 Art. 4:57 Algemene wet bestuursrecht (Awb).

47 Dutch Parliamentary Papers II 2007/2008, 31418, no. 3, p. 11.

48 Case C-310/99 *Italy v. Commission,* ECR I-2289, para. 91, Recovery Notice, para. 35, Bacon 2009, p. 485.

49 Case C-303/88, *Italy v. Commission* [1991] ECR I-1433, para. 58, Quigley 2009, p. 430.

50 A. Sinnaeve, 'Procedure regarding Unlawful Aid', *in* M. Heidenhain, *European State Aid Law* 2010, p. 656.

3.3.2 The Calculation of the Aid to Be Recovered

The calculation of the amount of aid may entail complex calculations which involve detailed provisions of national law and social security legislation.[51] The national authorities are best placed to make those calculations, particularly where an aid scheme is involved. For that reason the Commission is not required to identify the exact amount of aid to be recovered. Rather, it is sufficient for the Commission's decision to declare that there is an obligation to pay and to include information enabling the Member State to work out that amount without overmuch difficulty. The Commission can thus limit the Member States by clarifying in the decision how the amount is to be determined, provided that the method is sufficiently precise and leaves the Member State no discretion.[52]

Pursuant to Article 14(2) Procedural Regulation, state aid to be recovered pursuant to a recovery decision shall include interest at an appropriate rate fixed by the Commission. Interest shall be payable from the date on which the unlawful aid was at the disposal of the beneficiary until the date of its recovery. The payment of interest is necessary in view of the recovery's objective of restoring the competitive conditions prevailing prior to the grant of unlawful aid through removal of all monetary advantages derived therefrom.[53] The 'appropriate rate' refers to the customary Commission practice of calculating interest using a so-called 'reference interest rate'. The method for fixing the interest rate has been laid down in Regulation 794/2004[54] (hereinafter: Implementing Regulation), as amended by Regulation 271/2008.[55] The interest rate is in principle calculated by adding 100 basis points to the one-year market rate and is revised every year.[56] The interest rate in force at the time of the Commission's decision is normally applied to the whole period on which interest is charged.[57] However, if more than one year has passed between the date when the unlawful aid was first put at the disposal of the beneficiary and the date of the recovery of the aid, the interest rate shall be recalculated at yearly intervals, taking as a basis the rate in force at the time of recalculation.[58]

In addition, when determining the amount to be recovered, national authorities can take into account any tax paid by the beneficiary in respect of the aid, for instance by recovering only the net amount received by the beneficiary. The Commission considers that in such cases the national authorities should ensure that the beneficiary does not enjoy a further tax deduction by claiming that the

51 Bacon 2009, p. 481.

52 C-441/06 *Commission v. France* [2007] ECR I-8887, para. 29.

53 Sinnaeve 2010, p. 653.

54 Commission Regulation (EC) No 794/2004 of 21 April 2004 implementing Council Regulation (EC) No 659/1999 laying down detailed rules for the application of Article 93 of the EC Treaty, OJ L 140, 30.04.2004.

55 Commission Regulation (EC) No 271/2008 of 30 January 2008 amending Regulation (EC) No 794/2004 implementing Council Regulation (EC) No 659/1999 laying down detailed rules for the application of Article 93 of the EC Treaty, OJ L 82, 25.3.2008.

56 Art. 9 Recovery Notice.

57 Art. 11(1) Implementing Regulation.

58 Art. 11(3) Implementing Regulation.

reimbursement has reduced his taxable income, since this would mean that the net amount of the recovery was lower than the net amount initially achieved.[59]

Difficulties in determining the amount of aid are to be presented to the Commission and resolved in consultation with the Commission. Where the Commission is unable to determine either the amount granted or the parameters for calculating it, it will not require recovery. In practice, the Commission endeavours to quantify the aid amount in cases of individual aid, provided it has the necessary information to do so while for aid schemes it is usually left to the Member State to quantify the aid amount to be recovered in each individual case.[60]

4. Defences to a Recovery Order

4.1 Introduction

The Procedural Regulation provides for two exceptions from the Commission's obligation to order recovery of unlawfully granted State aid. First, pursuant to Article 14(1) the Commission shall not require recovery if doing so would be contrary to a general principle of Community law. Second, according to Article 15(1) the Commission's authority to order the recovery of aid is limited to ten years. Other justifications for the non-effectuation of the Commission's decision are the unlawfulness of the decision and the impossibility to implement the decision. This paragraph aims to provide more clarity as to the validity of the possible justifications of Member States as to the non-implementation of the Commission's decisions.

4.2 Time Limits

The recovery may be ordered by the Commission until ten years after the aid has been granted.[61] If the Commission or a Member State takes any action regarding the aid the limitation period is suspended. This is even the case when there was a simple request for information by the Commission.[62] In addition, the beneficiary does not have to be aware of the measures that caused a suspension of the period.[63] Finally, the limitation period is also suspended when proceedings are pending before the ECJ.[64] As national expiry dates to recover subsidies are often shorter according to administrative law, this might lead to difficulties. It is often argued that national expiry dates do not apply in case this would interfere with the efficient effectuation of Community law.[65] The ECJ has also made clear that Community interests must prevail over the national time limits where the

59 Recovery Notice, para. 50.
60 Sinnaeve 2010, p. 652.
61 Art. 15(1) Procedural Regulation.
62 Case T-369/00 *Département du Loiret v. Commission* [2003] ECR II-1789, paras 76-82.
63 Case T-366/00 *Scott v. Commission* [2004] ECR II-1763, paras 58-60.
64 Bacon 2009, p. 493
65 Adriaanse 2007, pp. 222-223.

Commission decision orders recovery of unlawful State aid. According to the ECJ, time limits are an expression of the principle of legal certainty. Once the Commission takes a recovery decision, the aid recipient is under no legal uncertainty as to the recovery of the aid. Accordingly, national authorities have no discretion in implementing the Commission's decision on this basis.[66]

4.3 Legitimate Expectations of the Recipient

The Commission has traditionally taken a restrictive position on the application of general principles of Community law that would prevent recovery.[67] The Commission is of the view that the most important principle, the principle of legitimate expectations, only applies where Community institutions, principally the Commission, have created such expectations.[68] According to the General Court an unofficial letter by a Member of the Commission outside the regular procedure for State aid control, according to which certain aid measures would have been approved, cannot lead to legitimate expectations that a certain aid measure has actually been approved.[69]

In most cases the Member States may thus not rely on the legitimate expectation of aid recipients that the aid will not be recovered, unless it has been granted in compliance with the procedure of Article 108(3) TFEU.[70] A 'diligent businessman' is regarded as being able to determine whether that procedure has been followed.[71] Otherwise, national authorities would in effect be able to rely on their own unlawful conduct in order to deprive decisions of the Commission of their effectiveness.[72]

The Procedural Regulation does not provide whether recovery is possible if an aid measure has been properly notified to the Commission, has been approved on that basis and has subsequently been implemented before the annulment of the favourable decision. The ECJ ruled that where an action for annulment has been brought against a positive Commission decision, the recipient of the aid cannot rely on any legitimate expectation of the lawfulness of the aid.[73]

Legitimate expectations as a means of preventing recovery have been an issue particularly in Germany. The German Administrative Act provides that an act whereby a sum of money is granted cannot be revoked, even if the aid granted was illegal.[74] Still, insofar as national law recognizes the legitimate

66 Case C-24/95 *Land Rheinland-Pfalz v. Alcan Deutschland (Alcan No. 2)* [1997] ECR I-1591, paras 33-38.
67 Sinnaeve 2010, p. 643.
68 T-129/96 *Preussag Stahl v. Commission* [1998] ECR II-609, paras 77-78.
69 *Ibid.*, paras 81-82.
70 Quigley 2009, p. 422.
71 Case C-5/89, *Commission v. Germany* [1990] ECR I-3437, para. 16.
72 *Ibid.*, para. 17.
73 Case C-199/06 *CELF/SIDE* [2008] ECR I-469, para. 68.
74 Enforcement study, p. 53.

expectations, those provisions should be interpreted in the light of the Community jurisprudence.[75]

4.4 Legal Certainty

Legal certainty is another principle that may be invoked to prevent the Commission from ordering a recovery decision, an unclear essential parameter of Article 108(2), such as the geographical scope of the Commission's decision, may pose a justification for Member States for the non-recovery of unlawful state aid.[76] In addition, the requirement of legal certainty prevents the Commission from extensively delaying the investigation as to the compatibility of the aid with the common market.[77] Cases in which this principle has been applied are rare.[78]

4.5 Proportionality

A third principle that may be invoked to prevent the Commission from issuing a recovery decision is the principle of proportionality. The Courts have, however, consistently held that this cannot frustrate recovery, as recovery is not a penalty but the logical consequence of the finding that an aid measure is unlawful. Consequently, the recovery of unlawful aid for the purpose of restoring the previously existing situation cannot in principle be regarded as disproportionate to the objectives of the Treaty with regard to state aid.[79]

4.6 Unlawfulness of the Decision

If a Member State wishes to avoid recovery of unlawful state aid on the basis that it disputes the lawfulness of the Commission's decision, it must both bring an action for annulment against the decision under Article 263 TFEU and obtain an order from the Court under Article 278 or 279 TFEU requiring interim suspension of the obligation to recover. This is because an action for annulment before the ECJ does not have automatic suspending effect.[80] Thus, in the absence of interim measures the obligation to recover remains.[81] If a Member State fails to bring an action for annulment on the basis of Article 263 TFEU, it will in principle not be able to raise the alleged illegality of the decision in subsequent proceedings.[82] Yet, in extreme cases there might be an exception to this rule, for instance where the Commission's decision contained particularly serious and manifest defects such that it could be deemed non-existent.[83] To date no state aid decision has been annulled on this ground.[84]

75 Adriaanse 2007, p. 223.
76 Case 70/72 *Commission v. Germany* [1973] ECR 813, para. 23.
77 Bacon 2009, p. 492.
78 Sinnaeve 2010, p. 646.
79 *Ibid.*, p. 647; Case C-148/04 *Unicredito Italiano* [2005] ECR I-11137, para. 113; Case C-372/97 *Italy v. Commission* [2004] ECR I-3679, paras 103-104.
80 Art. 278 TFEU.
81 Case 63/97 *Commission v. Greece* [1988] ECR 2875, paras 10-12.
82 Bacon 2009, p. 486.
83 Case C-404/97 *Commission v. Portugal* [2000] ECR I-4897, para. 35.
84 Bacon 2009, p. 486.

4.7 Impossibility to Implement the Recovery Decision

A Member State may resist an action for failure to comply with a decision if it is in practice absolutely impossible to carry out the recovery order.[85] The ECJ ruled that the only justification available to a Member State in opposing an infringement action by the Commission is to plead that it is absolutely impossible for it to implement the decision.[86] The exemption of absolute impossibility must be interpreted narrowly. The ECJ has consistently drawn a distinction between absolute impossibility and practical difficulties in recovery[87] and has rejected claims to impossibility where the aid entails examining the situation of a large number of undertakings.

The financial difficulties of a beneficiary do not render recovery impossible either. Since the ultimate objective of recovery is to end the distortion of competition, the ECJ has ruled that liquidation of the beneficiary can be regarded as an acceptable option for recovery.[88] It follows that it is only attainable to plead impossibility where the beneficiary company is liquidated and has no recoverable assets.[89] Notably, a Member State may not rely on legal provisions, practices or circumstances existing in its internal legal system in order to justify a failure to comply with its obligations under Community law.[90]

Originally, the time limit for compliance with a recovery order of the Commission was only two months. This was a rather short period for the Member States to implement the decisions of the Commission. The Commission has recognised that two months is too short in the majority of the recovery cases. Therefore, it has been decided to specify two time limits in recovery decisions: a first time limit of two months following the entry into force of the decision, within which the Member State must inform the Commission of the measures either taken or planned, and a second time limit of four months following the entry into force of the decision, within which the decision must have been actually executed.[91]

If the Member State faces unforeseen practical difficulties in the (timely) implementation of the recovery decisions or becomes aware of consequences of recovery which have been overlooked or were not envisaged by the Commission, the proper course is to submit these problems to the Commission together with proposals for suitable amendments to the decision. In such cases the Commission and the Member State are required by the principle of loyal cooperation to work together to overcome the difficulties while fully observing the European state aid rules.[92]

85 Case C-404/97 *Commission v. Portugal* [2000] ECR I-4897, para. 39.
86 Case C-348/93 Commission *v. Italy* [1995] ECR I-673.
87 Bacon 2009, p. 487.
88 Case C-52/84, *Commission v. Belgium* [1986] ECR 89.
89 Bacon 2009, p. 487.
90 Case C-5/89 *Commission v. Germany* [1990] ECR I-3437, para. 18.
91 Recovery Notice, paras 40-42.
92 Case 94/87 *Commission v. Germany* [1989] ECR 175, para. 9; Case C-404/97 *Commission v. Portugal* [2000] ECR I-4897, para. 40.

5. Insolvency of the Recipient

In the majority of the cases involving an insolvent or near-insolvent aid beneficiary it will not be possible to recover the full amount of the unlawfully granted aid as the beneficiary's assets will be insufficient to satisfy all creditor's claims. In the preceding paragraph it was established that such a situation does not constitute an exemption to the main rule that a recovery decision of the Commission must be implemented by the relevant Member State.

Still, it is observed that national insolvency laws may have a negative impact on the immediate and effective execution of the decision.[93] Likewise, the Commission held that the application of certain provisions of national bankruptcy laws may frustrate the effect of recovery decisions by allowing the company to operate despite the absence of full recovery, thus allowing the distortion to continue.[94] For this reason, the Commission has defined the obligations of Member States at the different steps of bankruptcy proceedings. First, recovery should be effectuated through the application of national insolvency laws and the Member States should immediately register its claims in the bankruptcy proceedings.[95] Second, in case the insolvency administrator refuses to register a recovery claim, the Member States should dispute that refusal.[96] Third, the authorities responsible for the execution of recovery decisions should appeal any decision by the insolvency administrator or the insolvency court which allows for a continuation of the insolvent beneficiary's activity beyond the time limits set in the recovery decision. The authorities can only support a continuation plan if they ensure that the aid will be repaid fully within the time limits foreseen in the Commission's decision. In addition, the national courts should not allow a continuation of an insolvent beneficiary in the absence of full recovery.[97] Fourth, in the case of liquidation, the Member State should oppose any transfer of assets that is not carried out on market terms and/or that is organized to circumvent the recovery decision. When the assets of the original beneficiary are transferred to a third party at a price lower than their market value or to a successor company which has been set up in order to circumvent the recovery order, the recovery order will need to be extended to that third party.[98]

6. Conclusion

In this paper it has been established that the Commission is entitled to order the recovery of unlawful and incompatible aid. In addition, the national courts must in principle order the recovery of aid where the aid had not been notified to the

93 Enforcement Study, p. 39.
94 Enforcement Notice, para. 63.
95 *Ibid.*, para 64; C-142/87 *Commission v. Belgium,* [1990] ECR I-959, para. 62.
96 Enforcement Notice, para. 65.
97 *Ibid.*, paras 66-67.
98 *Ibid.*, para. 68

Commission, irrespective of whether the aid is compatible with the common market. Recovery must always be ordered in total, regardless of subsequent events (section 2).

Difficulties may arise in relation to the identification of the competent national authority to recover unlawful aid (section 3.2). The existence of a central body in charge of implementing recovery decisions, which has ongoing contact with the Commission, may ensure the efficient implementation of recovery decisions. In addition, questions may arise as to the applicable procedural law. It was noted that administrative proceedings tend to be more efficient than civil law proceedings due to immediate enforceability. As a solution, the Dutch legislative proposal implements state aid law into the regular statutory rules applicable in the main branches of national law.

In certain cases there may be a lack of clarity as to the identification of the beneficiary and the amount of the aid (section 3.3). With respect to the identification of the beneficiary it is established that this might be problematic where assets of the recipient have been transferred to another undertaking or where the direct recipient of the aid was not the true beneficiary. In order to solve the problem that there might be no legal basis to recover the aid under such circumstances the Dutch legislative proposal allows addressing a recovery decision to third parties. In relation to the problem of the calculation of the aid it was explained that the Commission can limit itself to setting forth in its decision how the amount is to be determined, thereby leaving the issue to the Member State concerned. The method for calculating the interest on unlawfully granted aid is set out in the Implementing Regulation. In addition, the Member State should take into account any tax paid by the beneficiary in respect of the aid. Where the Member State is not able to identify the aid beneficiary or the amount of the aid it should consult the Commission, so that the problem can be solved on the basis of the principle of loyal cooperation.

Furthermore, it is questioned whether the Member States are obliged to effectuate a recovery order in every case. According the Procedural Regulation the time limit for the recovery order is ten years after the aid was granted (section 4.2). The ECJ ruled that national time limits cannot derogate from this principle. In addition, the Regulation provides that the Commission shall not require recovery if this would be contrary to a general principle of Community law. In this respect the principle of legitimate expectations (section 4.3), the principle of legal certainty (section 4.4) and the principle of proportionality (section 4.5) have been elaborated on. Generally speaking, the Commission takes a restrictive approach in the application of principles of Community law that would prevent recovery. Insofar national provisions recognize one of the principles (section 4.3-4.5), it may be argued that those provisions should be interpreted in the light of the Community jurisprudence.

If a Member State wishes to avoid recovery of aid on the basis of the alleged unlawfulness of the Commission's decision, it should both bring an action for annulment and obtain an order for suspension of the obligation to recover (section 4.6). Finally, a Member State may invoke the absolute impossibility to carry out the recovery order (section 4.7). In such case the Member State should also consult the Commission. Importantly, a Member State may not rely on legal provisions, practices or circumstances existing in its internal legal system in order to justify failure to comply with a recovery order.

Last, in case of the insolvency of the beneficiary the Member States should actively participate in the insolvency proceedings. The obligations of the Member States in such cases are laid down in the Enforcement Notice of the Commission (section 5).

Removing Obstacles in the Recovery of Unlawful State Aid

*P.C. Adriaanse**

1. The Need for Enforcement of EU State Aid Law

The financial and economic crisis of the last few years has put high pressure on EU competition policy, in particular on the application of the State aid rules. Voices were raised to relax competition rules in order to tackle problems encountered by business. Nevertheless, former Commissioner for Competition policy Neelie Kroes held on several occasions that State aid rules should be seen as part of the solution, not part of the problem.[1] Notwithstanding several initiatives to adapt its policy to the circumstances and urgent needs during the crisis, the Commission therefore continued to apply competition rules in accordance with the basic principles. Based on these principles is also a strict enforcement policy with regard to unlawfully granted State aid in the Member States.[2] Following on the State Aid Action Plan, which was adopted in 2005 as an indicative roadmap for State aid reform during the period 2005-2009, effective enforcement is considered to be essential for the effectiveness and credibility of the whole system.[3]

2. Unlawful State Aid and Recovery

State aid is considered to be unlawful when new aid (including alteration of existing aid) has been put into effect in breach of the procedural requirements as laid down in Article 108 TFEU.[4] In other words, an aid measure will be unlawful not only when it is implemented without being notified to the Commission, but also when, although notified to the Commission, it is implemented in breach of the

---

* Associate Professor of constitutional and administrative law at Leiden University. Coordinator of the Leiden Expert Group on State Aid (LEGSA) <http://law.leiden.edu/legsa>. The author can be contacted at p.c.adriaanse@law.leidenuniv.nl.

1 See *e.g.* Neelie Kroes, 'EU State aid rules – part of the solution', EStALI Conference Luxembourg 5 December 2008 (SPEECH/08/679).

2 See *e.g.* the Communication from the Commission - Temporary framework for State aid measures to support access to finance in the current financial and economic crisis (OJ 2009, C 83/1).

3 See the State Aid Action Plan, p. 13 and various Reports on Competition Policy by the Commission (*e.g.* 2004, Vol. I, pp. 4, 5 and 115; 2006, p. 18; State Aid Scoreboard spring 2006, COM(2006) 130 final, p. 33.) See also P. Anestis, S. Mavroghenis & S. Drakakakis, 'Recent developments in EC state aid policy', *The European Antitrust Review* 2005, pp. 68-72.

4 Art. 1(f) of Council Regulation (EC) No 659/1999 of 22 March 1999 laying down detailed rules for the application of Art. 93 [now Art. 108 TFEU] of the EC Treaty (OJ 1999, L 83/1).

standstill obligation as laid down in the last sentence of Article 108(3) TFEU, *i.e.* before the Commission has given its approval. According to consistent case law of the European Court of Justice and consistent practice of the Commission, it is recognised that the only way to restore the competition positions and to guarantee to all Member States an equal application of the State aid rules in situations of unlawful State aid, is to require recovery 'ex tunc' from the Member State concerned.[5] It has subsequently been confirmed that recovery could be considered as the logical consequence of the unlawful character of State aid.[6] Only through recovery, which means that the aid will have to be reimbursed by the recipient, will the latter forfeit the advantage that it enjoyed over its competitors on the market and will the situation as it existed prior to the grant of State aid be restored.[7]

3. The Ways to Recovery

Recovery can in the first place be the result of public enforcement measures initiated by the Commission. If the Commission, after closure of a formal investigation procedure, comes to a negative decision in case of unlawful aid, it shall according to Article 14 of Regulation (EC) No 659/1999 decide that the Member State concerned shall take all necessary measures to recover the aid from the beneficiary. The fact that Commission decisions are enforced not by Commission departments, but by the Member States under their national procedures, constitutes a weak point in the enforcement system. For various reasons Member States do not always give sufficient priority to the implementation of recovery decisions.

Recovery can in the second place be the result of so-called 'private enforcement' procedures initiated by private parties before national courts. Competitors and other interested parties may invoke the direct effect of the standstill clause within Article 108(3) TFEU and ask for recovery as soon as Member State authorities grant aid unlawfully. In the *CELF* case the Court of Justice also confirmed that interested parties that suffer a loss from the unlawfulness of State aid may claim for compensation for damage.[8] Such a claim may be combined with a request to the national court to order recovery of the unlawful State aid. When competitors are able to prove that they have suffered a loss caused by unlawful implementation of aid, the Member State might be obliged, according to the general principle of State liability for breach of Union law, based on cases like *Francovich* and *Brasserie du Pêcheur*,[9] to award damages against these

5 See Case C-70/72 *Commission v. Germany (Kohlegesetz)* [1973] ECR 813, para. 13.

6 See *e.g.* Case 310/85 *Deufil GmbH & Co. KG v. Commission (Deufil)* [1987] ECR 901, para. 24; Case C-142/87 *Belgium v. Commission (Tubemeuse)* [1990] ECR I-959, para. 66; Case C-305/89 *Italy v. Commission* [1991] ECR I-1603, para. 41.

7 See Case C-382/99 *Netherlands v. Commission* [2002] ECR I-5163, para. 89; Case C-298/00 P *Italy v. Commission* [2004] ECR I-4087, para. 76.

8 Case C-199/06 *CELF/SIDE* [2008] ECR I-469, paras 52-53.

9 Case C-6/90 and C-9/90 *Andrea Francovich et al. v. Italy* [1991] ECR I-5357; Case C-46/93 and C-48/93 *Brasserie du Pêcheur SA v. Germany* [1996] ECR I-1029.

competitors.[10] The effectiveness of private enforcement actions strongly depends on the willingness of interested private parties, like competitors of recipients of State aid, to start proceedings at the national level, and the willingness of national courts to rule in accordance with consistent case law of the Court of Justice.

4. Commission Initiatives

In the last few years the Commission has put particular emphasis on the importance of the recovery of unlawful State aid. In 2003, DG Competition set up a new unit within State Aid Directorate H, specifically charged with ensuring the enforcement of State aid decisions.[11] In 2007, the Commission issued a Notice which gives guidance to Member States as to how to achieve a more immediate and effective execution of recovery decisions.[12] Further guidance was provided in 2009 in a Notice on the enforcement of State aid law by national courts,[13] followed by a specific website to provide practical information to national courts and other parties involved,[14] and a Handbook on Enforcement of EU State aid law by national courts, which was issued in 2010.[15] It should be noted, however, that although the Commission itself plays an important role in this respect, it is not the only actor involved in the recovery process. As has been mentioned, Member State authorities, as well as private parties, and national courts have important roles to play, which can make the recovery process rather complex.

5. State of the Art of Recovery

Over the years the Commission has launched several studies on the enforcement of EU State aid policy at national level. A first study was carried out in 1999, followed by a comprehensive study consisting of two parts, which became available

10 See also J. Flynn, 'The Role of National Courts', *in* A. Biondi, P. Eeckhout & J. Flynn, *The Law of State Aid*, Oxford: Oxford University Press 2003, p. 333; K. Bacon, 'State Aids in the English Courts: Definition and Other Problems', *in* Biondi, Eeckhout & Flynn 2003, p. 354; U. Soltész, 'Der Rechtsschutz des Konkurrenten gegen gemeinschaftsrechtswidrige Beihilfen vor nationalen Gerichten', 7 *EuZW* 2001, p. 202-207; N. Sasserath, *Schadenersatzansprüche von Konkurrenten zur Effektivierung der Beihilfenkontrolle?*, Berlin: Ducker & Humblot GmbH 2001, p. 169.

11 The new unit has three main tasks: the effective enforcement of recovery decisions; ensuring a more coherent approach to the monitoring and control of implementation by Member States of other State aid decisions (especially conditional decisions); and procedural reform.

12 Notice from the Commission – Towards an effective implementation of Commission decisions ordering Member States to recover unlawful and incompatible State aid [2007] OJ C272/4 (Recovery Notice).

13 Commission notice on the enforcement of State aid law by national courts [2009] OJ C85/1.

14 <http://ec.europa.eu/competition/court/state_aid.html>. See also B. Brandtner, T. Beranger & C. Lessenich, 'Private State Aid Enforcement', 1 *EStAL* 2010, pp. 23-32 on p. 31.

15 <http://ec.europa.eu/competition/publications/state_aid/national_courts_booklet_en.pdf>.

in early 2006.[16] The purpose of the latter study was, amongst other things, to identify the strengths and weaknesses of national recovery procedures. In 2009, an update of the data on the application of State aid rules by national courts and their extension to the 27 Member States was presented.[17]

It should be noted that the effectiveness of the enforcement of EU law depends to a large extent on the availability of applicable and effective procedures in the Member States. The Union's legal order does not in general provide for EU law procedures.[18] Also in State aid cases, as a rule, therefore the actual enforcement will have to be carried out at the national level, depending on the applicable procedures of the Member State concerned.

While recovery has somewhat improved, it appears from these studies, however, that recovery of unlawful aid still faces a number of obstacles. To mention a few: lack of clarity as to the identity of the national body responsible for issuing a recovery decision, and of the beneficiary required to repay the aid, and as to the exact amount of the aid to be repaid; absence of a clear predetermined procedure to recover aid in some Member States; no availability or no use of interim relief to recover aid; stay of the recovery proceedings while an appeal is pending; difficulties experienced by the governmental authorities of a Member State when recovering aid at the local level; and the particular consequences for the enforcement of recovery decisions of insolvency of the beneficiary of unlawful aid. All this results, generally, in an excessive length of recovery proceedings.[19]

6. Procedures before National Courts

The recent studies also show that there has been a reasonably large increase in the number of court cases at national level in this field of State aid over the last few years in a wide variety of legal proceedings.[20] From the latest study, carried out in 2009, it appears that the increase of cases is not equally shared yet between Member States. Most of the cases before national courts deal with tax measures. In genuine private enforcement cases, initiated by competitors of recipients of

16 "Study of the Enforcement of State Aid law at the national level", reports coordinated by Jestaedt, Derenne, Ottervanger (to be downloaded from <http://bookshop.europa.eu/is-bin/INTERSHOP.enfinity/WFS/EU-Bookshop-Site/en_GB/-/EUR/ViewPublication-Start?PublicationKey=KD7506493>).

17 '2009 update of the 2006 Study on the enforcement of State aid rules at national level - FINAL REPORT', coordinated by Derenne, Kaczmarek & Clovin (<http://ec.europa.eu/competition/state_aid/studies_reports/enforcement_study_2009.pdf>).

18 See also P.C. Adriaanse *et al.*, 'Implementation of EU Enforcement Provisions: Between European Control and National Practice', 2008 *REALaw*, pp. 83-97.

19 For more extensive analysis of national State aid practice, see P.F. Nemitz (ed.), *The Effective Application of EU State Aid Procedures. The Role of National Law and Practice*, International Competition Law Series 29, Alphen a/d Rijn: Kluwer Law International 2007.

20 See the 2009 Update of the 2006 Study on the enforcement of State aid rules at national level, directed by J. Derenne, Lovells 2009 (<http://ec.europa.eu/competition/state_aid/studies_reports/enforcement_study_2009.pdf>).

unlawful State aid, only a number of competitors have been successful in their claims, in particular where they were seeking the suspension or the recovery of unlawful aid. No examples of successful claims for damages have been reported so far.[21] The way in which national courts deal with State aid cases varies.[22] The 2009 update Study on the enforcement of the State aid rules at national level shows several positive examples, as well as negative examples. A national court asked to safeguard the rights of private parties in the context of EU State aid control could face several difficult questions. One of these questions is whether a given measure should be qualified as State aid in the sense of the Treaty. Also questions on procedural issues, like time limits and aspects of evidence, may come up.

7. Loyal Cooperation

For questions on the interpretation of Union law national courts may request the European Court of Justice for a preliminary ruling on the interpretation of Article 107 TFEU.[23] It should be noted, however, that State aid questions will often concern factual questions for which reference to the European Courts will not be possible.[24] Therefore, national courts may also request assistance from the Commission by asking it to transmit to them relevant information in its possession. One could think of information concerning a pending Commission procedure, but also of other information, like copies of existing Commission decisions, factual data, statistics, market studies and economic analyses. Moreover, national courts can ask the Commission for an opinion concerning the application of the State aid rules.[25]

Since the Commission and national courts might have to decide on identical issues, like the characterisation of aid, and whether the aid should have been notified, they have, according to Article 4(3) TEU, a mutual duty of loyal cooperation in order to avoid conflicting decisions on the same issue.[26] This means that national courts will be bound by Commission decisions concerning new aid, the compatibility of aid or the (un)lawfulness of aid.[27] However, the Court of Justice confirmed in the *SFEI* case that a (preliminary) examination by the Commission cannot release the national courts from their duty to safeguard the

21 2009 Update of the 2006 Study on the enforcement of State aid rules at national level, Final Report, directed by J. Derenne, Lovells 2009, p. 2 (<http://ec.europa.eu/competition/court/state_aid_info.html>).

22 See the website of DG Competition with selected summaries of judgments from national courts: <http://ec.europa.eu/competition/court/state_aid_judgments.html>.

23 See Case C-39/94 *SFEI et al.* [1996] ECR I-3547, para. 51.

24 See J.P. Keppenne, *Guide des aides d'état en droit communautaire, Réglementation, jurisprudence et pratique de la Commission*, Brussels: Bruylant 1999, p. 313. See also M. Ross, 'State Aid and National Courts: Definitions and Other Problems – A Case of Premature Emancipation?', 37 *CMLR* 2000, pp. 401-423.

25 Enforcement Notice (OJ 2009, C 85/1), para. 77 *et seq.*

26 *Ibid.*, para. 77-78.

27 See Case C-312/90 *Spain v. Commission* [1992] ECR I-4117, para. 23. See also Keppenne 1999, p. 305.

rights of individuals in the event of a breach of the requirement to give prior notification.[28] In the *CELF* case the Court of Justice confirmed that a national court before which an application has been brought, on the basis of Article 108(3) TFEU, for repayment of unlawful State aid may not stay the adoption of its decision on that application until the Commission has ruled on the compatibility of the aid with the common market following the annulment of a previous positive decision.[29]

8. Concluding Remarks

Both public and private enforcement measures have been the subject of growing attention over the last few years. However, the enforcement of EU State aid rules, in particular recovery of unlawful State aid, still faces a number of obstacles. In order to remove these obstacles, it will be important to continue initiatives to raise awareness and understanding of the State aid rules at all levels, given the fact that the EU legal order and the national legal orders of the Member States strongly interact with respect to State aid control. Further advice and guidance by the Commission on both public and private enforcement measures should be welcomed. Member States should also make an effort to improve their efficiency, transparency and implementation of State aid policy, and as far as necessary, adapt their national laws to the requirements of EU law. Granting authorities should be helped in designing measures that are compatible with the Treaty rules, whereas national courts and other actors should be further informed about their tasks, rights, competences and obligations under the State aid regime.

28 Case C-39/94 *SFEI et al.* [1996] ECR I-3547, para. 44.

29 Case 1/09 *CELF/SIDE* [2010] ECR I-2099, para. 40.

Parallel Application of European and National Competition Law

*A. Gerbrandy**

1. Introduction

The topic of parallel application of European and national competition law can be viewed at least in two ways.

It can denote the *subsequent* application of national competition law by a national court (either a civil court, criminal court or, in appeal from a decision of a national competition authority, an administrative court) after European competition law has been enforced through Commission action on the European level. This sequential application may also occur more or less at the same time: in parallel with an action by the Commission on the European level the national competition authority or national court is confronted with the 'same' case. A civil court may be confronted with a claim for damages as a result of infringement of European competition law either after a Commission decision has been taken (a follow on action) or while the Commission is also dealing with the case. An order for injunctive relief may be asked at the national level, while at the European level a Commission decision is appealed. This subsequent application raises concerns in relation to the *ne bis in idem* principle that would prevent a company from being prosecuted twice for the same fact.[1] Civil claims for damages, either as follow-on action or stand-alone action, also raise many topics for discussion. This view on parallel application, however, is not the view I will take in this contribution to the conference "Removing Obstacles".

The second view of the topic of parallel application concerns the application by a national judge – either in appeal in administrative law proceedings or in civil or criminal law proceedings – of both European and national competition law *at the same time* to the case at hand. Because the facts of the case indicate a (possible) influence on interstate trade, next to the national competition law provisions European law provisions are applied *simultaneously*. This parallel – simultaneous – application of

* Anna Gerbrandy is Associate Professor in Public Economic Law at the Europa Institute of Utrecht University. This contribution was prepared for the conference Removing Obstacles, held in Utrecht, the Netherlands, on 20 and 21 October 2011. She would like to thank Merel Holtkamp for excellent research assistance.

1 See on this principle B. van Bockel, *The ne bis in idem principle in EU law, A conceptual and jurisprudential analysis* (Diss. Leiden), 2009.

European and national competition law provisions also raises many interesting aspects, of which I would like to discuss two: the influence this parallel application might have on national procedural law, and the possibility to ask or not to ask for a preliminary reference.

These issues will be discussed in this (short) contribution. The text is structured as follows: in the next paragraph I will consider some general starting points – well-known to all participants in the conference, but nonetheless useful as a reminder – that function as a backdrop to the discussion. In section 3 I will dwell a while on the issue of national procedural autonomy in relation to the parallel application of national and European competition law to a case at hand. In section 4 the choice to either ask or not to ask for a preliminary reference will be discussed in relation to the tensions that have become apparent in the discussion in section 3. Section 5 will contain a discussion of the *T-Mobile* case as this case provides an excellent example. I will end with some concluding remarks in section 6.

2. For Starters...

Some elements that form the backdrop to the discussion of the topic of parallel application of European and national competition law are fairly well established. To reiterate these points the following suffices.

First of all, throughout most of the EU national competition law regimes are substantively the same as the European competition law regime laid down in Articles 101 and 102 of the TFEU and in de merger control regulation. Most, though not all, national competition laws contain a provision dealing with anticompetitive agreements/cartels, a prohibition on abuse of dominant economic position and contain some form of ex-ante merger control. Merger control, of course, is slightly less relevant to the topic at hand, as in that area of competition law a one-stop shop regime is in place, in which *either* the national merger regime is applied *or* the European merger control regulation. Parallel application, in the sense of simultaneous application of national and European merger control, is therefore not very likely. This is different for the cartel prohibition and the prohibition on abuse of dominance, as the European and national prohibitions may be, or even have to be, applied simultaneously to a case that comes before a national court.

Secondly, the fact that most national competition laws are substantively the same as European competition law also brings with it that even if European law is not applicable – there is no possible effect on interstate trade – the substantive provisions being applied to a competition case are still similar (or even an exact copy) to the European competition law rules. This means that even in purely 'national' cases, European substantive competition law may play a role.[2]

2 See on this issue for Dutch Competition Law: A. Gerbrandy, 'Procedural Convergence in Competition Law', *in European Administrative Law, Top Down and Bottom up; Proceedings of the First REALaw Research Forum*, Groningen, Europa Law Publishing 2009a.

Thirdly, when applying national competition law, if there is indeed a possible interstate trade effect – that means: if both European and national law are applicable simultaneously – of course the national court is under an *obligation* to actually also apply European competition law.[3] The European competition law rules have, as is well-known, direct effect in their entirety and Regulation 1/2003 stipulates that national courts apply European competition law alongside their own competition law rules. In the course of these procedures, questions relating to the interpretation of the European competition law rules may come up, as may questions relating to conflict or tension between the application of national substantive competition law and European substantive competition law.

Fourthly, it must be pointed out that the national procedural setting in which the national judge applies both national and European competition law differs both from the procedural regime on the European level – the regime that covers the direct appeals against decisions of the Commission: European administrative law – and from the procedural regime of other Member States. Most often the application of competition law is set in general procedural law: general rules of administrative law apply to competition law cases as well as to other administrative law cases, as do general procedural rules governing civil disputes. Sometimes these administrative or civil procedural law regimes have a very long history, bound to the traditions of the Member State.

In reviewing these basic tenets of the application of national and European competition law, it becomes immediately clear that between the application of European and national competition law and the procedural rules governing the procedure at the national level, tensions and conflicts can arise. It is in this minefield that the concept of national procedural autonomy, which I will turn to in the next paragraph, plays an important role.

3. National Autonomy in Competition Law

When applying both European competition law and national competition law for some aspects of the case before the court, it has no room for autonomy (in respect of European law) at all. For example, a court will have to follow the interpretation of substantive European competition law as held by the European Court of Justice (the ECJ). It cannot contravene this interpretation without coming into conflict with European law obligations. Also, substantive national competition law cannot be interpreted contrary to European substantive competition law – at least, not in cases where European and national competition law are applied simultaneously. The principles of direct effect and supremacy govern these instances. Thirdly, the European principle of effectiveness (or the principles of effectiveness and equivalence) hems in the autonomy when applying national procedural law: the procedural environment in which the parallel application of substantive competition

3 Art. 3 Regulation 1/2003.

law takes place will have to conform to the requirements following from this European principle. Then, fourthly, there is the harmonising measure relating to procedural issues in competition law proceedings: Article 2 of Regulation 1/2003, concerning the burden of proof, is one of those harmonised rules. Although in most systems the same burden of proof follows from national procedural law (and through application of Art. 6 of the ECHR), the national court will have to follow this rule on the burden of proof in proceedings where European competition law is applied.

Finally, the national court may have to follow European substantive law, not as an obligation under European law, but as an obligation stemming from national substantive law: where national competition law explicitly refers to or is based on European competition law, the national court will also have to follow the European interpretation of the equivalent rules from the European level.

In these instances it is the European Court of Justice which, in final instance, provides the interpretation of the relevant provisions and principles.

This does not leave much room for 'autonomy' for the national courts, it seems. However, one important area where national law is relatively untouched by European law is the national procedural law governing competition law court procedures. It is here that the European Court of Justice has held that procedural autonomy is recognised: it is the national procedural environment governing procedures where parallel application of competition law is at stake. Although, of course, this procedural autonomy is fenced in by the principles of effectiveness and equivalence. Another area untouched by European law is the application of substantive law in cases without any European law aspect: competition cases which have no impact on interstate trade are governed solely by national competition law. In theory – but probably not often in practice – this means that the national substantive competition provision can be applied or interpreted in a way that is not in conformity with European substantive competition law. National procedural law, in such cases, is also left in peace by the European principles of effectiveness and equivalence of course.

This means that it is not the European Court of Justice, but the highest national court, which gives a final interpretation to the relevant provisions and principles (albeit within the limits of the principle of effectiveness). It is the ECJ, however, which decides on the limits of procedural autonomy.

However, in practice it will not be logical for a judge to keep to a 'national' interpretation of, for example, anti-competitive effect in purely national cases and conform to a 'European' interpretation of the same topic in cases where parallel application is at stake: this would mean that within one Member State the notion of anti-competitive effect, would be interpreted differently according to whether or not the case gives rise to an interstate effect. Unless national competition law explicitly refers to the possibility of, for example, an extra national exemption, this scenario is not very likely, especially not for courts involved with more than an occasional competition law case. The European interpretation of the notion of 'anticompetitive effect' will, most probably, also be used in purely national competition law cases: the interpretation will spill over from cases in which European and national competition law is applied simultaneously to purely national law cases.[4]

If it is for the ECJ to interpret substantive (competition) law, but for the national court to provide for the national procedural environment, it is important to decide whether a particular question is of a substantive or a procedural nature. The question also arises who has the final say on this matter: who decides what is substantive and what is procedural? I will come back to this point in section 4.

A very important way in which national procedural law may be influenced by European law is through parallelism: the national court finds solutions or interpretations of European administrative law – the procedural law that governs direct appeals against Commission decisions at the General Court and the ECJ – and uses these solutions in its own procedural environment. For example, a national court confronted with a question of how to review complex economic assessments, might find inspiration in the way the ECJ deals with the intensity of judicial review in proceedings against the Commission. The same may be true for issues of standing, hearing rights in the administrative stage of the proceedings, notions relation to the standard or burden of proof etc. In doing so, the national court spontaneously moves to using European procedural law solutions – there is no European obligation to do so. Also in this way national procedural law governing competition law cases will become Europeanised procedural (competition) law.

4. Preliminary References

When confronted with a question relating to the interpretation of European law, a judge may decide to stay the proceedings and ask for a preliminary ruling. Obviously, and as is well known, a highest court is under an obligation to refer a question to the ECJ when confronted with a matter of unclear interpretation of substantive European competition law. Other courts also have this possibility but are under no obligation. The same holds true for the interpretation of the principle of effectiveness: if a question arises as to the boundaries or interpretation of this principle, it is for the ECJ to provide a final interpretation.

On the other points, however, the situation is less clear-cut. It seems to be accepted that national courts may also ask for a preliminary ruling on the interpretation of *national* substantive competition law, where such national law is clearly based on European substantive competition law.[5] However, whether there is also

4 See on this effect also A. Gerbrandy, *Convergentie in het mededingingsrecht; de invloed van het EG-recht op materiële toepassing, toegang, bewijs en toetsing bij de Nederlandse mededingingsbestuursrechter in het licht van effectieve rechtsbescherming*, The Hague, Boom Juridische uitgevers 2009b and Gerbrandy 2009a.

5 See Case C-28/95, *Leur-Bloem, ECR* 1997, I-4161.

an obligation (for a highest court) is not clear. On the one hand, it can be argued that in a system where national and European substantive competition law are very much intertwined, and where its application by either Commission and/or national competition authorities is very much integrated to form 'European' enforcement of substantive national-European competition law, the obligation to refer an interpretative matter to the ECJ for final arbitration even when that interpretation relates to national competition law (where the competition law is a copy of or based on European competition law) can be extended to cover these instances as well. From the point of view of the effective enforcement of competition law throughout the European Union, this position can be defended. Also, as it is almost impossible in practice to have one interpretation of competition law for European law governed cases and another for national competition law cases, the distinction between national and European competition law becomes blurred.

On the other hand, it can be argued that it is not for the ECJ to claim for itself the function of giving the final interpretation of national substantive law, even where such law is based on European competition law provisions. Indeed, the choice to base national competition law on European competition law is still a choice – though apparently there is much less room for candidate Member States to choose not to copy the European competition law provisions into national law than there was for 'old' Member States. If it is a choice, it can also be undone. Therefore, this aspect of national substantive law is part of the national autonomy and therefore, also part of the autonomous room for national courts.

On matters of national procedural law – the heart of national procedural autonomy – there seems to be no obligation to refer questions to the ECJ as far as the boundaries staked by the principle of effectiveness are not in sight. The interesting question here is whether there is a possibility, in parallel with the possibility to ask preliminary questions on the interpretation of national substantive competition law, to ask questions relating to Europeanised national procedural law. Where national courts have copied – in parallelism as referred to above – a procedural 'solution' from European procedural law, such as the intensity of judicial review, matters of standing rights or burden of proof, would it not be possible to ask for a preliminary ruling of the ECJ relating to these issues of procedural law? For example, when confronted with a question relating to the intensity of judicial review in merger control cases where prospective economic analysis play a vital role in the evidence and the national court is pondering the exact scope, depth or width of the judicial review as undertaken by the ECJ in merger control cases of the Commission, might it ask a preliminary question to the ECJ?[6] Would it be different for merger control cases where a one-stop shop regime moves the national application slightly more away from the European application of merger control, as compared to cases relating to anti-competitive agreements or abuse of a dominant position?

---

6 See on the influence of the *Tetra Laval* judgment on national judicial review O. Essens, A. Gerbrandy & S. Lavrijssen (eds.), *National Courts and the Standard of Review in Competition Law and Economic Regulation*, Groningen, Europa Law Publishing 2009.

If a court has an obligation to refer a matter to the ECJ, because there is no *acte clair* nor *acte éclairé*, obviously the court has no room to decide differently. That being said, it is clear that in many cases it may be possible for the court to come to a judgment in which the issue on which the reference might have had to be made can be 'written away': in that way, the unclear issue is left undecided, while the case at hand is resolved. This route is not always possible or advisable, but there seems to be more room for deciding whether or not to ask a preliminary reference than the strict legal obligations may imply. Other courts, under no obligation to ask for a reference, may also be confronted with the question 'to refer or not to refer'.

If faced with such a choice there are several elements to be considered. On the one hand, reasons relating to legal certainty or legal clarity or the fact that there is a point of principle which needs to be decided, will play a role. Also, if parties explicitly ask for a preliminary reference, the judge may take that into account. Possibly, the idea of playing a role in the building of a *ius commune*, or the mere vanity of having a preliminary ruling to one's name, may be a factor in deciding to refer as well. On the other hand, there are procedural difficulties: not only does the ECJ take a long time to answer a preliminary question, but it also takes time to write the referring judgment. That brings extra work to the usually already overloaded work schedules of judges. The fact that the outcome may be uncertain – the ECJ may give an unexpected answer or seemingly no answer at all – adds to the mix. Lastly, procedural autonomy or the fact that there is a choice (and no obligation) at all may make a judge decide not to refer the matter to the ECJ.

5. The Interplay between European and National Substantive and Procedural Competition Law: An Example

The abovementioned tensions, questions and issues may be best illustrated by providing an example. Such an example can be found in the *T-Mobile* case, a preliminary reference procedure from the Dutch Appeal Tribunal for Tariffs and Trade, the highest administrative law court in competition law proceedings in the Netherlands.[7]

At issue is the question of proving a concerted practice – in this case between operators of mobile telecommunications networks – as prohibited by Article 101(1) TFEU. As may be known, the ECJ has held that for the Commission to prove a concerted practice three elements must be present: collusion, market behaviour and a causal connection between them. The Commission, the ECJ held, must prove the elements of collusion and market behaviour, but can then rely on a presumption that there is a causal connection between these elements.[8] In other words, the

7 Case C-8/08, *T-Mobile, ECR* 2009, I-4529. See also A. Gerbrandy, 'Case Note "Case C-8/08, T-Mobile Netherlands BV, KPN Mobile NV, Orange Nederland NV, Vodafone Libertel NV v. Raad van bestuur van de Nederlandse Mededingingsautoriteit, Judgment of the Court (Third Chamber) of 4 June 2009"', 47 *CMLR* 2010, pp. 1199-1220.

8 Case C-49/92 P, *Commission v. Anic Partecipazioni*, ECR 1999, I-4125.

presumption of proof of causal connection comes into play. The national court, confronted with the national authority also applying these three elements, including the presumption of causal connection, wonders whether this presumption of proof of causal connection is also valid for national competition authorities applying both national and European law. In other words: the principle is valid in European procedures – in European administrative law – but not necessarily in the national procedural surroundings in which the decentralised application of national and European competition law functions.

The Dutch Competition Act is silent on this point, although it does hold that the definition of a concerted practice is the same as the definition in Article 101(1) TFEU. There seems to be no clear statutory rule on the burden of proof or the standard of proof in national administrative procedures, though of course through case law there is a body of rules to be applied in these procedures as well.[9] It is, however, not clear whether there is a conflicting rule of national procedural law that would prohibit the parallel application of the presumption in national competition procedures.

The latter seems also to have been the opinion of the district court, who applied the presumption to the case at hand without explicitly dwelling on the possibility of either conflict or parallelism. The Appeals Tribunal, however, stays the proceedings and refers this matter (one of three questions) to the ECJ in a preliminary procedure. In its referring judgment the Appeals Tribunal points to two possible (alternative) solutions. One solution would be to look at the question through the lens of procedural autonomy and the principle of effectiveness: Is not applying the presumption of causal connection against this principle? In this view, the matter of presumptions is a procedural matter. The national rules on proof can be applied, albeit within the limits of effectiveness and equivalence. The other solution is to hold the presumption as being part of the substantive provision; part of the substantive concept of a concerted practice. In that view the presumption is removed from the procedural autonomy and put in the basket of the substantive application of European competition law in national courts: its final interpretation is in the hands of the ECJ.

It may not be surprising that the last route – the presumption of causal connection as part of the concept of a concerted practice – is the route chosen by the ECJ. Elsewhere, I have criticised this route,[10] so let me restrict my comment here by noting that this route is indeed to be welcomed from the view of the effective application of competition law throughout the Member States. In line with the theme of the conference, this solution does remove obstacles for the parallel application of national and European competition law and, moreover, removes obstacles in the application of competition law between Member States. All courts,

9 See Y.E. Schuurmans, *Bewijslastverdeling in het bestuursrecht* (Diss. Leiden), Deventer, Kluwer 2009.

10 See Gerbrandy 2010, pp. 1199-1220.

throughout the EU, are bound by this judgment to apply the presumption in cases relating to concerted practices.

There is one additional comment to make. Although the Appeals Tribunal does not explicitly refer to a possible conflict between the national rule on proof and the presumption of causal connection, it is only if such a conflict were to arise, that there would be an obligation to ask for a preliminary reference. This case, it seems to me, is an example of a case where the Appeals Tribunal would have been able *not* to ask the question but to apply either the national (similar) rule on burdens of proof, or apply the European rule on presumption of causal connection in parallel. The question of why that is possibly an important point to make, I would like to answer by pointing out that procedural autonomy and procedural differences may be a value in themselves, next to the value of effectiveness of application of European competition law.

6. Conclusions

The removing of obstacles for the parallel application of competition law can be found by developing *ius commune*: a body of procedural and substantive rules governing national court proceedings in which national and European competition law are applied simultaneously. By posing preliminary questions to the ECJ, such a *ius commune* may be helped along. There is a role for national courts, both the highest national courts and the courts in first instance, that they may choose to play in this development.

On the other hand, I would like to point out that values as national identity, diversity and autonomy are values not to be taken lightly. It is not certain that a 'harmonised' or 'unified' procedural law for competition law cases provides the best solution, while at the same time, it is unclear how insurmountable the obstacles (and for whom) are as a result of national procedural laws not being identical even where substantive law provisions are. As it is for the national courts to play their role in a developing *ius commune*, it is also here that national courts, maybe especially highest national courts, have a role to play in their respective Member States.

The Dichotomy between Object and Effect Restrictions under Article 101 TFEU and Slovenian Competition Law Enforcement Failures

T. Gross and M. Kovač

1. Introduction

As is well acknowledged, the text of Article 101(1) of the Treaty on the Functioning of the European Union (hereinafter: TFEU) makes a distinction between agreements (etc.) that have as their object a restriction of competition, and those that have as their effect a restriction of competition. This contribution maps the development of this distinction within the case law of the European Court of Justice and its Slovenian counterpart till its present day application. It also offers a doctrinal critique on the way the Slovenian Courts and Competition authority (hereinafter: UVK) apply the distinction and on possible alternatives that have been identified in the literature. The relationship with the more recently introduced category of 'hard-core' restrictions is surveyed too. Although Slovenia joined the European Union in 2004 and the history of the first competition legislation can be traced back to the mid 1990s, the coherent application and the use of economic evidence (and reasoning) is still lacking and can be improved further.

The presented survey of the economic and legal literature on the current EU competition law distinction between an "object" and "effect" as provided in Article 101(1) TFEU, derives several substantive principles for improved and coherent judicial application of this distinction. The provided analysis also shows that it might well be that the Slovenian national competition authority (and the court) has, while assessing the "object/effect" cases often misunderstood the core legal and economic concepts and theories, and also mishandled available economic evidence. Instructively, a path for a more coherent application of EU competition provisions, theory and the European Court of Justice case law appears as evident.

The first part of this contribution (section 2) starts with a survey of the relevant substantive EU law provisions and then offers a set of economic criteria which serve as the optimal distinction benchmark for agreements (etc.) that have as their object a restriction of competition, and those that have as their effect a restriction of competition. The second part (based on the provided set of legal and economic criteria) critically comments on the current Slovenian application (decisions, reports, Agency practices and enforcement standards), provisions and decisions where the need for statutory reform appears obvious (section 3). A conclusion is provided in section 4.

2. Optimal Distinction Benchmark

This section identifies several legal and economic principles, and tries to compress them into a single general "optimal distinction" principle.

2.1 The Substantive EU Law

Competition law has always played an important part in Community law where the enhancement of efficiency, protection of consumers and creation of a single European market have been advanced as some of the most relevant objectives and priorities.[1] A competitive economic system is also regarded in the EU as necessary for a prosperous, free and equitable society. The last few decades have thus witnessed the unprecedented success of such a policy, resulting in significant efficiency gains.

Moreover, substantial benefits for European consumers and the related improved overall social welfare have been marked as some of the most remarkable achievements of European integration. In this context one should also note that the economic analysis of competition law provisions has recently become central to the assessment of competition cases throughout all fields of EC competition rules.[2] The EC competition rules were set out in the Treaty establishing the European Community where, among other provisions,[3] Article 81 (now Art. 101 TFEU, OJ C115/47, 9.5.2008,) prohibiting anticompetitive agreements appears as the principal remedy to deter anti-competitive behaviour. Namely, Article 101 prohibits all agreements, decisions or concerted practices which could in any way prevent, distort or restrict competition and automatically voids all such prohibited agreements.[4] Obviously, the rationale for the broad, wide meaning of Article 101 TFEU,

---

1 Its precise role is, however, contestable and a number of differing objectives can be pursued by competition policy, not all of which are mutually compatible; P. Craig & G. De Búrca, *EU Law: Text, Cases and Materials* (4th ed.), Oxford University Press 2008, p. 950 *et seq*. Also see L. Ritter, D.W. Braun, F. Rawlinson, *European Competition Law: A Practitioner's Guide* (2nd ed.), Kluwer Law International 2000, p. 46 *et seq*.

2 See H.W. Friederiszick, "Economic Analysis in EU Competition Cases", *in* J. Drexl, L. Idot & J. Monéger (eds.), *Economic Theory and Competition Law*, Edward Elgar 2009.

3 This also includes the key Art. 102 (ex Art. 82) of the TFEU prohibiting the abuse of a dominant position.

4 The following shall be prohibited as incompatible with the common market; all agreements between undertakings, decisions by associations of undertakings an concerted practices which may affect trade between Member States and which have as their object or effect the prevention, restriction or distortion of competition within the common market, and in particular those which: (a) directly or indirectly fix purchase or selling prices or any other trading conditions; (b) limit or control production, markets, technical development, or investment; (c) share markets or sources

encompassing agreements, decisions or concerted practices, lies in the fact that if the competition rules were to operate only when an explicit, formal agreement has been made then they would have little practical use since undertakings would try to achieve their anti-competitive goals in less formal ways.[5] Moreover, even if there is no agreement at all, undertakings might be caught by the provisions of Article 101 if there is concerted practice (collusion).[6]

Yet, if price uniformity is really the result of rational action in an oligopoly[7], and there is no actual collusion, then such uniformity is exempted from the scope of Article 101.[8] Further, Article 101(1) also requires that the agreement, decision or concerted practice has the object or effect of preventing, restricting or distorting competition in the Common Market. The interpretation of those conditions has invoked intense scholarly debate in which a consensus has not yet been reached.[9] Yet, as commentators argue, a case law analysis shows that the European Court of Justice condemns certain types of agreements on the basis of their object or purpose without any extensive market analysis; in this sense, it effectively proscribes these agreements as *per se* illegal.[10]

To summarize, Article 101(1) prohibits agreements between undertakings which appreciably affect trade between Member States and which have as their object or effect the restriction of competition within the common market.[11]

---

of supply; (d) apply dissimilar conditions to equivalent transactions with other trading parties, thereby placing them at the competitive disadvantage; (e) make the conclusion of contracts subject to acceptance by the other parties of supplementary obligations which, by their nature or according to commercial usage, have no connection with the subject of such contracts. 2. Any agreements or decisions pursuant to this Article shall be automatically void;" Art. 101(1), (2), Treaty Establishing the European Community.

5 Craig & De Búrca 2008, p. 954. Also see *ACF Chemiefarma NV v. Commission,* C-41, 44, and 45/69 (1970), ECR 661; Dec. 86/398 (1986), OJ L230/1, (1988) 4 *CMLR* 347; Dec. 89/190 PVC (1989) OJ L74/1, (1990) 4 CMLR 345; *Commission v. BASF AG,* C-137/92 (1994) ECR I-2555; *Italian Flat Glass* (1989) OJ L33/44, (1990) 4 *CMLR* 535.

6 On the problems of concerted practices and on the theory of oligopolistic interdependence, see R. Whish, *Competition Law* (6th ed.), Oxford University Press 2009, p. 510 *et seq.*

7 Then the problem is actually structural since such a type of market will naturally generate this type of response. See *e.g. ICI v. Commission,* C-48/69 (1972) ECR 619; *Hüls AG v. Commission,* C-199/92 (1999) ECR I-4287.

8 For an economic discussion of the uniformity of prices in an oligopoly, see G. Stigler, "The Kinked Oligopoly Demand Curve", 55 *J. Pol. Econ.* 431, 1947.

9 See *e.g.* V. Korah, "The Rise and Fall of Provisional Validity – The Need for a Rule of Reason in EEC Antitrust," 3 *NW J. Int. L. and Bus.* 320, 1981; R. Whish & B. Sufrin, "Article 85 and the Rule of Reason", 7 *YBEL* 12, 1987.

10 The Court has also engaged in economic analysis within Art. 101(1), while it has not employed the language of the rule of reason; Craig & De Búrca 2008, p. 974. Also see P. Roth & V. Rose, *European Community Law of Competition* (6th ed.), Oxford University Press 2008; J.R. Barry, & A. MacCulloch, *Competition Law and Policy in the European Community and United Kingdom*, Cavendish Publishing Limited 1999, p. 157 *et seq.*; Whish 2009, p. 122, *et seq.*; V. Korah, V., "The Judgment in Delimitis A Milestone Towards a Realistic Assessment of the Effects of the Agreement – or a Damp Squib", 14 *E.I.P.R.* 167, 1992.

11 A. Jones & B. Sufrin, *EC Competition Law: Text, Cases and Materials*, (3rd ed.), Oxford University Press 2008, p. 205.

2.1.1 Object or Effect

The concepts object or effect have to be distinguished, since they should be applied as alternatives and not cumulative. As the ECJ decided in the case *Société Technique Minière v. Maschinenbau Ulm*[12] both words have to be read disjunctively. An agreement has to be first scrutinised to determine what is the object of an agreement, and only when this is not clear it is necessary to consider whether it might have a restrictive effect.[13] An agreement is caught under Article 101(1) either if its object or effect restricts competition.

2.1.1.1 Object

It is first necessary to scrutinize what is the object of the agreement by examining the aims of the agreement in the economic context in which the agreement is to be applied. A finding that an agreement has as its object a restriction of competition will not be undermined by an argument that an agreement pursues a legitimate object since the agreement constitutes a restriction of competition by its very nature.[14] Parties to such an agreement (a hard-core price fixing agreement) cannot simply argue that the fixing of prices does not restrict competition, when the Community Courts have decided on the basis of the wording of the Treaty and subsequent experience acquired through case law that it does.[15]

Several courts' decisions demonstrated that not every contractual restriction infringes Article 101(1).[16] An agreement which, *prima facie*, has as its object the restriction of competition can escape the prohibition of Article 101(1) if it has an insignificant effect on the market or on trade. This means that the restriction of competition has to be appreciable: if the impact on the market is minimal an agreement which restricts competition by object does not infringe Article 101(1). For an agreement that is plainly anti-competitive no negative effects on competition need to be proved since the seriousness of the nature of the restriction and experiences show that adverse effects are likely to be produced.[17]

Although economic analysis of effects is not needed, quantitative analysis as mentioned is required before determining that Article 101(1) is infringed. The ECJ also holds that it is irrelevant if the restriction was in the commercial interest of participants.[18]

12 Case 56/65 (1966) ECR 235, p. 249, (1966) *CMLR* 357, p. 375.

13 Whish 2009, p. 116.

14 Jones & Sufrin 2008, p. 220.

15 The Community Courts have decided, on the basis of the wording of the Treaty and subsequent experience acquired through case law; Whish 2009. But parties can argue that the agreement satisfies the criteria of Art. 101(3).

16 Whish 2009, p. 115.

17 This was first established in the *Société Technique Minière* judgement by the ECJ, soon it was repeated in *Consten and Grundig*.

18 Cases C-403/04 P *Sumitomo Metal Industries Ltd v. Commission* (2007) ECR I-729, (2007) 4 *CMLR* 650, paras 45-46.

2.1.1.2 Agreements that Restrict Competition by Object

In relation to horizontal agreements the Court of First Instance (CFI) stated in *European Night Services v. Commission* that agreements containing restriction of competition such as price fixing, market sharing or the control of outlets are considered due to their restrictive nature to be allocated in the object category.[19]

Beside mentioned there are also some other agreements. The CFI did not refer to them in *European Night Services* but they can also be put in the object category, for example agreements to limit output and other analogous agreements. The Commission has, likewise, added exclusive dealing.[20] In *Visa International-Multilateral Interchange Fee*,[21] where the agreement contained a provision to fix the MIF[22] paid by acquiring banks to issuing banks for each transaction with a Visa card, the Commission decided, that where an agreement involving price-fixing is not naked,[23] as it was in this case, it does not restrict competition by object. Here, it concluded that the agreement restricted competition by effect.[24]

2.1.1.3 Vertical Agreements

The CFI has in the *European Night Services* pointed at the control of outlets as one of the hardcore restrictions. This restriction is not specially referred to in Article 101(1), but the CFI most likely had in mind the imposition on distributors of export bans from one Member State to another.[25]

The Commission found that export bans in distribution agreements by *BASF*, constitute a restriction of competition by object. That was confirmed by the CFI in its judgment,[26] where it stated: *clauses designed to prevent a buyer from reselling or exporting goods he has bought is liable to partition the markets and consequently to affect trade between Member States*. But export bans, in the context of a specific type of agreement, do not always restrict competition. The ECJ concluded that in the *Erauw-Jacquery Sprl v. La Hesbignonne Société Coopérative* case, where it decided that a provision preventing a licensee from exporting so-called basic seeds protected by plant breeders rights could fall outside Article 101(1), where it was necessary to protect the right of the licensor to select its licensees.

But the judgment of CFI in *GlaxoSmithKline* case has obscured the clarity of the law in this area. Due to specific characteristics of the pharmaceutical sector, the

---

19 Category of agreements which restrict competition by object.

20 FEG and TU OJ (2000) L 39/1, (2000) 4 *CMLR* 1208, para. 105.

21 Participants in the Visa system agreed on the level of the multilateral interchange fee that acquiring banks pay to issuing banks for each transaction with a Visa card.

22 Multilateral interchange fee.

23 "Agreements are naked where they seek to restrict competition without producing any objective countervailing benefits." M. Monti, Jones & Sufrin 2008, p. 223.

24 Further, the Commission decided that the agreement satisfied the criteria of Art. 101(3).

25 Whish 2009, p. 120.

26 Case T-176/95 *Accinauto SA v. Commission of the European Communities* (1999) ECR II-1635.

Court decided that contractual measures designed to prevent parallel trade did not restrict competition by object, but by effect.

In the case *General Motor BV*, where an indirect export ban was imposed on exports of cars from the Netherlands, the CFI and ECJ concluded that agreements were restrictive by object. The ECJ emphasised that the lawful purpose, followed by such an agreement does not undermine the fact that the agreement constitutes a restriction of competition by its very nature.

Over a period of time a group of agreements can be reformed. Agreements which are now considered to restrict competition by object may be re-categorised due to changes in economic thinking and other developments. The process of categorization and re-categorization is a natural one and further fine-tuning is to be expected. The fact that such a process, however, takes place does not call into question the underlying object or effect distinction contained in Article 101(1).[27]

2.1.1.4 Effect

Where it is not possible to say that the object of an agreement restricts competition, an extensive analysis of an agreement's effect needs to be done before it can be found to infringe Article 101(1). The range of analysis undertaken in a certain case depends on the issue raised by an agreement. The same analysis is not deployed in different cases.

The need to examine an agreement in market context was stressed by the Community Courts on a number of occasions. One of the first cases in which it was required is *Brasserie de Haecht*,[28] where the ECJ said that:

> it would be pointless to consider an agreement's effect distinct from the market. An agreement should not be examined in isolation when determining whether it infringes Article 101(1), but could only be examined apart from the body effects, whether convergent or not, surrounding their implementation.

The importance to consider an agreement in the market context was, by the ECJ, also emphasised in *STM* and in *Metropole* by the CFI.

A case which demonstrates the depth of analysis required in determining whether an agreement has the effect of restricting competition, is *Delimitis*.[29] The analysis required in this case highlights the importance of looking at the agreement in the context in which it operates before its effect can be determined. The ECJ held that when determining an agreement's effect it is first necessary to define relevant product and geographic market. Further, the access to the market has to be considered: can a new competitor enter the market. If market access is impeded, it

27 Whish 2009, p. 122.
28 Case 23/67 (1967) ECR 407, (1968) *CMLR* 26.
29 Case C-234/89 (1991) ECR I-935.

is necessary to ask whether the agreement contributes to foreclosure effect. If it does Article 101(1) is infringed.[30]

For the purpose of examining whether the agreement restricts competition by effect it is necessary to consider what the position would have been in the absence of the agreement by comparing two situations. The CFI stressed the need to examine the counter-factual in *O2*.[31]

As emphasised, not every contractual restriction has anti-competitive effect. In this respect Whish[32] regards the *STM* and *Consten & Grundig* cases as the two most instructive judgments. In the first case the ECJ decided that simply granting exclusive rights to a territory may not infringe Article 101(1) if this is necessary to protect the investment of the licensee, where in *Consten & Grundig* the ECJ decided that an agreement imposing export bans and preventing a possibility of a parallel trade restricted competition by object.

In *Metro*[33] the ECJ held that where restrictive provisions in a selective distribution system satisfy objective, quantitative criteria and are applied in a non-discriminatory manner they do not infringe Article 101(1). In *Nungesser*[34] the ECJ held that the open exclusive license of a new technology to produce maize seeds did not infringe Article 101(1). Here, the licensee would not be prepared to take the license and incur the risk/expense of producing the patented product without some protection from intra-brand competition. A line of reasoning developed the ECJ in *Erauw-Jacquery Sprl*[35] where it accepted that in the context of the licensing of certain IP rights even export bans might, in certain circumstances, fall outside Article 101(1). When it is necessary to protect the investment of the licensee, an exclusive copyright license to exhibit a film in a Member State may fall outside Article 101(1).[36]

As the Commission has established in *Reuter/BASF* and the ECJ confirmed in *Remia BV*, restrictive covenants may also fall outside Article 101(1) if they satisfy the principle of proportionality.[37] The idea that unifies these judgments, is that the restrictions found were ancillary[38] to a legitimate commercial operation.

The Commission has to conduct, nearly in all cases, a market analysis of the effect of particular restrictions or agreements on the patterns of trade. However, on occasion that will not be needed, either because the restriction is of the type

30 Jones & Sufrin 2008, p. 241; Whish 2009, p. 123.
31 Case T-328/03 (2006) ECR II-1231, (2006) 5 *CMLR* 258.
32 Whish 2009, p. 124.
33 Case 26/76 (1977) ECR 1875, (1978) 2 *CMLR* 1.
34 Case 258/78 (1982) ECR 2015, (1983) 1 *CMLR* 278.
35 Case 27/87 (1988) ECR 1919, (1988) 4 *CMLR* 576.
36 Case 262/81 (1982) ECR 3381.
37 In *Pronuptia* the ECJ considered restrictions essential to the successful operation of the distribution franchise agreement to fall outside Art. 101(1).
38 Directly related and necessary to its implementation and proportionate to the main non-restrictive distribution or joint venture agreement.

(export ban), so clearly established as having the required effect on competition as not to need substantial proof of its individual effect on the particular market concerned or because the objective of the agreement is so anti-competitive that the Commission does not need to analyze the effects of the restrictions.[39]

2.2 The Optimal Effect/Object Distinction Criteria – A Synthesis of Law and Economics Scholarship

This section identifies several economic based principles which should provide the courts with an assessment tool for establishing whether there should be a distinction between effect and object.[40] Yet, as stressed by Motta, one must note that although industrial economics has been successful in identifying the mechanism through which collusion (anti-competitive behaviour) acts and the factors that facilitate it, it's practical implications for legal purposes (and hence for the related discussion on the optimal effect/object distinction benchmark) are less straightforward and require careful assessment.[41]

As stated, price fixing cartels or other agreements having as their object the restriction of competition are illegal *per se*. However, as Van den Bergh and Camesasca point out, there is no perfect harmony between previously discussed legal rules and economic insights.[42] Namely, a full scale economic analysis could show that prices are not above competitive levels, hence making antitrust intervention redundant.[43] Van den Bergh and Camesasca argue that even in markets that led themselves to a successful cartelisation[44] price fixing agreements may prove to be ineffective because of the presence of large buyers on the market and plenty of cheating on the cartel price.[45] In such circumstances (despite the explicit object to raise prices) cartels will be imperfect (*de facto* ineffective) and hence the price fixing actions will fail.[46] Moreover, the empirical assessment of the sector for liberal professions confirms the non-sustainability of such price cartels.[47] In

39 D.G. Goyder, *EC Competition Law* (4th ed.), Oxford University Press, 2003, p. 99.

40 For a synthesis see L. Kaplow & C. Shapiro, "Antitrust", *in* M.A. Polinsky, & S. Shavell (eds.), *Handbook of Law and Economics*, Vol. 2, Elsevier 2007, p. 1073 *et seq.*

41 M. Motta, *Competition Policy: Theory and Practice*, Cambridge University Press 2009, p. 185 *et seq.*

42 R. Van den Bergh & P.D. Camesasca, *European Competition Law and Economics: A Comparative Perspective* (2nd ed.), Thomson Sweet & Maxwell 2006, p. 182.

43 *Ibid.* See also Motta 2009.

44 *E.g.* homogenous products, mature market, predictable demand, no huge advances in technology, and high barriers to entry; *ibid.*

45 *Ibid.*

46 Recommended fees in the liberal profession's sector are discussed as a further illustration of such ineffective cartels; see Van den Bergh and Camesasca 2006, p. 182.

47 Cartel discipline is very difficult to maintain since there is large number of players and hence high monitoring and administration maintaining cartel's costs induce cheating. See *e.g.* R. Van den Bergh, "Towards Efficient Self-Regulation in Markets for Professional Services", *in* C.D. Ehlermann & I. Atanasiu (eds.), *The Relationship between Competition Law and Liberal Professions* 2006; F. Stephen & J. Love, "Regulation of the Legal Profession", *in* B. Bouckaert & G. De Geest (eds.), *Encyclopedia of Law and Economics*, No. 5860 Edward Elgar 2000; F. Stephen, *Effects of Deregulation in Professional Services Markets: Scottish Conveyance Markets*, 9 Strathclyde Economic Papers 2, 1993.

other words, such a wide interpretation would encompass almost all agreements regardless of the market position (market power) of the parties involved or of the economic impact of the agreement.[48] As Bishop and Walker point out, such a wide interpretation, not taking into account the real economic consequences, has little to do with a modern economic analysis of competition and if taken literally would be nonsensical.[49]

Economic analysis stresses the need to examine the real-life consequences of both explicit (object) and tacit (effect) collusion.[50] In addition, Van den Bergh and Camesasca argue that even though restriction of competition may be the proven object of cooperation (explicit collusion), market evidence may show that prices are not substantially above competitive levels, which makes antitrust intervention less compelling or even completely unnecessary.[51] Such an intervention would merely entail needless transaction costs (administration costs) and would represent pure welfare loss.

In addition, Posner argues further that one of the unintended consequences of such an "object" focused approach is that the cartels most likely to be discovered and prosecuted are those in which the price and output effects are small.[52] Hence, the smoothly functioning cartels (with substantial negative competitive outcomes) are less likely to generate evidence of actual agreement.[53]

Yet, despite these economic arguments current EU competition law enables the relevant economic arguments to be pushed aside if the objective to fix prices or control output can be proven and the lack of economic impact on the market will only be taken into account when determining the ultimate fine.[54]

48 S. Bishop & M. Walker, *The economics of EC Competition Law: Concepts, Application and Measurement*, University ed., Sweet & Maxwell 2010, p. 158.

49 *Ibid.*

50 Object/effect distinction can be in economic terms regarded as the explicit/tacit collusion distinction. Firms can either collude explicitly by setting up formal cartels, or they can collude tacitly. Tacit collusion exists where in the absence of any formal attempts to implement a collusive outcome, firms understand that if each firm competes less vigorously they might all be able to enjoy higher prices and higher profits; Bishop and Walker 2002, p. 164. See also Kaplow & Shapiro 2009, p. 1098 *et seq.*; M. Whinston, *Lectures on Antitrust Economics*, MIT Press 2006; and C. Shapiro, "Theories of Oligopoly Behavior", *in* R. Schmalensee & R. Willing (eds.), *Handbook of Industrial Organization*, Vol.1, North-Holland 1989, p. 329 *et seq.*

51 In general, agreements such as price fixing, market sharing, quotas and rigging bids having as their object the restriction of competition will mainly entail enforcement related issues such as leniency, fines and damages; Van den Bergh and Camesasca 2006, p. 202.

52 "They are the cartels with many members, so there is a better chance that one will become disgruntled and inform on the others; that depend on explicit and reiterated negotiation and agreement, which provide the essential evidence of violation; and that are likely to be riddled with cheating and collapse shortly amidst mutual recrimination – circumstances that create opportunities to obtain willing witnesses to offer evidence of agreement; R.A. Posner, *Economic Analysis of Law* (6th ed.), Aspen Publishers 2002, at p. 289.

53 What law mainly punishes is the attempt to fix prices, whereas completed conspiracy often escapes attention; Posner 2002, p. 289.

54 From the economic perspective such fine's determining procedure represents needless litigation and administration costs (transaction costs) and also wastes scarce resources which are devoted to the competition law enforcement. See also *ibid,*, at p. 182.

However, one should also note that even if good and reliable data exists, econometric techniques might not always provide completely straightforward answers as to the existence of collusive pricing (prices substantially above market level) and consequent intervention urge. According to Motta inferring illegal collusive behaviour in such circumstances might not be desirable, and the legal approach which requests some hard evidence as proof of collusion (object) might be a sensible, cost saving practice.[55] Along this line he argues further that firms should be convicted for anti-competitive behaviour only insofar as there is proof that they have communicated with each other to sustain collusion. In all instances of interchangeable communication[56] and if there is evidence that firms have not acted unilaterally, Motta calls for antitrust enforcement procedures.[57]

Although Motta's arguments on *ex post* verifiability problems should be taken into account the prevailing view in modern law and economics literature differs substantially.[58] Posner, for example, argues that the enforcement policy in which emphasis has been placed on proving an agreement to fix prices (and not on the effect) rather than on proving the effects of the seller's conduct on price and output is simply a non-economic and inefficient one.[59] Such an approach is actually harmful to an effective competition policy.[60] If the economic evidence presented in a case warrants an inference of collusive pricing, there is neither legal nor practical justification for requiring evidence that will support the further inference that the collusion was explicit.[61] Moreover, there is now ample empirical evidence that the traditional "object" approach to price fixing resulted in a significant distortion of the enforcement efforts.[62]

Furthermore, Posner offers several additional arguments in favour of the "economic effects" concept.[63] First, although businesspeople would not attempt to fix

55 Motta 2009, p. 185 *et seq.*

56 Such communication encompasses minutes of meetings, e-mail messages, memos, other written (or recorded) evidences, open discussion on prices or quantities, forum price announcements, maintenance price schemes/practices; Motta 2009, p. 189.

57 In such instances firms should be found guilty of collusion. Such approach has according to Motta also the advantage that it is based on observable elements *ex post* verifiable at courts; Motta 2009, p. 189.

58 See *e.g.* Kaplow and Shapiro 2009; D.W. Carlton & J.M. Perloff, *Modern Industrial Organization* (3rd ed.), Prentice Hall 2000.

59 R.A. Posner, *Antitrust Law* (2nd ed.), Chicago University Press 2001.

60 Many attempts to fix price may have negligible consequences, while much serious price fixing may escape detection altogether because detectable overt communication is necessary for proof of an attempt but is not always necessary to bring about a concerted increase of price above the competitive level; *ibid.* at p. 53.

61 From an economic standpoint it is a detail whether the collusive pricing scheme was organised and implemented in such a way as to generate evidence of actual communication (object); Posner 2001, p. 94.

62 See H.P. Marvel, J.M. Netter, & A.M. Robinson, "Price Fixing and Civil Damages: An Economic analysis", 40 *Stanford Law Review* 561, 1988; P. Asch & J.J. Seneca, "Is Collusion Profitable", 58 *Review of Economics and Statistics* 1, 1976; D.F. Lean, J.D. Ogar & R.P. Rogers, "Does Collusion pay...Does Antitrust Work?", 51 *Southern Journal of Economics* 828, 1985; and M.F. Sproul, "Antitrust and Prices", 101 *Journal of Political Economy* 741, 1993.

63 Offered as his arguments towards several reasons in favour of the law's emphasis on the attempt to fix prices rather on the completed act; Posner 2001, p. 54.

prices in situations where they were unlikely to succeed,[64] they may sometimes be mistaken, and such mistakes, even if occasional, could account for a large proportion of the small number of price-fixing cases that the public enforcement agencies bring.[65] Second, budget constraints may be offered as an additional argument towards a common legal perception that pursuing attempts to fix prices that would actually not succeed can be done without any harm and cost. Namely, enforcement resources employed and consumed in marginal cases may afterwards be, due to budget constraints, unavailable for more important ones.[66] Third, even if methods of litigation would be ill-suited to the resolution of the complex economic arguments that an "effect" case would frequently involve, this shall, however, not empower enforcement agencies to refuse such a use.[67] Fourth, even if some authors express doubts towards economic analysis of cartels, economic data can be used to identify serious limitations of output due to either explicit or tacit collusion, both by identifying those markets whose characteristics predispose them toward price fixing and by applying certain tests in the suspect markets to determine whether the market price is in fact substantially above the competitive level.[68]

Moreover, such a formalistic approach would be generally at odds also with the economic reality where economic theory advances that unless firms posses and exercise market power, they are unable to affect competition adversely.[69] In other words, in the absence of the market power, agreements between firms will not give rise to anti-competitive outcomes (effects).[70] A competition authority's intervention would in such instances imply pure waste of scarce resources (inefficiency). This economic reasoning is explicitly utilised also by the European Commission's Horizontal Guidelines which admits that the anti-competitive outcomes of the agreement depends on the economic context, taking into account the nature of the agreement as well as the parties' combined market power.[71]

Yet, most competitor cooperation, however, does not have as its object a restriction of competition. As previously stated, for triggering the applicability of Article 101 in such cases an economic analysis of the agreement's effects is required.[72]

---

64 And by forbidding the attempt one would prevent the actual price fixing.

65 In addition, if the costs of price-fixing cases (including punishment cost – expected punishment cots – discounted by the probability that the conspirators will actually be caught and punished) are low, conspiracy may be a rational business strategy even if most attempts fail; Posner 2001, p. 54.

66 This also assumes both that public enforcement budgets are constrained and that the investigative capacities of the private plaintiffs' competition bar are limited in relation to those of the EU Commission and national competition authorities; Posner 2001, p. 54 *et seq.*

67 It could at most justify the refusal of the courts to apply such economic criteria; *ibid.*

68 *Ibid.*

69 Bishop & Walker 2010, p. 158.

70 According to Bishop and walker this distinction also explains why it is perfectly consistent for a given contract clause (restriction of competition as an object) in one agreement to have benign outcomes whilst the same clause in other agreements is anti-competitive; *ibid.*

71 EC Horizontal Guidelines.

72 Van den Bergh & Camesasca 2006, p. 185.

Such an agreement must be able to limit competition between parties involved and it must be likely to affect the competition in the market to such an extent that negative market effects as to prices, output, innovation or the variety or quality of goods and services can be expected.[73] The economic object of Article 101(1) TFEU is according to commentators in creating a distinct concept of "effect" is to prevent the possibility of undertakings evading the application of this article by colluding in a manner which does not involve an agreement, *per se*, but still has an adverse impact on competition.[74] Such an adverse impact on competition can be achieved either by setting up formal cartels or by tacit collusion.[75] The latest mimicking of monopoly outcomes has been extensively studied by several economists[76] showing that the interaction over time may enable firms to increase their profits relative to the one shot non-cooperative outcomes.[77] In addition, it should be noted that generally firms prefer to collude tacitly rather than explicitly since explicit cartel behaviour lays firms open to more severe legal penalties.[78]

However, the possibility that firms can engage in tacit collusion raises difficult policies issues – the workable discrimination between anti-competitive tacit collusion and normal effective competition being the most obvious one. Commentators note that policy should not as a general rule attempt to intervene in a market on suspicion that firms are competing tacitly without there being very good reasons to believe that the market outcome is substantially different to the effective competitive one.[79] The identified risk lies in misinterpreting the firms' legitimate competitive interactions in the market with them consciously trying to support some form of implicit coordination.[80] Instructively, the EU Courts have in line

73 The EU Commission's Horizontal Guidelines hold that this depends on the economic context of the agreement, taking into account both (a) the nature of the agreement and (b) the parties' combined market power, as this determines the capability of the cooperation to affect overall competition; *ibid.*

74 Bishop & Walker 2010, p. 163; Van den Bergh & Camesasca 2006, p. 186 *et seq*.

75 Tacit collusion exists where in the absence of any formal attempts to implement a collusive outcome, firms understand that if each firm competes less vigorously they might all be able to enjoy higher prices and higher profits; Bishop & Walker 2010, p. 164.

76 See *e.g.* E.J. Green, "Continuum and Finite-Player Noncooperative Models of Competition", 4 *Econometric Society* 52, 1984; M. Slade, *Conjectures, Firm Characteristics, and Market Structure: An Analysis of Vancouver's Gasoline Price Wars*, Mimeo 1987; and S. Borenstein & A. Shepard, "Dynamic Pricing in retail Gasoline Markets", 27 *Rand Journal of Economics* 3, 1996.

77 Yet, according to Jacquemin and Slade total industry profit falls short of the monopoly profits and this might suggest that co-ordination and communication difficulties are probably greater in practice than most theoretical treatments assume; A. Jacquemin & M. Slade, "Cartels, Collusion and Horizontal Merger", *in* R. Schmalensee & R. Willing (eds.), *Handbook of Industrial Organization*, North-Holland D. 1989.

78 Implying that firms should only engage in explicit collusion where tacit one would not be successful; Bishop and Walker 2010, p. 165.

79 Van den Bergh and Camesasca 2006, p. 190. See also Bishop and Walker 2010, p. 165 *et seq*.

80 D. Neven, P. Papandropoulos & P. Seabright, *Trawling for Minnows: European Competition Policy and Agreements between Firms*, 1998. See also J.B. Baker, "Two Sherman Act Section 1 Dilemmas: Parallel Pricing, the Oligopoly Problem, and Contemporary Economic Theory", 38 *Antitrust Bull.* 143, 1993.

with economic arguments acknowledged that the law does not deprive firms of the right to adapt themselves intelligently to the conduct of their competitors.[81]

To conclude, recently the EU Commission and Courts have recognised increasingly that the previous formalistic approach (object) has no place in a modern effects-based competition regime and, the need for a detailed substantive analysis of the impact of an agreement under Article 101 TFEU has become even more relevant.[82] Since 1999, the EU Commission has recognised these inadequacies and has implemented a move towards an economic-based approach that focuses on market power and market outcomes.[83]

2.3 The Problem of Economic Evidence

Economic science will stress the difficulties of drawing conclusions with certainty. Obviously the risk lies in misinterpreting the firm's legitimate competitive interactions in the market with them consciously trying to support some form of implicit coordination.[84] However, as previously stated economic analysis can be utilised in two ways: first, it can play a role in providing evidence as to whether it is plausible that an industry was cartelised; and, secondly, it can provide estimates of the impact that a cartel has on price.[85] As to the first, Posner offers a set of possible indicators of a market's predisposition to effective price fixing: a) the number of (major) sellers; b) no fringe of small sellers; c) the homogeneity of the product; d) the elasticity of demand with respect to price; e) the condition of entry; f) the relative importance of price *versus* non-price competition; g) is the market growing, declining, or steady over time; h) high ratio of fixed to variable costs; i) if prices can be changed quickly; and j) the structure of the buying side of the market.[86]

As to the latter, law and economics literature suggest a set of economic evidence[87] that can be used to indicate the existence of collusive pricing even though no overt acts of collusion were detected (a market is being successfully cartelised): a) fixed relative market shares; b) a market-wide price discrimination; c) exchanges of price information; d) regional price variations; e) identical bids; f) a decline over time in the market share of the largest firms in the market; g) an industry-wide resale price maintenance; h) price, output and capacity changes at the formation of the cartel; i) amplitude and fluctuation of price changes; j) demand elastic at the market price; k) the presence or pattern of abnormally high rates of return;

81 See *Cooperatieve Vereniging Suiker Unie VA and others v. Commission* (1975) ECR 1663.
82 Van den Bergh & Camesasca 2006, p. 202. See also Bishop & Walker 2002, 164 *et seq.*
83 Bishop & Walker 2010, p. 162.
84 See *e.g.* R. Sugden, "A Theory of focal Points", 105 *Econ. J.* 535, 1995.
85 Bishop & Walker 2010, p. 183 *et seq.*
86 Posner 2002, p. 289 *et seq.* For a longer list and a fuller discussion see Posner 2001, p. 69 *et seq.*
87 For a general methodology and for the estimating "effects" techniques applied in the EU competition law see Bishop & Walker 2010, p. 699 *et seq.*

l) a negative correlation between the number of firms in the market and the price level in the market; m) basing-point pricing; and n) exclusionary practices.[88]

However, as commentators note, heavy reliance on economic evidence in competition cases may seem indicated, or contraindicated, by the many economic mistakes that courts have made in those cases.[89] Moreover, the courts have often misunderstood the core concepts and theories, and also mishandled economic evidence.[90]

3. Analysis of Slovenian Application and Enforcement Practices

The following part surveys Slovenian literature and case law on the dichotomy between "object" and "effect" and while comparing them with related substantive EU jurisprudence, not surprisingly though, offers several substantive insights.

3.1 Assessment of Current Slovenian Doctrine and Statutory Provisions

The comparison of the Slovenian competition/antitrust statute *Zakon o preprečevanju omejevanja konkurence* (hereinafter: ZPOmK-1)[91] with Article 101(1) TFEU reveals doctrinal coherence. Slovenian Article 6(1) ZPOmK-1 forbids those agreements, decisions or concerted practices that have the object or effect of preventing, restricting or distorting competition in the territory of Republic of Slovenia. Obviously, this provision merely resembles the provision of Article 101(1) TFEU. Slovenian literature in this respect quotes related EU guidelines, relevant cases[92] and discusses the effective goals of the competition policy (*allocative efficiency v. consumer welfare*).[93] Slovenian legal commentators note that the distinction between "object" and "effect is according to Article 6 ZPOmK-1 a very substantive one, and that both conditions must be applied alternatively and not cumulatively.[94] Hence, as legal commentators argue, the

88 Posner 2002, 291 *et seq*. For a longer list and a fuller discussion see Posner 2001, p. 79 *et seq*. See also A. Shepard, "Price Discrimination and Retail Configuration", 99 *Journal of Political Economy* 30, 1991; J. Tirole, *The Theory of Industrial Organization*, Harvard University Press 1988; D.W. Carlton, R.H. Gertner & A.M. Rosenfield, "Communication among Competitors: Game Theory and Antitrust", 5 *George Mason Law Review* 423, 1997; D.W. Carlton, "A Reexamination of Delivered Pricing System", 23 *Journal of Law and Economics* 51, 1983; K.S. Corts, "On the Competitive Effects of Price-Matching Policies", 15 *International Journal of Industrial Organization* 283, 1997.

89 Posner 2002, p. 294.

90 G.J. Stigler, "The Dominant Firm and the Inverted Umbrella", *in The Organization of Industry* 39, 1968.

91 An approximate English translation would be the: Statue on prevention of competition's limitations.

92 *E.g. Grundig-Verkaufs Gmbh v. Commision.*

93 See M. Repas, *Konkurenčno Pravo v Teoriji in Praksi: Omejevalna Ravnanja in Nadzor Koncentracij*, Uradni List 2010. However, this dilemma is to the ones familiar with the law and economics concepts a superfluous one. See *e.g.* Posner 2001.

94 See Repas 2010, p. 169.

"effect" is actually irrelevant, insignificant and the "object" alone should trigger the competition law authority's intervention.[95]

According to current Slovenian enforcement practice the UVK should at first assess whether an agreement has as its object the prevention, restriction, or distortion of competition.[96] If such an "object" is established then further inquiry and the need for any evidence of adverse "effect" on the competition becomes unnecessary.[97] Those adverse effects are, according to Slovenian legal literature, simply assumed (without any economic evidence), and there is, since those agreements have *per se* such a great probability of adverse effects, no need for any evidence at all.[98] Hence, there is no need for any economic analysis of "effects" which would establish that a distortion of competition has occurred.[99] Moreover, the decisions of the Slovenian competition authority confirm this doctrinal view almost unanimously.[100]

Obviously, such a doctrinal position and UVK enforcement policy which focuses solely on "object" and disregards "effect" is at odds with previously listed economic and legal arguments. As argued, whenever market evidence shows that prices are not substantially above competitive levels (effect based intervention), antitrust intervention may be less compelling or even completely unnecessary.[101] Such an intervention would merely entail needless transaction costs (administration costs) and would represent pure welfare loss.

Posner, as previously stated, argues that such an enforcement policy in which emphasis has been placed on proving an agreement to fix prices (and not on the effect) rather than on proving the effects of the seller's conduct on price and output is simply a non-economic and inefficient one.[102] Such an approach is actually harmful to an effective competition policy.[103] If the economic evidence presented in a case warrants an inference of collusive pricing, there is neither legal nor practical justification for requiring evidence that will support the further inference that the collusion was explicit.[104] Furthermore, there is now ample empirical evidence that

95 To pomeni, da zadošča že, da je cilj sporazuma omejevanje konkurence in učinek ni pomemben (literally: the effect is not important); *ibid.*

96 Repas 2010, p. 169.

97 *Ibid.*

98 *Ibid.*

99 See *e.g.* UVK 306-14/2006, 26.2.2007.

100 See *e.g.* UVK 306-51/2005, 27.10.2006; UVK 306-21/2005, 1.2.2006; UVK 306-62/2005, 15.11.2006; UVK 306-83/2005, 18.1.2006; UVK 306-77/2005, 25.11.2005 *etc.*

101 Van den Bergh & Camesasca 2006, p. 202.

102 Posner 2001.

103 Many attempts to fix price may have negligible consequences, while much serious price fixing may escape detection altogether because detectable overt communication is necessary for proof of an attempt but is not always necessary to bring about a concerted increase of price above the competitive level; *ibid.* at p. 53.

104 From an economic standpoint it is a detail whether the collusive pricing scheme was organised and implemented in such a way as to generate evidence of actual communication (object); Posner 2001, p. 94.

the traditional "object" approach to price fixing resulted in a significant distortion of the enforcement efforts.[105] To sum up, competition authority's intervention would in such instances imply pure waste of scarce resources (inefficiency).

Moreover, this economic reasoning is explicitly utilised also by the European Commission's Horizontal Guidelines which admits that the anti-competitive outcomes of the agreement depend on the economic context, taking into account the nature of the agreement as well as the parties' combined market power.[106] Recent EU Commission and Courts' decisions have increasingly recognised that the previous formalistic approach (object) has no place in a modern effects-based competition regime and, the need for a detailed substantive analysis of the impact of an agreement under Article 101 TFEU has become even more relevant.

3.2 *Assessment of the Slovenian Law in Action*

As previously stated, the vast majority of UVK and Slovenian courts' decisions are concerned with the "object" and not with the "effect". The survey of relevant cases[107] indeed reveals the UVK's focus on the "object" where the actual distortion, effect on competition has not been assessed at all. Moreover, the UVK has in the *Združenje turističnih agencij Slovenije*[108] case actually established that there was no effect on the competition between tourist agencies, or on consumer prices charged, since there was merely a unified registration fee (which was part of the final price). In other words, the UVK established that the tourist association agreement on the unified registration fee did not give rise to an anti-competitive effect. Yet, the fact that the Association of tourist agencies prescribed the unified registration fee (for association's registration services abroad), has been regarded as an association's "object" to restrict the competition and represented sufficient ground for the UVK's intervention (imposed sanctions). Obviously, UVK's enforcement policy in cases where market evidence actually show that prices are not substantially above competitive levels (effect based intervention), makes antitrust intervention less compelling or even completely unnecessary. Such an intervention merely imposes needless transaction costs (administration costs), represents pure waste of resources and is also not coherent with recent EU Commission and Courts' decisions.

However, in one case the UVK has investigated whether the "effect" of an agreement is a distortion of competition. In the *Lekarniška zbornica Slovenije*[109] case the

105 For further arguments see *supra*.

106 EC Horizontal Guidelines

107 *Nova Ljubljanska banka/Banka Celje/Nova KBM/Abanka Vipa v. UVK*, UVK 306-14/2007, 26.2.2007; *Združenje turističnih agnecij Slovenije v. UVK*, UVK 306-77/2005, 25.11.2005; *Gospodarska zbornica Slovenije & Združenje za tisk in medije ter Strokovno združenje založnikov in knjigotržcev v. UVK*, UVK 306-21/2005, 1.2.2006.

108 UVK 306-77/2005, 25.11.2005. In this case the association of Slovenian tourist agencies prescribed to its members a unified registration fee for its registration services.

109 UVK 3072-11/2003, 1.2.2005. In this case Slovene Chamber of Pharmacies has in Art. 27 Code determined rules regarding restrictions about advertising pharmacy services.

UVK has investigated whether the pharmacy's restriction of prescription medicine advertisement may as its effect distort competition.[110] The UVK has in order to demonstrate the adverse effect of such advertisement restriction employed a questionnaire on the pharmacies' advertisement practices. The performed analysis demonstrated that the internal advertisement practice (informative advertisements between pharmacies), which actually never reached the public and where there was actually no "outside" advertisement, did not distort competition. Such a "questionnaire economic analysis" performed by the UVK is at least dubious and should be open to criticism. First, such an analysis of the advertisement's type has nothing to do with a serious economic analysis of anti-competitive effects. Second, the available facts of the case show that indeed there might be an "effect" based distortion of competition. A profound economic analysis (in accordance to previously established principles) may well reveal a rise in prices above the competitive level (distortion of competition) and stress the irrelevance of internal advertisement procedures.

To conclude, it is obvious that the UVK (and the court) has in this case misunderstood the core legal and economic concepts and theories, and also mishandled available economic evidence. Moreover, a path for more coherent application of EU competition provisions, theory and the European Court of Justice case law appears evident.

4. Conclusion

This contribution represents a survey of the economic and legal literature on the current EU competition law distinction between an "object" and "effect" as provided in Article 101(1) TFEU, and derives several substantive principles for improved and coherent judicial application of this distinction. It discusses the development of the distinction between "object" and "effect" within the case law of the European Court of Justice and its Slovenian counterpart till its present day's application. It also offers a doctrinal critique on the way Slovenian Courts and Competition authority (UVK) apply the distinction and on possible alternatives that have been identified in the literature. Moreover, it also assesses related Slovenian statutory provisions and doctrinal comments where a path for possible improvements appear evident.

The main findings can be summarised as follows: (1) modern EU competition policy has implemented a move towards an economic, effect-based approach that focuses on the market power and market outcomes; (2) growing law and economics literature shows that, in the absence of market power, agreements between firms will not give rise to anti-competitive outcomes; (3) law and economics literature

110 More accurately, the disputable issues were the restraints of advertisements provided in Art. 27 of The codex of pharmaceutical deontology – the restrain of trade on the cost of other pharmacies and the preclusion of any additional (and free-of-charge) services.

offers a set of economic evidence that can be used to indicate the existence of collusive pricing even though no overt acts of collusion were detected; (4) the Slovenian doctrinal position and enforcement policy which focuses solely on "object" and disregards "effect" is incoherent with modern EU competition law practice; (5) an assessment of Slovenian competition policy and related case law reveals a lack of economic understanding, ineffective competition policy, and imposition of needless transaction costs representing pure waste of resources; and finally (6) economic evidence is applied rarely, inaccurately and is very often misunderstood or mishandled.

Instructively, the provided analysis also shows that it might well be that the Slovenian national competition authority (and the court) has, while assessing "object/effect" cases often misunderstood the core legal and economic concepts and theories, and also mishandled available economic evidence. Finally, a path for a more coherent application of EU competition provisions, theory and the European Court of Justice case law appears evident.

The Dichotomy between Object and Effect Restrictions under Article 101(1) TFEU and the Relationship between the Articles 101(1) and 101(3) TFEU against the Backdrop of the Economisation of European Competition Law

D. Abdoelkarim

1. Introduction[1]

Competition policy can be used to pursue a number of different objectives all of which are not mutually compatible.[2] The main objectives and priorities of European competition policy have not remained static since the introduction of competition law. Traditionally, the main objectives of European competition law are to facilitate the creation of a single European market and to protect individual economic freedoms. More recently, however, there has been a trend towards placing a standard of consumer welfare at the heart of competition policy.[3] The two most important goals of EU competition law at this time, being the market integration goal and the economic goal relating either to consumer welfare alone or a broader perspective on competition law, carry a large potential for conflict. This on-going debate and criticism about the application and interpretation of Article 101(1) TFEU has been stirred up again by the recent judgments in the *T Mobile* case[4] and the

1 Due to the entry into force of the Lisbon Treaty on the 1 December 2009, Art. 81 TEC is now referred to as Art. 101 TFEU and the Court of First Instance will be referred to as the General Court.

2 P. Craig & G. de Búrca, *EU Law; Text Cases and Materials* (4th ed.), Oxford 2008, p. 950.

3 Commission guidelines on the application of Art. 101(3) TFEU.

4 Judgment of the Court (Third Chamber) of 4 June 2009, Case C-8/08 (*T-Mobile Netherlands BV, KPN Mobile NV, Orange Nederland NV and Vodafone Libertel NV v. Raad van bestuur van de Nederlandse Mededingingsautoriteit*), ECR 2009, p. I-04529. This case concerned a meeting between five mobile telecommunication operators which entered into an agreement or concerted practice relating to remuneration for dealers with regard to telephone mobile post subscriptions. Postpaid subscriptions are characterised by the fact that the number of minutes called in a particular period is invoiced to the customer subsequently; generally there is, in addition, a fixed subscription price which may also include a credit in respect of call minutes. The Dutch Competition Authority qualified the conduct as an anti-competitive concerted practice and found that in addition to an infringement of Art. 6(1) of the Dutch Competition Act, the conduct concerned constituted an infringement of Art. 101(1) TFEU.

GlaxoSmithKline case.[5] In the latter case, the General Court referred to the goal of consumer welfare as to establish a restriction of competition, whereas the European Court of Justice (hereinafter: the ECJ) in appeal reminded us of the broader objectives of competition law: competition law is not only about consumer welfare, but also about competition on the market as such. While the goal of market integration may sometimes take precedent over the more economic goal, this does not imply that no attention should be given to the economic efficiency of agreements, even if those agreements clearly seek to restrict cross-border trade. By ignoring the impact on consumer welfare, decisions which focus purely on the market integration goal may have unpersuasive outcomes.[6]

Tied to the discussion on the goals of competition law is the dichotomy between object restrictions and effect restrictions. As is well known, this distinction is made in the text of Article 101(1) TFEU itself. Until recently, it was presumed that 'appreciable'[7] object restrictions have by definition negative effects on consumer welfare and competition. Therefore, in case of object infringements, no analysis of the effects of the restriction is required under European law (and therefore usually also by national courts and national competition authorities). This approach is called a form-based approach, in that – though it looks beyond the pure legal form of an agreement – the economic effects on the market are not researched. In the *GlaxoSmithKline* case[8] the General Court introduced a more economic analysis of object restrictions. The ECJ, however, put this possible new trend to a stop in the *T-Mobile* case.[9] These cases will be repeatedly addressed throughout this paper, since they are illustrative for the on-going debate concerning Article 101(1) TFEU.

The consequence of a form-based assessment of object restrictions under Article 101(1) TFEU is that we are left with a legal structure that appears contradictory. The traditional interpretation under Article 101(1) TFEU entails a legal formalistic interpretation of whether an agreement is said to affect competition. To add a

---

5 Judgment of the Court of First Instance (Fourth Chamber, extended composition) of 27 September 2006, Case T-168/01 (*GlaxoSmithKline Services Unlimited v. Commission of the European Communities*), ECR 2006, p. II-02969. The case concerned a dual pricing system by GlaxoSmithKline in its General Sale Conditions to some of its medicines. Only medicines reimbursed by the Spanish health authorities and marketed through pharmacies and hospitals did not exceed the maximum industrial price, while other medicines were priced according objective and non-discriminatory economic conditions. This dual pricing system meant that pharmaceutical products purchased by Spanish wholesalers, and re-sold in other Member States, would cost more than those destined for the Spanish market. The differences in pricing restricted parallel trade in the pharmaceutical products. Therefore the Commission held that the agreement limiting parallel trade had as its *object* of restricting competition.

6 S. Bishop & M. Walker, *The Economics of EC Competition Law: Concepts, Application and Measurement*, University ed., Sweet and Maxwell 2010, p. 7.

7 Case 5/69 *Völk v. Vervaecke* (1969), ECR 295.

8 Judgment of the Court of First Instance (Fourth Chamber, extended composition) of 27 September 2006, Case T-168/01 (*GlaxoSmithKline Services Unlimited v. Commission of the European Communities*), ECR 2006, p. II-02969.

9 Judgment of the Court (Third Chamber) of 4 June 2009, Case C-8/08 (*T-Mobile Netherlands BV, KPN Mobile NV, Orange Nederland NV and Vodafone Libertel NV v. Raad van bestuur van de Nederlandse Mededingingsautoriteit*), ECR 2009, p. I-04529.

third element of discussion to this background paper – the relationship between the first and the third paragraph of Article 101 TFEU – the assessment of the compatibility of the agreements under Article 101(3) TFEU, on the other hand, seems to return to an economic view of the impact on competition.[10] The ECJ endorses a formalistic approach under Article 101(1) TFEU with the use of object restrictions where solely the objective intent, and not its effect, is sufficient to establish a restriction of effective competition.[11] Due to this controversy agreements which fall under the scope of Article 101(1) TFEU may have both features that enhance and features that restrict competition. Regardless of the European Commission's (hereinafter: Commission) leniency towards crisis cartels,[12] horizontal agreements such as horizontal price fixing, horizontal market division and boycotts are clear examples of per se illegalities in the sense that no beneficial results may be acquired from them. However, certain horizontal agreements and especially certain vertical agreements are more complicated and an economic assessment is necessary to determine whether those agreements actually – in effect– restrict competition.

Although the European Courts never formally acknowledged the application of a rule of reason for the assessment of object restrictions,[13] the ECJ stated that in assessing agreements under Article 101(1) TFEU, particular account must be taken of the economic context and actual structure of the market in which the undertakings operate.[14] This requirement has recently been reiterated by the Court in the *T-Mobile* case.[15] In subsequent cases the ECJ resorted to a substantive evaluation of the agreements and appraisal of beneficial economic effects, encouraging the consideration of agreements outside the scope of Article 101(1) TFEU, regardless of some of its restrictive effects on pricing.[16] On the one hand, the General Court denies the existence of a rule of reason,[17] while on the other hand the ECJ

10 Bishop & Walker 2010, p. 160.

11 Judgment of the Court (Third Chamber) of 4 June 2009, Case C-8/08 (*T-Mobile Netherlands BV, KPN Mobile NV, Orange Nederland NV and Vodafone Libertel NV v. Raad van bestuur van de Nederlandse Mededingingsautoriteit*), ECR 2009, p. I-04529.

12 The Commission has shown leniency towards crisis cartels in which firms co-ordinately reduced capacity due to declining demand and permitted restructuring cartels, when competition was not substantially eliminated. See for example: *Synthetic fibres*, Official Journal 1984, L 207/17. *Stichting Baksteen*, Official Journal 1994, L 131/15. *Bayer/BP Chemicals*, Official Journal 1988, L 150/35.

13 Rule of reason in the sense of US Antitrust law, meaning balancing the pro-competitive effects against the anti-competitive effects of an agreement.

14 Judgment of the Court of First Instance (Second Chamber) of 15 September 1998, Joined cases T-374/94, T-375/94, T-384/94 and T-388/94 (*European Night Services and others*) ECR 1998, p. II-03141, para. 136.

15 For the establishment of an anti-competitive object of an agreement, it is sufficient that it has the potential to have a negative impact on competition. Case C-8/08 *T-Mobile*, paras 31, 33.

16 A. Pera & V. Auricchio, "Consumer welfare, standard of proof and the objectives of competition policy", *European Competition Journal*, March 2005, Vol. 1 , p. 158. Case 78/70 *Metro v. Deutsche grammophon*, Case 258/78 *Nungesser v. Commission*, Case 161/84 *Pronuptia v. Schillgallis*, Case C-234/89 *Delimitis v. Henninger Brau.*

17 Judgment of the Court of First Instance (First Chamber, extended composition) of 11 July 1996, Joined cases T-528/93, T-542/93, T-543/93 and T-546/93 (*Métropole and others*), ECR 1996 p. II-00649.

provides for a 'less formalistic' application of Article 101 TFEU by weighing the pro- and anti-competitive effects. This is confusing in light of the relevance of Article 101 (3) TFEU. Should the inclusion of an economic rule of reason within 101(1) TFEU without casting aside Article 101(3) TFEU be considered?

This contribution focuses on criticism on the assessment of agreements under Article 101 TFEU. This criticism is still present after the modernisation of competition law in 2004[18] which indicates that the traditional strict legalistic approach to the enforcement of competition law by the Commission is considered a ship sailed. Nevertheless, the trend towards economisation of the assessment of agreements under Article 101 TFEU raises the following issues:

- First, there is a concern of what the ultimate goals of European competition law should be. As will be illustrated by the *GlaxoSmithKline* case and the *T-Mobile* case, there is a divergence between on the hand, the approach taken by the ECJ and on the other hand, the approach taken by the General Court and the Commission.
- Also, it is questionable whether the formalistic approach to object restrictions under Article 101(1) TFEU established by the ECJ, still bears grounds against the backdrop of economisation of competition law.
- Finally, it seems unclear whether the adoption of an 'economic' rule of reason under Article 101(1) TFEU, which seems consistent with the case law of the ECJ, will still preserve a role for Article 101(3) TFEU.

2. Background

2.1 The Concept of 'Economisation'

To understand the nature of the debate, it must be explained what in this paper are considered to be the underlying concepts of economisation of competition law. Many different schools of thought have evolved with respect to competition economics.[19] The Chicago School has undeniably changed competition law thinking profoundly in the sense that it placed economic analysis at the centre of competition law.[20] The basic underlying concept of this 'economisation' is the belief that competition must be understood as the maximization of consumer welfare, or economic efficiency, and that this requires economic reasoning.[21] Post-Chicago analysis acknowledges the efficiency goal but at the same time recognizes real-life

18 The criticism on the legalistic approach of the Commission in its decisions, where the European Courts required sound economic reasoning is no longer a major issue since the introduction of the modernisation of competition law. Therefore the overly broad application of Art. 101 TFEU before the modernisation is not taken into consideration.

19 For a good description and understanding of these schools of thought, see D. Hildebrand, *The role of economic analysis in the EC Competition rules* (3th ed.), International Competition Law Series, Kluwer 2009, p. 4.

20 A. Jones & B. Sufrin, *EC Competition Law: Text Cases and Materials* (3th ed.), Oxford 2008, p. 30.

21 R.H. Bork, *The Antritrust Paradox: A Policy at War with Itself*, Basic books 1978 (reprinted 1993), pp. 426-429. See excerpt Jones & Sufrin 2008, p. 26.

difficulties in the application of competition rules to achieve this.[22] Although the theoretical framework of the Chicago School cannot be applied to European integration, in the European school of thought, initiated and developed by the Commission,[23] the same underlying concept seems to have crawled into the enforcement of competition law by the Commission.

2.1.1 Economisation of European Competition Law

A direct cause of the trend towards economisation of the enforcement of European competition law is that the European Courts have emphasised the role of economic analysis in the decision making process of the Commission. Annulments of Commission decisions by the General Court,[24] based on a lack of economic reasoning have been an important reason for the adoption of a more economics based approach to the enforcement of European competition law. This more economic approach is a rather evolutionary development of competition law enforcement in the European Union; so far, there has been a shift from a competitive assessment which emphasizes the consideration whether competitors are harmed towards an assessment which focuses on whether competition is harmed to the detriment of consumers. This change to a more economic approach is illustrated by the revised Block Exemption Regulations (hereinafter: BERs) and corresponding guidelines with regard to both Articles 101 and 102 TFEU. Economists have played a significant role in the transformation of BERs from a form-based approach to an effects based approach.[25] Furthermore, the newly drafted Merger Regulation (139/2004) and state aid provisions also underline this economisation.

Due to the economisation the Commission has placed consumer welfare and economic efficiency at the heart of European competition law. The economisation of European competition law is strongly connected to the debate on what the actual goals of European competition law are or what they should be.[26] If in this economisation of competition law, economic efficiency and consumer welfare are seen to be of central importance, the establishment of the anti-competitive object of an agreement under Article 101(1) TFEU should not be based on its form, but on

22 Jones & Sufrin 2008, p.32.

23 Hildebrand 2009, p. 169.

24 See cases: Judgment of the Court of First Instance (Fifth Chamber, extended composition) of 6 June 2002, Case T-342/99 (*Airtours v. Commission*) ECR 2002 p. II-02585. Judgment of the Court of First Instance (First Chamber) of 25 October 2002, Case T-5/02 & T-80/02, (*Tetra Laval v. Commission*) ECR 2002 p. II-04381. Judgment of the Court of First Instance (Fourth Chamber, extended composition) of 11 July 2007, Case T-351/03 (*Schneider Electric SA v. Commission of the European Communities*), ECR 2007 p. II-02237. Judgment of the Court of First Instance (Third Chamber) of 13 July 2006, Case T-464/04 (*Independent Music Publishers and Labels Association (Impala, association internationale) v. Commission of the European Communities*), ECR 2006 p. II-02289.

25 I. Lianos & I. Kokkoris, *The Reform of EC Competition Law, New Challenges*, International Competition law series, Kluwer Law International 2010, p. 186.

26 A. Gerbrandy, "Case C-8/08, T-Mobile e.a. v. Raad van Bestuur vd NMa, Judgment of the Court (Third Chamber) of 4 June 2009", 47 *CMLR* 1206, 2010.

its likely impact on the market.[27] For this reason object restrictions, regardless of whether their form implies anti-competitive effects, should be assessed in their legal and economic context, where emphasis is on the economic context. In this approach, it is essential to evaluate the actual impacts on competition in order to determine whether the assessed conduct represents effective competitive behaviour or anti-competitive behaviour.[28]

2.2 Inconsistent Application

The ruling of the General Court in the *GlaxoSmithKline* case,[29] suggests a trend to effect analysis of object restrictions. The General Court reasoned that although agreements which seek the restriction of parallel trade must in principle be regarded as having as their object the prevention of competition, the application of Article 101(1) TFEU requires an analysis designed to determine whether it has as its object or effect the prevention, restriction or distortion of competition on the relevant market, to the detriment of the final consumer.[30]

In the *T-Mobile* case, the ECJ was called upon 'to clarify whether and to what extent assessment of the specific market circumstances, the market conduct of the undertakings concerned and the effects of that conduct on competition is required for presumption of an anti-competitive object.'[31] In this case the ECJ overturned the General Court's judgement in the *GlaxoSmithKline* case. While previously the General Court ruled that an agreement can only be restrictive by object if the agreement will have *detrimental effects on consumers*, the ECJ reasoned in the *T-Mobile* case that Article 101 TFEU is not designed to protect only the interests of competitors and consumers, but also 'to protect the structure of the market and thus competition as such'.[32] Afterwards, this view has been reiterated by the ECJ in *GlaxoSmithKline*. The ECJ held that there is no indication in Article 101(1) TFEU, nor in case law, that only those agreements which deprive consumers of certain advantages may have an anti-competitive object.[33]

There are opposite flanks with respect to the assessment of object restrictions under Article 101(1) TFEU. Advocate General Kokott and the ECJ find such an assessment unnecessary, whereas the General Court engaged in an effect based

27 *Ibid.*

28 Bishop & Walker 2010, p. 4.

29 Judgment of the Court of First Instance (Fourth Chamber, extended composition) of 27 September 2006, Case T-168/01 (*GlaxoSmithKline Services Unlimited v. Commission of the European Communities*), ECR 2006, p. II-02969.

30 *Ibid.*, paras 115-119. Still, when analyzing the effects, the General Court came to the conclusion that the agreement had as effect the restriction of competition.

31 Opinion of Advocate General Kokott delivered on 19 February 2009, Case-8/08 *T-Mobile*, ECR 2009, p. I-04529, para. 2.

32 Judgment of the Court (Third Chamber) of 4 June 2009, Case C-8/08 (*T-Mobile Netherlands BV, KPN Mobile NV, Orange Nederland NV and Vodafone Libertel NV v. Raad van bestuur van de Nederlandse Mededingingsautoriteit*), ECR 2009, p. I-04529, para. 38.

33 Judgment of the Court (Third Chamber) of 6 October 2009, Joined cases C-501/06 P, C-513/06 P, C-515/06 P and C-519/06 P (*GlaxoSmithKline*), ECR 2009, p. I-09291, paras 62, 63.

approach to object infringements. The *T-Mobile* case illustrates the confusion on a decentralized level around the 'object' requirement against the trend of economisation of competition law. The Netherlands Trade and Industry Appeals Tribunal (hereinafter: the Appeals Tribunal) held the view that it may be concluded from the competition case law of the ECJ that the anti-competitive object of an agreement is established, if experience shows that by virtue of that agreement, 'irrespective of economic circumstances, competition is always, or most always, prevented, restricted or distorted.'[34] According to the Appeals Tribunal, this is the case when the actual detrimental effects are unmistakable and will occur irrespective of the characteristic features of the relevant market. In the view of the Appeals Tribunal, it is therefore always necessary 'to examine the effects of a concerted practice in order to ensure that conduct is not regarded as pursuing the object of restricting competition when it is clear that it does not have any restrictive effects'.[35]

Legal commentators have defended the proposition that in *every* case the actual effects of the agreement must be determined; consequently also in the case of object restrictions.[36] The problematic aspects of the application of competition law has instigated the debate about the interpretation and application of Article 101(1) TFEU. There is great uncertainty because the meaning and function of the object requirement remain unspecified.[37] What exactly are these notions of 'structure of the market' and the protection of 'competition as such' as referred to by the ECJ in *T-Mobile*? What should be the ultimate goals of competition law? What is meant by a restriction of competition under Article 101(1) TFEU and how should object restrictions be established?[38] Although it is not the purpose of this paper to provide definite answers to these questions, this paper aims to provide some useful insights to substantiate the debate.[39]

34 Judgment of the Court (Third Chamber) of 4 June 2009, Case C-8/08 (*T-Mobile Netherlands BV, KPN Mobile NV, Orange Nederland NV and Vodafone Libertel NV v. Raad van bestuur van de Nederlandse Mededingingsautoriteit*), ECR 2009, p. I-04529, para. 20.

35 *Ibid.*

36 B. Baarsma & J. Poort, "Mededingingseconomisch perspectief op het leerstuk van de doelbeperking: toepassing op het BIDS-arrest", *NTER*, Vol. 15, No. 2, 2009, pp. 50-58. See also: H.M. Cornelissen, "General Motors BV/Commissie – Het HvJ EG bevestigt het arrest van het GvEA: Gevolgen van een doelbeperking blijven desondanks een aandachtspunt voor de Commissie", *NTER*, Vol. 12, No. 8/9, 2006, p. 185.

37 O. Odudu, *The Boundaries of EC Competition Law, the Scope of Article 81*, Oxford 2006, p. 3.

38 Alternative questions but not the focus of this paper: Does the examination of the legal and economic context in cases of object restrictions encompass a counterfactual assessment? How much examination should take place before, by an economic approach, sufficient evidence is provided for the establishment of an object restriction? E.M.H. Loozen, *Het begrip mededingingsbeperking zoals neergelegd in artikel 101(1) VWEU: een beslismodel*, Boom Juridische uitgevers 2010, pp. 44, 48.

39 Despite the fact that Art. 102 TFEU is beyond the scope of this paper, it must be noted that the challenging duality between forms and effects based approaches in the application of Art. 102 TFEU has also become a recent subject of debate. The Commission has taken an effect based approach to abuse of dominant position in its Guidance Paper on Enforcement Priorities in the Application of Article 102 TFEU. See A. Ezrachi, "Form and effects based approaches: A challenging duality in the application of Art. 102 TFEU", *Concurrences Review of Competition Laws*, No. 2, 2010.

3. The Goals of EU Competition Law

The interpretation of Article 101(1) TFEU has been the subject of a debate about the multitude of competition goals and the many objectives that have been pursued by the European Courts and the Commission over the last decades in the area of competition law.[40] This discussion is highlighted by the judgements in the *GlaxoSmithKline* case and the *T-Mobile* case.

3.1 Competition Goals

Ever since the case of *Consten and Grundig*,[41] the traditional objective of European competition law has been to facilitate the creation of a common market. Initially, the competition provisions were introduced in view to their role in the process of market integration.[42] Competition law plays both a positive and negative role in the integration of the common market. The negative role is illustrated by preventing measures to isolate domestic markets from each other. The positive role is reflected in the way that competition law encourages trade between Member States by providing a level playing field in Europe and by facilitating cross border trade and integration.[43] Another goal in European competition law has been the protection of individual economic freedom. Individual freedoms are observed as an important benefit from preserving competition.[44] It follows from this ordoliberal approach that competition law should create and protect the conditions of competition, and should not solely be a means by which pure economic objectives are to be achieved.[45] An ordoliberal approach to competition policy leads to the protection of competitors, 'regardless of the effects on efficiency, rather than the protection of competition, as it prizes the freedom of all citizens to be able to enter and compete on markets.'[46]

The more modern goals of competition law interpreted by the Commission are (amongst others) reflected in the guidelines on the application of Article 101(3) TFEU. The Commission stresses that the aim of the European competition rules is to protect competition on the market as a means of enhancing consumer welfare and the efficient allocation of resources.[47] The predominant importance of an efficient allocation of resources is explicitly mentioned in Article 120 TFEU. Subsequently in

40 R. Wesseling, *The Modernisation of EC Antitrust Law,* Hart Publishing 2000, p. 80. See also: R. Whish, *Competition Law* (6th ed.), 2009, p. 19. Even the statements of the European Commission in its Annual Reports on Competition Policy show that there are a multitude of goals attributed to competition policy which have shifted in emphasis over time. For an overview of these statements, see: R.J. Van den Bergh & P.D. Camesasca, *European Competition Law and Economics: A Comparative Perspective,* Sweet & Maxwell 2006, pp. 5, 38.

41 Judgment of the Court of 13 July 1966, Joined Cases 56 and 58/64 *Consten Grundig, European Court Reports*, English special edition, p. 00299.

42 Wesseling 2000, pp. 48-49.

43 See Whish 2009, pp. 22-23.

44 Van den Bergh & Camesasca 2006, p. 48. Also, the European Commission held in its Fifteenth Annual Report on Competition Policy in 1985, that effective competition preserves the freedom of individual economic operators and therefore it fosters the spirit of enterprise.

45 Jones & Sufrin 2008, p. 35.

46 *Ibid.*

47 Guidelines on the application of Art. 81(3), para. 33.

its Annual Report on Competition Policy of 2008, the Commission emphasized that it 'considers it essential that the main thrust of competition policy should be on maximizing consumer welfare.'[48]. This pursuit of economic efficiency and consumer welfare is consistent with the underlying concept of 'economisation' of competition law.

3.2 Higher Goals

Exemptions from competition rules were granted by the Commission to forms of cooperation between undertakings which were desirable, to promote either the market integration or the attainment of 'higher goals'.[49] The Commission previously indicated that the effects of competition policy in other areas always have to be taken into account.[50] It seems, however, that the view of the Commission has shifted since the Commission now attributes a secondary role to other goals pursued by the Treaty provisions. In the guidelines on the application of Article 101(3) TFEU the Commission stated that these other goals *can* be taken into account in the assessment under Article 101(3).[51] There should be interaction between the competition goals and other 'higher' goals pursued by the Treaty. It is not uncommon that these different goals conflict, resulting in difficult trade-offs.

3.3 Conflicting Goals and the Goal of Market-Integration

In *GlaxoSmithKline*, the goal of market integration was undermined due to a restriction of parallel trade.[52] European competition law is aimed to promote intra-brand competition and parallel trade to reduce price differences across the European Union. Parallel trade allows rivalry between distributors which will result in lower prices to the benefit of consumers. Intra-brand competition will be significantly hampered if manufacturers vertically integrate with a few or only one distributor(s) for a specific territory. This will prevent other distributors from operating in that territory, meaning that the official distributor is shielded from other distributors' competitive pressure. Consequently, consumers will pay higher prices. As has been pointed out: 'in EU competition law, the rationale for prohibiting market partitioning lies in the policy objective to ensure the integration of the internal market, rather than the aim to protect consumers from being

---

48 Commission of the European Communities, *Report on Competition Policy 2008*, Brussels, 23.7.2009, COM(2009) 374 final, par. 108.

49 See for example OJ L187/47, 2000 5 *CMLR* 635 (CECED), OJ L131/15, 1995, 4 *CMLR* 646 *Stichting Baksteen*, and OJ L144/20, 1994, *Exxon/Shell*. Goals include environment, industrial policy, employment, cultural policy and national interests.

50 Statement former Commissioner for Competition van Miert in 'Die Wettbewerbspolitik der neuen Komission' (1995), 45 *WuW* 553, 554.

51 Guidelines on the application of Art. 81(3), para. 42.

52 According to the glossary of the European Commission, parallel trade is 'trade in products, which takes place outside the official distribution system set up by a particular firm. Through their own distribution system, firms may handle differences in prices for different countries, taking advantage of the national differences in the different behaviour of consumers. Parallel traders buy products in countries where they are sold at lower prices and sell them in high-price countries. The flow of products thereby created is called parallel trade.' See: <http://ec.europa.eu/competition/publications/glossary_en.pdf>.

impoverished by lack of intra-brand competition.'[53] The ban on absolute territorial protection and price discrimination lie at the core of the *GlaxoSmithKline* case. These examples are illustrative of the conflict between the objective of market integration and the goals of economic efficiency and consumer welfare.[54] On the one hand, territorial protection is prohibited because it is meant to segregate markets along national borders. But on the other hand, this means that efficiency savings resulting from these intra-brand restrictions, such as coping with free riding[55] and incentives to increase sale efforts, are lost.[56] As mentioned above, in both the *T-Mobile* case and the *GlaxoSmithKline* case the ECJ held that Article 101(1) TFEU is not designed only to protect the interests of competitors or consumers, but also to protect the market and thus competition as such.[57] Herewith, the Court whistled back the General Court, and indirectly the European Commission, in its pursuit of consumer welfare.[58] A very far-reaching interpretation of this judgment suggests that the ECJ considers market integration to be the overriding goal of European competition law, although this is not explicitly expressed. A more realistic interpretation suggests that these goals must be balanced and that the choice of one goal at the expense of the other must be well substantiated with convincing argumentation.[59] Whereas the General Court in GlaxoSmithKline applied the standard of consumer welfare, the ECJ ruled that a restriction of parallel trade is contrary to the market-integration objective and is therefore anti-competitive.[60]

---

53 C. Petrucci, "Parallel trade of pharmaceutical products: the ECJ finally speaks - comment on GlaxoSmithKline", 35 *European Law Review* 2, 2010, p. 276.

54 Some authors adhere to the view that the only goals of competition law should be efficiency and consumer welfare. They indicate that the objective of market integration is a perfectly legitimate goal, but it must be pursued by other instruments. They question the appropriateness of competition law as an instrument to further market integration. See Van den Bergh & Camesasca 2006, p. 47.

55 The distributor's incentive to make investments for the promotion of the manufacturers products would be undermined if distributors in other Member States where the brand has also been introduced, to ' free ride' on the investments. To avoid free-riding, distributors active in other markets should be restrained from selling in a new market. See Van den Bergh & Camesasca 2006, p. 236.

56 See Van den Bergh & Camesasca 2006, p. 46.

57 Judgment of the Court (Third Chamber) of 4 June 2009, Case C-8/08 (*T-Mobile and others v. Nma*), ECR 2009, p. I-04529, para. 38.

58 Judgment of the Court (Third Chamber) of 6 October 2009, Joined cases C-501/06 P, C-513/06 P, C-515/06 P and C-519/06 P (*GlaxoSmithKline*), ECR 2009, p. I-09291, para. 63. See, by analogy, *T-Mobile Netherlands and Others*, paras 38, 39.

59 These cases illustrate the vagueness of the prevailing goals and the potential for conflicting competition goals As mentioned above, pharmaceutical producer GlaxoSmithKline attempted to prevent parallel trade in its pharmaceuticals out of Spain and Greece. Pharmaceutical prices throughout Europe are set by the government of the Member States. The government-set prices are low in Spain and Greece compared to the rest of Europe. The result is that it is profitable for wholesalers in Spain and Greece to import pharmaceuticals into Spain and Greece and then re-export them to higher priced countries such as France and the UK. GlaxoSmithKline has attempted to stop this trade by refusing to fulfil all the demand from wholesalers in Spain and by bypassing the use of wholesalers at all in Greece. The Commission has argued that this is contrary to the single market objective, therefore anti-competitive by object.

60 Earlier a clear sign may have been given in the *Bayer/Adalat* case that the goal of market integration is of smaller importance. (see Van den Bergh & Camesasca 2006, p. 46. See also excerpt: D. Geradin, A. Layne-Farrar & N. Petit, *EU Competition Law and Economics*, June 2010). In this case, the General Court and ECJ refused to consider that a unilateral action by a pharmaceutical supplier of rationing supplies in order to limit parallel trade amounted to an anti-competitive

The Commission itself has acknowledged the positive effects of vertical restraints, in particular in promoting non-price competition and improving the quality of services.[61] In the Guidelines on vertical restraints, the Commission recognises that exclusive distribution or similar restrictions may be helpful to solve the free rider problem or to 'open up and enter new markets'.[62] These are only two efficiencies of the eight identified by the Commission which prove that under certain conditions vertical agreements are likely to realise efficiencies and the development of new markets and that these efficiencies may offset possible negative effects.[63] As will be discussed in section 4, it is unlikely that these efficiencies will be revealed by only looking at the clauses of an agreement to establish a restriction of competition in the case of anti-competitive object.

Another example of tension between conflicting goals relates to price discrimination across the EU. Different prices in different geographical areas pose a threat to the common market.[64] From an economic perspective however, (perfect) price discrimination leads to maximized consumer welfare and may have beneficial consequences for consumers if overall output is increased. From a legal perspective however, price discrimination is flawed because 'discrimination as such' suggests negative effects.[65]

Furthermore, it follows from the Guidelines on the application of Article 101(3) TFEU that the objective of Article 101 TFEU is to protect competition on the market as a means of enhancing consumer welfare and to ensure an efficient allocation of resources.[66] A question then is how consumer welfare itself relates to the different concepts of efficiency.[67] Although allocative efficiency and consumer welfare are considered to be synonyms,[68] the concepts of economic efficiency are diverse and not immune to internal conflict. On the one hand, a conflict between dynamic efficiencies and consumer welfare is unlikely because consumers generally benefit from innovations, but on the other hand, a conflict is more likely to arise between consumer welfare and productive efficiency.[69]

---

agreement (Judgment of the Court (full Court) of 6 January 2004, Joined cases C-02/01P and C-03/01P (*Bundesverband der Arzneimittel-Importeure eV and Commission of the European Communities v. Bayer AG*), ECR 2004, p. I-00023. Judgment of the Court of First Instance (Fifth Chamber, extended composition) of 26 October 2000, Case T-41/96 (*Bayer AG v. Commission*), ECR 2000, p. II-03383). Although this observation is of less importance against the background of *T-Mobile*, it may explain the approach taken by the General Court in *GlaxoSmithKline*.

61 Guidelines on vertical restraints, para. 115.

62 *Ibid.*, para. 116.

63 *Ibid.*, para. 117. These efficiencies have also been reiterated by the Commission in the new Vertical Agreement Block Exemption Regulation which entered into force on 1 June 2010.

64 See Van den Bergh & Camesasca 2006, pp. 46, 47.

65 The tension in the area of price discrimination is much harder to solve in competition policy because here the standard of consumer welfare may run into theoretical difficulties. See J. Wallenberg, "Challenges in EU Competition Policy", in *Competition Policy Report*, 8 March 2010, European Round Table of Industrialists, p. 14.

66 Guidelines on the application of Art. 81(3), para.13.

67 See Van den Bergh & Camesasca 2006, p. 29 *et seq.*

68 P. Craig & G. de Búrca, General editors' preface in O. Odudu, *The Boundaries of EC Competition Law, The Scope of Article 81*, Oxford 2006, p. 3.

69 See also Wallenberg 2010, p. 15.

Also in the literature the question of whether competition is valued to promote efficiency, to achieve the objective of market integration, or to promote certain market freedoms is addressed.[70] It is acknowledged that the pursuit of one value may come at the expense of another, but a shift in favour of placing efficiency on top of the hierarchy of competition goals may be identified. The reasoning here is that since it is the purpose of integration to unlock efficiencies, that efficiency cannot be sacrificed to promote integration.[71] Despite the fact that this notion does not fit in the judgment of *GlaxoSmithKline* where efficiency and consumer welfare were sacrificed at the altar of market integration, an establishment of a hierarchy of goals would enable a consistent enforcement of Article 101 TFEU.

3.4 Restriction of Competition and Conflicting Goals

The debate about the goals of competition law is closely related to the establishment of a restriction of competition. If the ECJ is considering market integration to be the supreme goal of European competition law, it is indeed unnecessary to include an effect analysis of object infringement under Article 101(1) TFEU since it is fairly easy to demonstrate whether agreements will divide markets along national borders. If against the backdrop of economisation of competition, the focus were, however, to be placed on consumer welfare and economic efficiency, it will be necessary to include an economic analysis of the market conduct, specific market circumstances and the effects on competition to demonstrate detrimental effects of the market conduct on consumer welfare. From a goal-oriented perspective, the case of *GlaxoSmithKline* is a setback since the traditional goal of market integration does not fit well into the more modern concept of economisation of European competition law, let alone an overriding goal of market integration. Subsequently, in *T-Mobile*, the ECJ referred to the notion that competition law aims to protect 'competition as such'.[72] Some legal commentators have argued that the emphasis on the protection of competition implies that competition policy should aim to enhance competition, and not integration, thereby challenging agreements containing territorial restrictions.[73]

4. Article 101(1) TFEU and the Object & Effect Differentiation

Article 101(1) TFEU prohibits anti-competitive behaviour by cartels. The solid dichotomy between object and effect restrictions has evolved over the years in the well-established case law of the ECJ.[74] When analysing this dichotomy, the main

70 Odudu 2006, p. 2.

71 *Ibid.*, p. 22.

72 Judgment of the Court (Third Chamber) of 4 June 2009, Case C-8/08 (*T-Mobile Netherlands BV, KPN Mobile NV, Orange Nederland NV and Vodafone Libertel NV v. Raad van bestuur van de Nederlandse Mededingingsautoriteit*), ECR 2009, p. I-04529, para. 38.

73 Wesseling 2000, p. 81. He refers to Korah who continuously opposed the lack of economic reasoning in Commission decisions and ECJ case law with respect to restrictions to free cross border trade. V. Korah, "EEC Competition Policy – Legal Form or Economic Efficiency", 39, *Current Legal Problems* 1986, pp. 85-109.

74 For an historical and extensive overview of the dichotomy between object and effect restrictions, see Jones & Sufrin 2008, p. 219 *et seq*. See also: Whish 2009, p. 116 *et seq*.

focus is on the inconsistent application of Article 101 TFEU in this respect, and the debates arisen from this inconsistent application.

The starting point for this discussion lies in the *Société La Technique Minière (STM)* case (1966),[75] in which the ECJ stated that for agreements to be caught by the cartel prohibition in Article 101(1) TFEU, they must have as their object or effect the prevention, restriction or distortion within the common market.[76] The ECJ stressed that these requirements are not cumulative, but must be seen as two alternatives. This is indicated by the conjunction 'or'; it is thus necessary to first consider the precise purpose of the agreement in the economic context in which it is to be applied. Where the anti-competitive object of an agreement cannot be revealed by an analysis of the clauses of the agreement, the consequences of the agreement should then be considered. In order for the agreement to be caught by the prohibition, it is then necessary that those factors must be present which show that competition has in fact been prevented, restricted or distorted to an appreciable extent.[77]

It has been stressed by the European Courts in a number of cases that where the anti-competitive object of the agreement cannot be established, it is necessary to conduct an extensive analysis of the effect on the markets before it can be concluded whether the agreement has the effect of restricting competition.[78] The Court introduced a counterfactual when analysing the effect on competition, since the competition in question must be understood within the actual context in which it would occur in the absence of the agreement.[79] The need to establish this counterfactual was stressed by the General Court in the case *O2*.[80]

4.1 Object Requirement

The anti-competitive effects of some types of agreements can be determined based on their object; 'object' relating not to the subjective intention of parties entering into an agreement but the objective meaning and purpose considered in the economic context in which an agreement is to be applied.[81] In the *STM* case the

---

75 A French undertaking STM and a German undertaking MBU had signed an exclusive supply contract. This contract contained a clause entailing that STM had the exclusive right to sell grading equipment produced by MBU in France. However, STM could sell the goods outside France and parallel imports could be obtained from other countries. Due to a conflict between the two parties, STM argued that the contract was invalid under the cartel prohibition.

76 Since the dichotomy between object and effect restrictions is the central theme of this paper, it is assumed that there is in fact an agreement in its pure form, a decision by an association of undertakings or a concerted practice between undertakings which has an appreciable impact on competition or inter-state trade.

77 Judgment of the Court of 30 June 1966, Case 56/65 *Société Technique Minière v. Maschinenbau Ulm GmbH*, *European Court reports*, English special edition p. 00235, p. 249.

78 Examples: case 23/67 (1967) *Brasserie de Haecht v. Wilkin*, ECR 407, Case C-234/89 (1991) *Delimitis v. Henninger Bräu*, ECR, p. I-935.

79 Judgment of the Court of 30 June 1966, Case 56/65 *Société Technique Minière v. Maschinenbau Ulm Gmb*, European Court reports, English special edition p. 00235, p. 250.

80 Case T-328/03, O2 *GmbH & Co v. Commission* (2006), ECR, p. II-1231.

81 Whish 2009, p. 116.

ECJ held that the interference with competition must be inferred from all or some of the clauses of the agreement itself. In this early case, the ECJ indicated that agreements from which its precise purpose could be derived from all or some of its clauses, are condemned without further analysis of the market circumstances.[82] Two weeks later in the *Consten and Grundig* case,[83] the Court of Justice established a legal anti-competitive presumption of object restrictions, considering that Article 101(1) applies to agreements which have as their object the restriction of competition irrespective of their alleged effects.[84] Apart from establishing that Article 101(1) applies to both horizontal as well as vertical agreements, the Court of Justice ruled that 'for the purpose of applying Article 101(1) TFEU, there is no need to take account of the concrete effects of an agreement once it appears that it has as its object the prevention, restriction or distortion of competition.'[85] Ever since, the *Consten and Grundig* case has been marked as a landmark case for the dichotomy between object and effect restrictions and the legal presumption of anti-competitiveness of object restrictions has been reiterated by the European Courts in subsequent case law. Although these object restrictions do not require a qualitative analysis, there is a quantitative component to Article 101(1) TFEU which means that any restriction of competition must be appreciable.[86] This means that if it appears that an agreement whose anti-competitive object has been established does not have an appreciable impact on either competition or interstate trade, this agreement will not be caught by the prohibition in Article 101(1) TFEU.

Agreements containing obvious restrictions of competition such as price fixing, market sharing and/or the control of outlets are considered to be anti-competitive. In *European Night Services v. Commission*, the General Court indicated that due to their nature these types of agreements should be allocated into the 'object' box.[87] This object box is extended to the category of hardcore restrictions listed in the Block Exemption Regulations. In contrast with the tenets of economisation of competition law, the *actual effects* on consumer welfare and economic efficiency of these object restrictions are not considered within Article 101(1) TFEU for object restrictions. The case law of the Courts as well as the Commission Guidelines on

82 Judgment of the Court of 30 June 1966, Case 56/65 *Société Technique Minière v. Maschinenbau Ulm Gmb, European Court reports*, English special edition p. 00235, p. 249.

83 Cases 56 and 58/64, *Consten Grundig v. Commission* (1966) ECR 299. The case concerned absolute territorial protection. Grundig had granted the sole distributorship of its products to Consten in France. In order to obtain a trademark from Grundig which Consten could use against unauthorized sales in France, Consten agreed on taking a minimum amount of products and not to sell the products of competing manufacturers. Another distributor, UNEF bought Grundig products in Germany and sold them for a lower price than set by Consten in France. Consten alleged an infringement of its trademark and UNEF held that the agreement between Consten and Grundig violated Art. 85(1) EC, now Art. 101(1) TFEU.

84 Jones & Sufrin 2008, p. 230.

85 Judgment of the Court of 13 July 1966, Joined Cases 56 and 58/64 *Consten Grundig, European Court Reports*, English special edition, p. 00299, para. 342.

86 This minimum doctrine was formulated by the ECJ in case 5/69 *Völk v. Vervaecke* (1969), ECR p. 295.

87 Other hardcore restrictions are blacklisted in the Block Exemption Regulations. Whish 2009, p. 119.

the application of Article 101(3) indicate that if the object of an agreement is to restrict competition, the restrictions may be weighed against their claimed pro-competitive effects under Article 101(3) TFEU,[88] causing the burden of proof to shift to the undertakings concerned. This shift in analysis has the effect that the economic goal of competition law may come at the expense of other goals pursued by the Treaty. This will be discussed in section 5.

Critics also claim that the notion of competition employed by the Commission and the Courts overlooks the fact that competition can take a variety of forms.[89] The point is best illustrated by the so called beneficial restrictions of competition, meaning that in some circumstances restrictions of competition can have beneficial results. Many commentators have criticized the consequence that certain business conduct with the same economic effects have received dissimilar treatment under Article 101 TFEU.[90]

4.2 Opening the Debate

The cases of *STM* and *Consten and Grundig* opened the debate about the economic substance of Article 101(1) TFEU.[91] Where both cases concerned agreements entailing absolute territorial protection, the two cases appear to point in different directions. In the *STM* case, the ECJ indicated that it may be doubtful whether there is an interference with competition if the agreement seems really necessary for the penetration of a new area by an undertaking. The ECJ listed a number of factors which should be taken into account in order to decide whether an agreement has anti-competitive effects by its object or its effect.[92] This seemed to suggest that even in the case of absolute territorial protection the pro-competitive effects must be balanced against the anti-competitive effects. Advocate General Roemer pointed out that it would be artificial to apply 101(1) TFEU, as is shown by the *STM* case, based on purely theoretical considerations of situations, which upon closer examination reveal no appreciable adverse effects on competition, in order then to grant exemption on the basis of Article 101(3) TFEU.[93] However, the ECJ stuck to a formalistic consideration and held that absolute territorial

88 Judgment of the Court of First Instance (Fourth Chamber, extended composition) of 27 September 2006, Case T-168/01 (*GlaxoSmithKline Services Unlimited v. Commission of the European Communities*), ECR 2006, p. II-02969, para. 233. Joined cases 56 and 58/64 *Consten Grundig v. Commission*, 1966, ECR 299, p. 343. Judgment of the Court of First Instance, case T-17/93 *Matra Hachette v. Commission* (1994), ECR, p. II-595, para. 85. C-101/8 Commission Guidelines on the application of Article 81(3) of the Treaty, OJ 2004, para. 46. See also Judgment of the Court of First Instance (First Chamber, extended composition) of 11 July 1996, Joined Cases T-528/93, T-542/93, T-543/93 and T-546/93 (*Métropole and others*), ECR, p.1996 p. II-00649.

89 Wesseling 2000, p. 81.

90 Odudu 2006, pp. 3-4.

91 R. Nazzini, "Article 81 EC between the time present and time past: a normative critique of 'restriction of competition' in EU law", 43 *CMLR* 2006, p. 506.

92 Judgment of the Court of 30 June 1966, Case 56/65 *Société Technique Minière v. Maschinenbau Ulm Gmb*, *European Court reports*, English special edition p. 00235, p. 250.

93 Opinion of Mr Advocate General Roemer delivered on 27 April 1966, Cases 56 and 58/64 *Consten Grundig*, *European Court reports* English special edition p. 00299, p. 358, para. a.

protection has as its object the restriction of competition so that an assessment of the effects was unnecessary. Hence, the agreement assessed in the *STM* case contained less severe clauses with respect to the single market perspective than the agreement clauses assessed in the *Consten and Grundig* case which contained export bans. Restrictions of parallel trade are qualified as object restrictions.[94]

It has been argued that the cases of *STM* and *Consten and Grundig* are *consistent* and can be reconciled as being expressions of the principle that Article 101(1) TFEU prohibits collusive behaviour which leads to a reduction in consumer welfare, either by a limited output and high prices or through the partitioning of the common market, which is consistent with the objectives of the Treaty.[95] If this were to be the case, then it may be suggested that it would have been even more consistent to engage in an effect-based assessment under Article 101(1) TFEU, as advocated by AG Roemer in 1966.[96]

4.3 Rebuttable Presumption of Anti-Competitiveness

It has also been illustrated that the cases of *STM* and *Consten and Grundig* are *inconsistent* from an efficiency perspective. The argument runs that there is a legal presumption that certain types of conduct cause allocative inefficiency. The *STM* case suggests that this presumption is rebuttable, whereas *Consten and Grundig* suggests that this legal presumption is conclusive.[97] Accordingly, 'the ability to cast doubt on the applicability of the presumption that competition is restricted makes it clear that the presumption of necessary consequences is rebuttable rather than conclusive'.[98] In this light the most recent examples of the rebuttable presumption are the *O2* case and the *GlaxoSmithKline* case: in these cases this presumption was successfully rebutted, at least, in the cases before the General Court.[99]

More specifically, in the *O2* case, the General Court annulled part of the Commission's decision on a network sharing agreement between O2 and T-Mobile, because the agreement could not be qualified as restrictive by object. O2 pleaded that a restriction of competition could only be established on the basis of the actual effects of the agreement. The General Court ruled in favour of O2, stating that

94 Judgment of the Court of 13 July 1966, Joined cases 56 and 58-64 (*Établissements Consten S.à.R.L. and Grundig-Verkaufs-GmbH v. Commission of the European Economic Community) European Court reports*, English special edition, p. 00299, para. 340.

95 The objective of consumer welfare as indicated by Art. 2 in conjunction with Art. 3(1)(g) EC. Nazzini 2006, p. 507.

96 Opinion of Mr Advocate General Roemer delivered on 27 April 1966, Joined Cases 56 and 58-64 (*Établissements Consten S.à.R.L. and Grundig-Verkaufs-GmbH v. Commission of the European Economic Community) European Court reports*, English special edition, p. 00299. A trade-off between anti- and pro-competitive effects might have resulted that absolute protection was legitimate due to the necessity of enabling manufacturers to penetrate new markets, thereby enhancing interbrand competition.

97 Odudu 2006, p.119.

98 *Ibid.*, p. 14.

99 *Ibid.*

where it is accepted that the agreement does not have as its object a restriction of competition, the effects should be considered so that the competition in question is understood within the actual context in which it would occur in the absence of the agreement in dispute.[100]

In the *GlaxoSmithKline* case, the General Court cast serious doubts on the strict distinction between the alternatives of infringements by object or effect. The Court was of the opinion that in the specific case of GSK, the restrictive nature of the agreement could not be inferred from its clauses, and therefore it was necessary to consider the effects of the agreement. The judgment appears to suggest that in order to establish the anti-competitive object of an agreement account needs to be taken of its effects. Such an interpretation would seriously contradict the sharp distinction between object and effect restrictions as established by the ECJ.[101] However, on appeal in the *GlaxoSmithKline* case, the ECJ pointed out that, 'by requiring proof that the agreement entails disadvantages for final consumers as a prerequisite for a finding of anti-competitive object and by not finding that that agreement had such an object, the General Court committed an error of law.'[102]

In line with the reasoning that the legal presumption of negative effects on competition *should* be rebuttable, Advocate General Trstenjak pointed out in the *Beef Industry Development Society* case, that 'it is clear that classification as a restriction of competition by object cannot depend on whether that object is clear at first sight or becomes evident only on closer examination of the circumstances and the intentions of the parties.'[103] A-G Trstenjak advocates that in order to assess whether an agreement has as its object the restriction of competition, account must not only be taken of its content but also of its legal and economic context which could cast doubt on the existence of a restriction of competition and that this requirement must be taken seriously.[104] Three categories are listed in which the assumption of a restriction of competition may be doubtful on the basis of the legal context.

- The first category concerns cases in which it is doubtful whether there is actually sufficient competition which might be restricted by the agreement.[105]

100 Judgment of the Court of First Instance (Fourth Chamber) of 2 May 2006, Case T-328/03, (*O2 (Germany) v. Commission*) ECR 2006, p. II-01231.

101 M. Hofmann & F. Bremer, "Relationship between Anti-competitive Practices by <<Object>> and <<Effect>> and the Requisite Standard of Proof (T-mobile Netherlands and Others v. Raad van Bestuur vd NMa, ECJ (Third Chamber), Judgment of 4 June 2009, Case C-8/08", *European Law Reporter*, no 7-8, July/August 2009, p. 240.

102 Judgment of the Court (Third Chamber) of 6 October 2009, Joined cases C-501/06 P, C-513/06 P, C-515/06 P and C-519/06 P (*GlaxoSmithKline*), ECR 2009, p. I-09291, para. 64.

103 Opinion A-G Trstenjak delivered on 4 September 2008, C-209/07 BIDS, ECR 2008, p. I-08637, para. 47.

104 *Ibid.*, para. 50.

105 The Advocate General points to the case of GlaxoSmithKline which casts some doubts regarding the effects on price competition, because prices charged to the final consumer are free from the market mechanism, since prices for pharmaceuticals are set on government level: Opinion A-G Trstenjak delivered on 4 September 2008, C-209/07 BIDS, ECR 2008, p. I-08637, para. 52, including reference to footnote 33.

- The second category concerns agreements the object of which is to promote competition. Examples are exclusive rights of sale for market penetration and the grant of licences for the distribution of a new technology.[106] When matters are viewed as a whole, such agreements may give rise to the promotion of competition.
- The third category concerns ancillary restraints which are necessary for the attainment of the primary objective of the agreement.[107]

This case will be returned to below.

4.4 Balancing Effects

There have been a number of cases in which agreements containing contractual restrictions were found *not* to have anti-competitive effects. Already in the *STM* case, the ECJ recognized *positive* effects of agreements containing vertical restraints, since the Court stated that exclusive distribution agreements may not infringe Article 101(1) TFEU if this restraint was really necessary for the penetration of a new area by an undertaking. Also ancillary restraints may exclude the application of the Article 101(1) TFEU. With respect to this doctrine, it is necessary to balance pro and anti-competitive effects of agreement clauses to determine whether a contractual restriction is in fact related and necessary to the implementation of a main operation.[108] The cases in this area indicate that even absolute territorial protection may not infringe Article 101(1) TFEU, even though the Court adopted a per se rule against absolute territorial protection.[109] In the *Pronuptia* case, the ECJ even recognized that competition may actually be reduced because of the requirement of free parallel trade under EU competition law.[110]

The implications of these cases are difficult, as the exclusion of an effect assessment of object restrictions cannot be easily reconciled from the perspective that

106 *Ibid.*, para. 53. Case 56/65 *LTM* [1966] ECR, p. 250: exclusive right of sale for market penetration, Case 258/78 *Nungesser and Eisele v. Commission* [1982] ECR 2015, paras 44-58: grant of an open licence for the distribution of a new technology, *MetroSB-Großmärkte v. Commission* (cited in footnote 16 paras 20-22): channels of distribution which are adapted to high-quality and technically advanced products.

107 Opinion A-G Trstenjak delivered on 4 September 2008, C-209/07 BIDS, ECR 2008, p. I-08637, para. 54. Example of ancillary arrangements are no-competition clauses without which a transfer of a business would not be possible (Case 42/84 *Remia and Others v. Commission* [1985] ECR 2545, paras 19 and 20), prohibitions on participation or restrictions on activities, in so far as these are necessary to ensure the functioning of a company with a purpose which is unobjectionable in terms of competition (Case C-250/92 *DLG* [1994] ECR I-5641, paras 30-45), and restrictions on activities which are necessary for determining professional ethics (Case C-309/99 *Wouters and Others* [2002] ECR I-1577, para. 97), or eliminating doping in sport (Case C-519/04 P *Meca-Medina and Majcen v. Commission* [2006] ECR I-6991, paras 42- 44).

108 Judgment of the Court of First Instance (First Chamber, extended composition) of 11 July 1996, Joined Cases T-528/93, T-542/93, T-543/93 and T-546/93 (*Métropole and others*), ECR 1996, p. II-00649.

109 Literature indicate as the most prominent cases: Pronuptia, Remia, Nungesser and Gøttrup-Klim. In particular, Cases 262/81 (*Coditel II*) 1982, ECR 3381, paras 15-20; 27/87 (*Erauw-Jacquery*) 1988, ECR 1919. See V. Korah, *An Introductory Guide to EC Competition Law and Practice* (7th ed.), Oxford 2000, p. 287.

110 Judgment of the Court of 28 January 1986, Case 161/84, (*Pronuptia*), ECR 1986, p. 00353, para. 384.

restrictions may be necessary for the implementation of a main operation. It has therefore been commented that the anti-competitive object procedure of vertical relationships does not conform to a more economics based approach.[111] It has been suggested that a functional approach should be followed, in line with the General Court's assumption in the *GlaxoSmithKline* case that a restriction of competition is present when there is proof that the agreement has negative effect on consumers, meaning that 'restrictive agreements will only be prohibited when they *on balance* lead to a decrease of consumer welfare.'[112]

4.5 Necessity Effect Analysis

To determine whether an agreement between undertakings constitutes a breach of Article 101(1) TFEU, courts and competition authorities have made extensive use of the 'object box'. Until recently it was assumed that hardcore restrictions were automatically captured by the cartel prohibition in Article 101(1) TFEU. However, the recent cases of *T-Mobile* and *GlaxoSmithKline* may show that these assumptions cannot be followed without further assessment. In the light of the economic approach required by the case law of the European Courts, competition authorities and in particular *national* courts have to cope with the proposition that no balancing of anti and pro-competitive effects may be carried out within the application of Article 101(1) TFEU. For example, as mentioned before, Dutch competition courts seem to have shifted away from the object approach to the more effect based approach in their case law.[113]

Although the judgment of the General Court in the *GlaxoSmithKline* case was overruled by the ECJ, it has been suggested that it was *not* in conflict with the settled case law of the ECJ. It has been brought forward that 'although both alternatives have a different scope of application, they are not completely unconnected with each other.'[114] Agreements can only be considered anti-competitive by object, if when the agreements were carried out, they would have resulted in

111 Loozen 2010, p. 86.

112 E.M.H. Loozen, "The workings of article 101 TFEU in case of an agreement that aims to limit parallel trade (GlaxoSmithKline Services (C-501/06 P, C-513/06 P, C-515/06 P and C-519/06 P))", 31 *ECLR 9*, 2010, pp. 349-353.

113 A. Ottow, "Observations on Economic Proof in Economic cases", in O. Essens, A. Gerbrandy & S. Lavrijssen, *National Courts and the Standard of Review in Competition Law and Economic Regulation*, Europa Law Publishing 2009, p. 44. In the case of Secon (CBb 7 dec. 2005, AWB 04/ 237, 04/249, *Secon Group and G-Star International v. NMa*, para. 6.5. See also: Cbb 28 oktober 2005, AWB 04/794 en 04/829 *Vereniging Modint en Modint Credit & Finance v. NMa*), the Dutch competition court required an examination by the Dutch Competition Authority of the concrete effects of the agreement, including an effect analysis to situations where the object of the agreement is to restrict competition. More recently, in the case that gave rise the preliminary proceedings, the Trade and Industry Appeal Tribunal considered the question of whether it is always necessary to examine the effects of an object restriction to ensure that the agreement is not qualified as having an anti-competitive object when it is clear that it does not have any negative effects on consumers (ECJ C-8/08 *T-Mobile*, para. 20. See also: CBB, 31 december 2007, AWB 06/657, 660, 661, 662 *T-Mobile and others*, LJN BC1396, see paras 9.5.3.1-9.5.3.5).

114 Hofmann & Bremer 2009, p. 240.

anti-competitive effects.[115] This implies that in fact an assessment of the effects is necessary to indicate that the anti-competitive object of an agreement may be lacking and should not be qualified as an object infringement in the first place, albeit in limited circumstances, meaning only in cases in which the negative impact on economic efficiency and consumer welfare is doubtful.

This line of reasoning seems consistent with earlier case law of the General Court, such as the *General Motors* case.[116] Though in this case the General Court held that there is no need to take into account the concrete effects of an agreement when it has a restrictive object,[117] it nevertheless did examine the effects of a restrictive bonus policy to determine that the rebate policy by its nature was an object restriction and consequently anti-competitive.[118] Although the ECJ seems to have suggested that the General Court performed this effect assessment within the framework of effect restrictions,[119] it can be deduced from this case that examination of the concrete effects on competition is necessary in order to establish the nature of the restrictive measure. The case of *General Motors* has caused some confusion because it seems to imply that the anti-competitive object of the restrictive bonus policy was established by means of a counterfactual analysis, though it has also been brought forward that the assessment by the General Court relates to the legal and economic context in which an agreement must be placed.[120] The subsequent judgment of the General Court in *GlaxoSmithKline*, however, confirms that the General Court may in fact have been analysing the effects of the 'restriction by object' to determine its actual nature.

In a case prior to *T-Mobile*, the ECJ was already called upon to clarify the issues regarding restrictions of competition by object. This preliminary reference by the Irish Supreme Court, the case *Beef Industry Development Society*,[121] concerned an agreement between Irish meat processors to reduce structural overcapacity in order to sustain profitability of all those present in the meat processing sector. Although BIDS argued a lack of anti-competitive object requiring an assessment of the effects,[122] the ECJ considered this a restriction by object because the

115 *Ibid.*, p. 241.

116 Judgment of the Court of First Instance (Second Chamber) of 21 October 2003, Case T-368/00 (*General Motors Nederland BV and Opel Nederland BV v. Commission of the European Communities*) ECR 2003, p. II-04491, para. 104. In this case Opel Nederland, owned fully by General Motors and responsible for the sole national sales of the Opel brand in the Netherlands, concluded dealership agreements for sales and service with about 150 dealers. As a result, the dealers are integrated in the Opel distribution network in Europe as authorised resellers. The agreement contained a restrictive supply policy, a restrictive bonus policy and instructions to dealers to refrain from export sales in general.

117 *Ibid.*, para. 104.

118 Cornelissen 2006, p. 185.

119 *Ibid.* See also: Judgment of the Court (Third Chamber) of 6 April 2006, Case C-551/03P *General Motors BV v. Commission*, ECR 2006, p. I-03173, paras 72-74.

120 Loozen 2010, p. 68.

121 C-209/07 *Competition Authority v. Beef Industry Development Society*, 2008, ECR, I-8637.

122 Judgment of the Court (Third Chamber) of 20 November 2008, C-209/07 (*Competition Authority v Beef Industry Development Society Ltd and Barry Brothers (Carrigmore) Meats Ltd*), ECR 2008, p. I-08637, para. 19.

agreement would lead to a reduction in rivalry between the parties to an agreement,[123] so there was no need to take account of its actual effects.[124] The Court equated a restriction of competition with any restriction on rivalry and that any agreement lessening rivalry between competitors is restrictive by object.[125] This implies that any agreement between competitors is restrictive by object and that analysis of these agreements is immediately shifted to Article 101(3) TFEU. It has been pointed out that this interpretation of a restriction of competition is inconsistent with the Guidelines on the application of Article 101(3), 'which define a restriction of competition on the basis of the impact of an agreement either directly on consumer welfare or indirectly in terms of a negative effect on market structure.'[126]

The interpretation of a restriction of competition is striking. Where the Commission relies on competition as an instrument for the outcome of maximized consumer welfare, the ECJ is using competition as a process of rivalry, suggesting that competition is an end itself by means of protecting competitors. Nevertheless, an assessment of the effects may illustrate that a reduction in rivalry could have a negative impact on consumer welfare and the market structure as such. A restriction of competition interpreted by a reduction in rivalry does not fit well in the line of reasoning of the ECJ in *T-Mobile* and *GlaxoSmithKline*, where it was reiterated that Article 101 TFEU was not primarily designed for the protection of competitors and consumers.

Commentators have concluded that although in the *BIDS* case the agreement was restrictive by object, this does not mean that every capacity restraint is an object infringement, so that effect analysis remains essential.[127] They identified two similar situations in which a capacity restraint from an economic perspective appeared justified,[128] although an object box is desirable on account of legal certainty and process efficiency. Besides, as mentioned earlier, even object restrictions may be exempted by the cartel prohibition by means of Article 101(3) TFEU. This means that legal certainty and process and cost efficiency are not automatically served. Therefore, it is arguable to adopt a *per se* illegality in the sense of US antitrust law, so that agreements can only be considered illegal *per se* if there has been experience with similar or identical agreements of which the anti-competitive effects have been established

123 *Ibid.*, para. 35.

124 *Ibid.*, para. 16. See also: Joined Cases 56/64 and 58/64 *Consten and Grundig v. Commission* [1966] ECR 299, 342, and Case C-105/04 P *Nederlandse Federatieve Vereniging voor de Groothandel op Elektrotechnisch Gebied v. Commission* [2006] ECRI-8725, para. 125). That examination must be made in the light of the agreement's content and economic context (Joined Cases 29/83 and 30/83 *Compagnie royale asturienne des mines and Rheinzink v. Commission* [1984] ECR 1679, para. 26, and Case C-551/03 P *General Motors v. Commission* [2006] ECR I-3173, para. 66.

125 J. Kallaugher & A. Weitbrecht, "Developments under the Treaty on the Functioning of the European Union, articles 101 and 102, in 2008/2009", *ECLR*, 8, 2010, p. 312.

126 *Ibid.*

127 Baarsma & Poort 2009, p. 50.

128 Other cases which concerned crisis/restructuring cartels were two Dutch cases: *Stichting Baksteen* and *Stichting Saneringsfonds Varkensslachterijen*. See: Baarsma & Poort 2009, pp. 55, 56.

based on an effect analysis.[129] The adoption of such a rule of experience has led to opposing views in the legal doctrine.[130] Nonetheless, a rule of experience inserts to a certain extent economic insights within the legal formalistic framework under Article 101(1) TFEU, meaning that we are still left with an object box and an effect box, but the boxes have evolved from 'economic' experience and will eventually contribute to the benefit of process and cost efficiency. Although such an approach would be more acceptable from the perspective of economisation, there is no indication in case law that the European Courts are inclined to adopt such an approach.

4.6 Recategorisation

Due to beneficial restrictions of competition, the object box may require refinement from time to time to exclude some types of agreements from the object box which are not unquestionably restrictive of competition as certain other agreements.[131] Whish has listed numerous examples which suggest that a 'blanket prohibition' of agreements that restrict competition deprives the public of substantial beneficial advantages.[132] He argues that the emphasis on the protection of parallel trade disregards the difference between inter-brand and intra-brand competition.[133] Restrictions imposed by a producer on its distributors to ensure the best possible promotion of his products might lessen competition in his own goods and therefore may restrict intra-brand competition, but the net effect may be to enhance its competiveness against products from its competitors, thereby enhancing inter-brand competition as such.[134]

As suggested by Wesseling, the declaration of restrictions on parallel trade invariably prohibited by EU competition law may in fact reduce competition, since there are no obvious objections from a competition policy perspective to restrictions on the freedom to trade in a particular brand when there is intensive inter-brand competition in the markets.[135] Agreements should be categorised and recategorised periodically, based on convincing economic effects. This process will not jeopardise the sharp distinction between object 'or' effect restrictions under Article 101(1) TFEU.[136] Consequently, the existence of two distinguishable boxes will not undermine process efficiency and legal certainty.

---

129 This process has a parallel with the US Antitrust system where competition courts are called upon to determine whether a particular type of agreement should be tested according the per se application or the rule of reason standard. Agreements of which experience illustrate per se negative effects on competition, the agreements are qualified per se illegalities.

130 This latter view is also in line with the Guidelines on Art. 81(3), para. 21, the Opinion of A-G Kokott in *T-Mobile*, para. 46. Also CBB in *T-Mobile*, para. 20. However, Loozen indicated that such a rule of experience is superfluous when the interpretation of the cartel prohibition would be aligned with economic insights, and that restrictions by object can easily be established when the agreement by its object will result in a dead weight loss. See Loozen 2010, p. 62.

131 Whish 2009, p. 122.

132 *Ibid.*, p. 13.

133 *Ibid.*

134 *Ibid.* See also Wesseling 2000, p. 81.

135 *Ibid.*

136 Whish 2009, p. 122.

4.7 Need for Clarification

The above mentioned preliminary judgments illustrate that there is uncertainty among national courts as to the application of the cartel prohibition, indicating that the national competition courts are inclined to adopt a more economic approach consistent with the backdrop of economisation of competition law. An assessment of the actual effects of competition may be necessary in order to establish the nature of the restrictive measure, in particular of the increasing number of 'innovative' agreements. These decentralised conceptions indicate that the interpretation and application of Article 101(1) TFEU is not self-evident and they emphasize the need for a consistent and more coherent application of Article 101 TFEU with the corresponding clarification. Although the impression is that the market conduct, specific market circumstances and consequently the effects of that market conduct on competition need to be established, the legal approach taken by the ECJ and A-G Kokott in the *T-Mobile* case is a step backwards in the development of a more economic interpretation of competition enforcement.[137] The result of these rulings does not mean that consumer welfare is completely disregarded in European competition law. Instead, Article 101(3) TFEU must be used in the sense that the balancing of pro-and anti-competitive effects of both object and effect restrictions under Article 101(3) TFEU must be to the benefit of the consumers.

5. Article 101(3) TFEU

The aforementioned cases raise the question whether the European Courts in fact applied a rule of reason under Article 101(1) TFEU. Craig and de Búrca indicated that according to them the Courts have engaged in an economic analysis under Article 101(1) TFEU.[138] In its White Paper on the Modernisation of Competition law the Commission indicated that it already adopted this approach to a limited extent and carried out an assessment of the pro and anti-competitive aspects of some restrictive practices under Article 101(1) TFEU.[139] The Commission also indicated that this approach has been endorsed by the ECJ. Although in the *Métropole* case the General Court denied the existence of a rule of reason within Article 101(1) TFEU, there is evidence that European Courts have done some weighing of the pro-competitive and anti-competitive effects when agreements did not have the object to restrict competition.[140] As indicated by Craig and de Búrca, the reasoning in the *Métropole* judgment is problematic. The rationalisation of the General Court is inconsistent with prior case law, because the Union Courts considered the entire economic context. Due to this consideration, it was only

137 Loozen has argued that the interpretation by the ECJ is generally in line with a more economics approach. See E. Loozen, 'The application of a more economic approach to restrictions by object: no revolution after all (T-Mobile Netherlands (C-8/08))', 31 *ECLR* 4, 2010, p. 146.

138 Craig & de Búrca 2008.

139 *White Paper on modernisation of the rules implementing Articles 81 and 82 of the EC Treaty* (formerly Articles 85 and 86 of the EC Treaty) *Official Journal* C 132 of 12.5.1999, para. 57.

140 Craig & de Búrca 2008, p. 974.

then possible to tell whether a clause restricting competition should be allowed, because it enabled parties to break into new markets. In this sense, the Union Courts have balanced the pro and anti-competitive effects of an agreement.[141] The reasoning by the General Court assumes that a rule of reason is incompatible with the existence of Article101(3) TFEU. It has been suggested in the literature that the *Wouters* case has incorporated a rule of reason into Article 101(1) TFEU, since the court balanced negative effects on competition against both pro-competitive effects and non-competition interests.[142] Nazzini extensively argued that the test of the *Wouters* case is inconsistent with the test adopted by the General Court in the *Métropole* case and that the *Métropole* judgement has implicitly been overruled by the *Wouters* judgement, which is consistent with the economic purpose of Article 101 TFEU.[143]

5.1 The Modernisation

Regulation 1/2003 has given a greater role to national competition authorities and national courts with regard to the enforcement and application of European competition law, by which they are allowed to apply Articles 101 and 102 TFEU in full, including the power to withdraw the benefit of a Block Exemption Regulation.[144] In its White Paper on Modernisation of European competition law the Commission sets out the general direction EU competition policy should take. Regarding the interpretation of Article 101 TFEU, the Commission stated that the current division between Article 101(1) and 101(3) TFEU in the implementation of Article 101 TFEU is artificial and runs counter to the integral nature of Article 101, which requires economic analysis of the overall impact of restrictive practices.[145]

In the context of the debate around the interpretation and application of Article 101(1) TFEU, the Commission indicated in its White Paper that the inclusion of a rule of reason under Article 101(1) TFEU would cast aside Article 101(3) TFEU and would run the risk that Article 101(3) TFEU would be diverted from its purpose, which is to provide a legal framework for an economic assessment of restrictive practices and not to allow the application of competition rules to be set aside due to political considerations.[146] These rejections can be criticised. Pro 'rule of reason' commentators have argued that competition authorities and courts should weigh the anti-competitive and pro-competitive effects of agreements when they consider Article 101(1)TFEU because there is no legitimate rationale for exempting agreements from the prohibition to restrict competition if their ultimate effects is not a restriction but, on the contrary, enhancement of competition.[147] Therefore,

141 *Ibid.* See also: Nazzini 2006, p. 487.

142 Nazzini 2006, p. 525.

143 *Ibid.*, pp. 505, 526.

144 Council Regulation 1/2003 of 16 December 2002, On the implementation of the rules on competition laid down in Articles 81 and 82 of the Treaty, Official Journal L1/2, paras 7, 10.

145 *White Paper on modernisation of the rules implementing Articles 81 and 82 of the EC Treaty* (formerly Articles 85 and 86 of the EC Treaty) Official Journal C 132 of 12.5.1999, para. 49.

146 *Ibid.*, para. 56.

147 Wesseling 2000, p. 82.

an economic rule of reason should be inserted within Article 101(1) TFEU, in line with the case law of the European Courts.[148] The inclusion of such an economic rule of reason would lead to the result that competition goals are balanced within 101(1) and the pursuit of other treaty goals and non-competition interests are absorbed by Article 101(3) TFEU. This exclusion of an economic rule of reason within Article 101(1) when balancing economic effects under 101(3) TFEU will result in the higher goals being shifted out.

5.2 Non-Competition Interests

The European Courts have endorsed Commission decisions which took into account non-competition interests in the determination of an exemption of Article 101(3) TFEU.[149] In this regard, Wesseling holds that the assessment of an agreement's overall impact on competition under Article 101(3) TFEU runs counter to the purpose of that Article.[150] The purpose of Article 101(3) is to provide a legal framework within which the competent institutions competent to apply Article 101(3) TFEU may pursue non-competition interests. The inclusion of non-competitive interests within Article 101(3) TFEU is confirmed by the Commission Guidelines on the application of Article 81(3) EC, in which the Commission stated that the other goals pursued by the Treaty provisions can be taken into account in the assessment under Article 81(3) EC.[151] It seems that the Commission held on to this approach in the draft revision of the guidelines on horizontal agreements. To restrict the application of Article 101(3) TFEU to the application of an economic rule of reason implies that social considerations cannot be taken into account under Article 101(3) TFEU, contrasting the Commission's decisional practice in the application of Article 101(3) TFEU as endorsed by the European Courts.[152]

Odudu reasons in a purely economic way. He argues that Article 101(1) TFEU is the principal domain of allocative efficiency, while 101(3) TFEU is the domain of productive efficiency.[153] He argues that Article 101(3) TFEU allows a trade off between the losses flowing from allocative efficiency and the gains that may be forthcoming in terms of productive efficiency.[154] Odudu questions the legitimacy of considering additional goals under Article 101(3) TFEU and advocates a unitary goal to ensure effectiveness.[155] The prevention of balancing Treaty goals within

148 *Ibid.*, p. 103.

149 See for example OJ L187/47, 2000 5 *CMLR* 635 (CECED), OJ L131/15, 1995, 4 *CMLR* 646 *Stichting Baksteen*, and OJ L144/20, 1994, *Exxon/Shell*.
For further reading about the role for national competition authorities in the protection of non-competition interests after the entry into force of the Lisbon Treaty, see S.A.C.M Lavrijssen, "What Role for National Competition Authorities in Protecting Non-Competition Interests after Lisbon?", *European Law Review*, October 2010.

150 Wesseling 2000, p. 82.

151 Guidelines on the application of Art. 81(3), para. 42.

152 Wesseling 2000, p. 82.

153 This line of reasoning can in fact be deduced from the Chicago School line of thinking, see Jones & Sufrin p. 24: H. Hovenkamp, "Antitrust policy after Chicago", 1985 *Univ. Mich. LR* 213, pp. 226-229.

154 Odudu 2006, pp. 125, 137.

155 *Ibid.*, p. 164, 170.

Article 101 TFEU would enhance legal certainty, transparency and accountability. Wesseling submitted that the interpretation of Article 101(1) TFEU must be revised and be brought in line with that of the European Courts. There is practical experience that it is feasible to divide the application of Article 101(1) and 101(3) in such a manner that Article 101(3) allows that public policy considerations can be considered where competition is not eliminated completely and does not go further than necessary to achieve the pursued policy objectives.[156]

6. Conclusion

The interpretation and application by the European Courts of Article 101(1) TFEU is inconsistent and obscure. The ECJ has given a formalistic reading to the concept of restriction of competition under Article 101(1) TFEU. The General Court has been more inclined to engage in an economic assessment of the pro and anti-competitive effects of an agreement with respect to object restrictions under Article 101(1) TFEU.[157] Where the ECJ in the *T-Mobile* case reiterated the classical dichotomy between object and effect restrictions, the General Court in the *GlaxoSmithKline* case appeared to have suggested that it is necessary to take account of the effects before the anti-competitive object of an agreement may be established. European competition law as-it-stands does not require the consideration of the actual effects of agreements of which the anti-competitive object has been established based on its clauses, which does not fit well with the trend of economisation of European competition law. As a consequence, an agreement which is considered anti-competitive under Article 101(1) TFEU may only be determined pro-competitive under Article 101(3) TFEU. In this respect, excluding an assessment of the effects of object restriction under Article 101(1) TFEU feels counterintuitive, since absence of anti-competitive effects could indicate that an anti-competitive object is lacking.[158] Due to the multitude of goals ascribed to European competition law, guidance is needed to clarify the interaction between goals. Especially since the debate about the objectives of competition law is linked to the debate about whether to adopt an effect based approach to object restrictions. A feasible solution is desirable, since the legal formalistic approach to object restrictions will raise serious difficulties as illustrated by the preliminary questions by the Netherlands Trade and Industry Appeals Tribunal and the Irish Supreme Court. The preliminary judgments illustrate that the solid dichotomy between object and effect restrictions established by the ECJ is not self-evident against the backdrop of economisation of competition law. The consideration of a rule of experience, in which agreements can only be considered illegal *per se* if there has been experience with similar or identical agreements of which the anti-competitive effects have been established based on an effect analysis, seems a feasible solution. This 'per se box' will in the long run meet the criteria of legal certainty and process and cost efficiency. It is argued that the Commission and the European Courts should include

156 Wesseling 2000, p. 105.
157 Craig & de Búrca 2008, p. 1003.
158 Hofmann & Bremer 2009, p. 245.

an economic rule of reason within Article 101(1) TFEU. This rule of reason should moreover be consistent with the case law of the courts and should still preserve a role to play for Article 101(3) TFEU in the sense of pursuing other Treaty goals, as long as competition under Article 101(1) is not fully eliminated and the restrictive effects do not go further than necessary to attain the policy objectives.

Removing Obstacles: The Competition Law Regime of Slovenia

K. Zajc

Slovenia's Constitution sets out the guarantee of freedom of economic initiative and prohibits acts of unfair competition and acts contrary to the law restricting competition (Art. 74 of the Constitution of the Republic of Slovenia). Protection of competition is the responsibility of the State, as fair competition is in the public interest, while companies operating in the free market are undoubtedly interested in restricting competition or abusing their dominant position and thereby increasing their operating profit in this market.

In Slovenia, the most important laws in the field of competition law are the Protection of Competition Act (ZVK, Official Gazette of the Republic of Slovenia, No. 18/1993, with amendments) and the Competition Restriction Prevention Act (ZPOmK-1, Official Gazette of the Republic of Slovenia, No. 56/1999, with amendments). The area of unfair competition is governed by ZVK, which in 13 articles defines an act of unfair competition as an act of a company in the market, which is contrary to good business practices and which causes or may cause damage to other market participants. The act goes on to list exhaustively the cases of unfair competition. Monitoring of the implementation of the ZVK is done by the Market Inspectorate of Slovenia. ZPOmK-1 regulates restrictive practices, concentration of companies, governmental restrictions of competition and measures to prevent restrictive practices and concentrations, which significantly restrict effective competition (Art. 1 of ZPOmK-1). Monitoring the implementation of the ZPOmK-1 is the responsibility of the Office for Protection of Competition. The area of competition law also includes for instance State aids and consumer protection. However, this article is limited primarily to the presentation of conduct of proceedings before the Office for Protection of Competition, in particular the shortcomings of dual process as essentially the same legal and factual issues are resolved in the administrative process and separately in the misdemeanour proceedings and as a result there is a difference in legal protection against both types of decisions of the Office.

The Office for the Protection of Competition (UVK) is responsible for supervising the implementation of ZPOmK-1, Articles 81 and 82 TEC, which are now Articles 101 and 102 TFEU, and also serves as the minor offence authority for misdemeanours identified by the ZPOmK-1. The Office therefore on the one hand, leads the administrative process and determines whether a concentration is compatible with competition rules on the basis of an application and on its own initiative or at the request of a party investigates alleged cartels (Art. 6 ZPOmK-1), alleged abuse of dominant position (Art. 9 ZPOmK-1) and identifies violations of Articles 101 and 102 TFEU. On the other hand, the UKV as a minor offence authority leads the offence proceedings for infringement of the provisions of ZPOmK-1 and TFEU and gives the prescribed penalty for the offence. In all these cases the assessed conduct is largely identical (abuse of dominance, restrictive agreements) or closely related (*e.g.* identifying application of concentration).

ZPOmK-1 partially covers both the administrative process and the misdemeanour procedure (UVK powers). To process the misdemeanour it is further necessary to consider the Minor Offences Act (ZP-1, Official Gazette of the Republic of Slovenia, No. 7/2003 with amendments). There is no appeal against decisions of the Office (administrative and misdemeanour), but it is possible to demand judicial protection, depending on the nature of the decision either on the basis of the ZPOmK-1 or the Law on Administrative Disputes (ZUS-1, Official Gazette of the Republic of Slovenia, No. 105/06 with amendments) or ZP-1.

In the administrative process the Office assesses whether there has been a breach of the provisions on restrictive agreements and abuse of dominant position and assesses compliance of the concentration with the law. In the case of assessment of restrictive agreements (Article 6 ZPOmK-1) and abuse of dominant position (Art. 9 ZPOmK-1) the Office issues a decision finding an infringement and demands that the company cease the breach, with the possibility of the imposition of additional measures (Art. 37 ZPOmK-1), a decision on the acceptance of obligations (Art. 39 ZPOmK-1) or the decision to suspend the proceedings if it finds no violations of Articles 6 and 9 ZPOmK-1 or if the procedure would not be expedient and in the case when the European Commission initiates proceedings for infringement or if it has already issued a decision, the procedure is also suspended if the procedure has commenced, or a body responsible for protecting competition has already issued a decision in another Member State (Article 40 ZPOmK-1).

In the case of assessment of concentrations the UVK may issue a:[1]

- Decision on non-subordination of the concentration (Art. 46(2) ZPOmK-1);
- Decision on compliance of the concentration in the first phase (Art. 46(3) ZPOmK-1);
- Decision on compatibility of the concentration with corrective measures in the first phase (Art. 46(3) ZPOmK-1 in conjunction with Art. 51 ZPOmK-1);
- Decision on compliance of the concentration in the second stage (Art. 50(1), first indent ZPOmK-1);
- Decision on compatibility of the concentration with corrective measures in the second phase (Art. 50(1), first indent ZPOmK-1 in conjunction with Art. 51 ZPOmK-1);
- Decision on non-compliance of the concentration (Art. 50(1), second indent ZPOmK-1);
- Decision on non-compliance of the concentration with measures to eliminate the effects of the concentration (Art. 50(1), second indent ZPOmK-1 in conjunction with Art. 53 ZPOmK-1); or a
- Decision on measures to eliminate the effects of the concentration (Art. 53 ZPOmK-1).

1 Based on webpage Urada: <www.uvk.gov.si/>.

Judgments and other decisions issued by the UVK in the administrative proceedings are final, but it is possible to request judicial protection. For judicial protection against UVK decisions ZUS-1 is applied *mutatis mutandis*. The action must be filed within 30 days after service (notification) of the decision at the Supreme Court of the Republic of Slovenia. The Supreme Court decides judicial protection cases in a panel of three judges. A judgment or decision of the Supreme Court issued in the process of judicial protection cannot be challenged by a further appeal.

Protection of competition is the subject of protection in the field of criminal law as well. Given the intensity of unlawful conduct we separate crimes and misdemeanours. Since economic activity is predominantly driven by legal entities, in order to assess accountability for crimes and offences it is necessary to consider the Liability of Legal Persons for Criminal Offences Act (ZOPOKD, Uradni list RS, št. 59/1999, with amendments) which determines when a legal entity may be held liable for a misdemeanour or criminal offence.

The Criminal Code (KZ-1, Official Gazette of the Republic of Slovenia, No. 55/2008, with amendments) prescribes criminal offences. The interference with effective competition is incriminated in the form of abuse of dominant position under article 225 KZ-1. The offence of abuse of dominant position is committed by anyone in business activity who in contravention of the regulations governing the protection of competition, infringes the prohibition of restrictive agreements between companies, abuses dominant position of one or more companies or creates a prohibited concentration of companies and thereby prevents or significantly hinders or distorts competition in the Republic of Slovenia or the European Union market or its significant part, or significantly effects trade between Member States, resulting in big material benefit to this company or companies or significant financial loss to another company. For such an offence imprisonment from six months to five years has been prescribed.

Criminal conduct with a lower degree of risk to the society is prescribed as offences in sector-specific laws, and is generally governed by the Minor Offences Act (ZP-1, Uradni list RS, št. 7 / 2003, with amendments). In the field of competition, protection violations are prescribed particularly in the ZPOmK-1 and ZVK. ZP-1 provides general conditions for the prescription of offences and penalties for them, the general conditions of liability for violations, the imposition and enforcement of sanctions for violations, the procedure for misdemeanours and the authorities and courts to rule on violations. ZPOmK-1 in part VIII contains provisions on penalties and Articles 73 and 74 define offences and penalties for them. In accordance with Articles 73 and 74 ZPOmK-1 persons liable for violations include legal entities, individual sole trader and self-employed individuals who perform professional activity as well as the responsible person of the legal entity and responsible person of individual sole trader. The fines prescribed by the ZPOmK-1 do not have restrictions on amount, as defined by ZP-1 (Art. 17(5) ZP-1). Using an expedited procedure the Office may also give a fine of any amount within the limits set out in ZPOmK-1, and not just the minimum fine (Arts. 77 ZPOmK-1 and 52 ZP-1). ZPOmK-1 also prescribes a longer limitation period and allows for dismissal or reduction of fines in case of cooperation of the offender with the Office (Arts. 75 and 76 ZPOmK-1 and Art. 42 ZP-1). Articles 73 and 74 ZPOmK-1 prescribe for a legal entity a fine of up to 10% of annual turnover of the company or enterprises involved in the concentration in the previous financial year and for the responsible person of the legal entity a fine from 5,000 to 10,000 Euros or in the case of a particularly serious nature of the offence from 15,000 to 30,000 Euros. In the case of concentrations, for violations under Article 74 ZPOmK-1 a person who has managed at least one company can also be punished by a fine ranging from 3,000 to 5,000 Euros, or due to the particularly serious nature of the offence from 10,000 to 15,000 Euros. ZPOmK-1 specific provisions concerning the calculation of the fine do not include, therefore, the general provisions of the ZP-1 for imposing sanctions under Article 26.

There is an eight-day period to apply for judicial protection after the service (notification) of the decision on the offence by the UVK. To hear the request for judicial protection against the decision of the UVK exclusive authority in the field of competition is given to the Local Court in Ljubljana (Art. 214(5) ZP-1). On receiving a request for judicial protection, based on Article 63 ZP-1 the UVK itself can annul or replace the decision on the offence or it forwards the decision to the competent court – Local Court in Ljubljana. Against a court decision on the request for judicial review an appeal is allowed if the offender was fined more than the minimum prescribed, or if he was ordered forfeiture of proceeds in excess of 400 Euros, (Art. 66 ZP-1). The appeal must be filed within eight days after being served with the court judgment and may be made on all grounds, except by reason of erroneous and incomplete findings of fact (for this reason, an appeal may be filed in the case of dismissal of an application for judicial review). The appeal shall be decided by a higher court – the Higher Court in Ljubljana. Against any decision issued in the second stage, or any final decision, the prosecutor can file a request for protection of legality if the ZP-1 or regulation which prescribes the offence is violated (Art. 169 ZP-1). The request is assessed before the Supreme Court in a panel of three judges. The Attorney General files requests for protection of legality *ex officio* or based on the request of the person who has the right to appeal the first instance judgment.

From the described decision-making process in administrative proceedings deciding on compliance of a concentration, restrictive agreements and abuse of dominant position it can be seen that in the first stage the Office makes the decision, against which a lawsuit before the Supreme Court can be filed. In minor offence cases the authority is also given to the Office at the first stage, which in a fast offence proceeding issues a decision on the offence with which it imposes a fine. The offender may request judicial protection against that decision, which is heard before the Local Court in Ljubljana. An appeal against the ruling of the Court can be filed, which is heard by the Higher Court in Ljubljana. Against a final judicial decision on the offence, the prosecutor is entitled to apply for protection of legality which is heard before the Supreme Court. The Office decides on identical or substantially similar and related issues in two different procedures, the difference is also in the judicial protection. From the definitions of offences in Articles 73 and 74 ZPOmK-1 it can be clearly seen that the factual and legal issues in administrative matters on the one hand and minor offence cases on the other hand are closely related or even identical. Thus, for example, if after assessment of the abuse of dominant position and restrictive agreements on the basis of Articles 6 and 9 ZPOmK-1 the UVK issues a decision finding an infringement and a request that the company ceases the breach this is essentially identical to the assessment of an offence under Article 73 ZPOmK-1, as acting in violation of Articles 6 and 9 of the ZPOmK-1 is prescribed as an offence. In the case of concentrations, for example, Article 74 prescribes the failure to notify and delayed notification of a concentration as offences, which is also strongly linked to assessment of compliance of concentration. Under current law, first the UVK starts separate procedures and then the courts separately assess the legality of administrative and offence decisions, which makes the formation of adequate and uniform legal practice very difficult. Preferably, the UVK should have the authority to issue a decision which would assess cartels, abuse of dominant position and, as appropriate, also impose a misdemeanour fine. If the Office were to decide with a single decision, this would also allow the judicial branch of government more rational and uniform control over the administrative branch of government, especially because the Office when imposing fines has a very broad margin of discretion as methods for calculating the amount of the fine are not definitely prescribed, but subject to the general provisions for the assessment of violation fines.

Removing Obstacles: The Competition Law Regime of Hungary

M. Veenhuizen

1. Introduction and Background

In October 2011, Utrecht University will organize a two day conference. For this conference Competition Law Judges from a selection of countries, consisting of new Member States and future Member States, will be invited. The main goal of this conference is to disseminate knowledge of competition law to judges who in practice are confronted with competition cases in a mutual learning process.

This contribution provides background information for the upcoming conference by giving an overview of the competition law regime in Hungary.

2. Research Questions

This contribution focuses on the following questions: (1) How is competition law regulated in Hungary?; (2) What is the relation between Hungarian competition law and European competition law?, and (3) How is competition law enforced by Hungary?

3. Legislation

3.1 Introduction

With Hungary's accession to the European Union, Community competition law is directly applicable to Hungarian cases relating to restrictive agreements and abuses of a dominant position that may affect the trade between Member States.[1] Commission notice 2004/C 101/07 provides for guidelines on the effect on trade concept with regard to Articles 101 and 102 of the Treaty on the Functioning of the European Union (hereafter: TFEU). Among others, it states that the effect on trade is an autonomous Community law criterion which has to be assessed separately in each case.[2] The notice also defines the scope of the application of

1 I. Solyom, 'Hungary', *in* M. Dabbah and B. Hawk, *Anti-Cartel enforcement Worldwide volume II: France - Norway*, Cambridge, Cambridge University Press 2009, pp. 532 -556.
2 Commission Notice 2004/C 101/07, para. 12.

Community competition law. An effect is presumed to be present when it is "possible to foresee with a sufficient degree of probability on the basis of objective factors of law or fact that it might have an influence, direct or indirect, actual or potential on the pattern of trade between Member States".[3] Within this assessment lies the (fine) line between the applicability of Community law, Hungarian law or both. However, the preamble of the Hungarian Competition Act (see further: 3.1 and 3.2) states that when amending the Act, Community law has been taken into account. This follows from the words:

> In order to attain these objectives (. . .) taking into consideration (. . .) the law of the European Community and the conventions of domestic competition law (. . .).

3.1 Hungarian Legislation

3.1.1 Primary Legislation

Before its accession to the European Union, Hungary had already rendered operative several acts relating to competition law.[4] Currently, Act LVII of 1996[5] on the Prohibition of Unfair Market Practices and Restrictions of Competition ('Competition Act') is the main source of Hungarian competition law.[6] It regulates unfair market practices, unfair manipulation of consumer's choice, cartels, abuse of a dominant market position, merger control and the position of the Hungarian Competition Authority (hereafter: HCA).[7]

Presently, the Hungarian Competition Act is fully harmonised with EU law. The preamble of the Competition Act underlines the importance of the process of harmonisation:

> (. . .) In order to attain these objectives – also taking into consideration the requirements of the approximation to the law of the European Community and the conventions of domestic competition law – the Parliament passed the following Act.

On 1 May 2004, the same date as Hungary's accession to the European Union, an important amendment of the Hungarian Competition regime came into force.[8] One of the changes introduced was on the procedural regulations of the HCA, to ensure conformity with Council Regulation No. 1/2003.[9] Article 1(2) of the Competition Act now states that in any proceeding for the application of Article 101

3 Commission Notice 2004/C 101/07, para. 23.
4 Act V of 1923 on Unfair Competition, Act XX of 1931 on Cartels, Statute on Unfair Market Practices 1990, as amended in 1996.
5 Act LVII of 1996 entered into force on 1 January 1997.
6 Solyom 2009, pp. 532-556.
7 *Gazdasagu Versenyhivatal.*
8 Established by Act XXXI of 2003; entering into force as of 1 May 2004.
9 Council Regulation (EC) No. 1/2003 on the implementation of the rules on competition laid down in Articles 101 and 102 TFEU.

or 102 TFEU, the procedural rules laid down in this Act shall also apply to market practices falling under the scope of Regulation 1/2003. It also provides that the Hungarian Competition Authority or the Hungarian court may proceed. Another amendment was (again) on Regulation 1/2003 and Regulation 139/2004.[10] The most recent amendment came into force in April 2010.

3.1.2 The Competition Act

The Competition Act contains all the substantive provisions of Hungarian competition law. In addition to antitrust rules, it also covers unfair competition and competition-related consumer protection provisions. The Act also provides for rules relating to enforcement, instructions and procedural law applicable to the HCA and the courts.[11] The scope of the Competition Act is defined in Article 1 which states that the Act:

> shall apply to market practices carried out on the territory of Hungary by natural and legal persons and companies with no legal personality (. . .), except where otherwise regulated.

With the exception of Chapters II and III of the Act, the Competition Act also applies to market practices of undertakings carried out abroad if they may have effect on the territory of Hungary. Additionally, the Act contains provisions relating to the following areas: Prohibition of unfair competition,[12] prohibition of unfair manipulation of business decisions,[13] prohibition of agreements restricting economic competition,[14] prohibition of abuse of a dominant position,[15] and finally the control of concentration of undertakings.[16] The other chapters, on procedures, are dealt with in chapter 4 of this contribution.

Additional legislation, which goes beyond substantive competition law, has also been adopted,[17] such as the European Accession Treaty of 16 April 2003, which entered into force on 1 May 2004, and Act CLXIV 2005 on Commerce, which is effective from June 2006. Furthermore, various (additional) rules are formulated in the Hungarian Civil Code, the Act on Business Associations, the Act on Business Advertising Activity, the Act on Price Setting, the Act on Trade,[18] the Act on Capital Markets, the Act on Prices and the Criminal Code.[19]

---

10 Council Regulation (EC) No. 139/2004 of 20 January 2004 on the control of concentration between undertakings.
11 Chapters II and III Competition Act.
12 Arts. 2-7 Competition Act.
13 Arts. 8-10 Competition Act.
14 Arts. 11-20 Competition Act.
15 Arts. 21-22 Competition Act.
16 Arts. 23-32 Competition Act.
17 Solyom 2009, pp. 532-556.
18 June 2006.
19 Solyom 2009, pp. 532-556.

Closely related to the Competition Act is the aforementioned Act on Trade. This Act introduced rules that are intended to influence the conduct of large retailers, which have significant market power. The Trade Act prohibits abusive conduct with respect to suppliers by traders having significant market power. The HCA, however, proceeds pursuant to the procedural and other provisions concerning the abuse of a dominant position of the Competition Act.

2.1.3 Secondary Legislation

Maher and Hawk,[20] furthermore, mention secondary legislation, such as government decree 54/2002 on the exemption from the general prohibition on restricting competition on certain categories of research and development agreements,[21] a decree on exemptions of insurance agreements (18/2004),[22] a decree on specialization agreements (53/2002)[23] and a decree on technology transfer agreements (86/1999).[24] With regard to vertical agreements the so-called 'Umbrella Decree' (55/2002)[25] can be mentioned and also a decree on car industry[26] was implemented.

2.1.4 Other

Certain legal norms are not directly part of the Hungarian competition regulation but nonetheless contain provisions in connection with competition and (to some extent) with the activities of the HCA. Some of these legal norms are included in 'sectoral rules'. For example in Hungary there is an Electronic Communications Act, the Act on Electricity and the Act on Railway Transport. The HCA is also entitled to start and/or perform sectoral inquiries (III.3, Chapter VIII Art. 43/B). The provisions of Articles 49 to 51 shall then be applied *mutatis mutandis* as well as the provisions of Act CXL of 2004 on the General Rules of Public Administrative Procedures and Services (PAPA).

Finally, the HCA is competent to issue notices. At the request of the Government, ministers or international organizations, the President of the HCA shall report on experience gained in the course of his activities relating to economic competition and on issues relating to economic competition. Notices are not legally binding and do not impose any obligations on undertakings.[27] The main goal is to reflect the general approach and to state how the law enforcer will apply the legal provisions. The HCA has issued three notices in relation to cartels; a notice on the calculation of fines,[28] a notice on leniency[29] and a notice on differentiating between

20 *Idem.*
21 In accordance with EC Regulation no. 2659/2000 of November 2000 on research and development.
22 In accordance with EC Regulation no. 358/2003 of 27 February 2003.
23 In accordance with EC Regulation no. 2658/2000 of 29 November 2000.
24 In accordance with EC Regulation no. 86/1999, 240/96 and 772/2004.
25 In accordance with EC Regulation no. 2790/1999 of 22 December 1999.
26 Implemented EC Regulation 1400/2002.
27 Art. 36(5) Competition Act.
28 Notice no 2/2003: Notice Repealed: The Method of Setting Fines in Antitrust Cases (2009).
29 Notice no 3/2003: The application of a leniency policy to promote the detection of cartels (until 31 May 2009).

concentrations subject to authorization in simplified or full procedure. The competition council has a similar competence. It can make position statements which reflect the competition council's law interpretation with regard to the Competition Act. The position statements are currently only available in Hungarian.

3.2 European Legislation

Since Hungary's accession to the European Union, Community competition law is directly applicable to Hungarian undertakings. This is implemented in Hungary, among others (see preamble), by way of the Competition Act. Article 91/A of Chapter XVI ("Procedures for the Application of European Community Competition Rules"), refers to Regulation 1/2003.

Article 3 of Regulation no. 1/2003 describes the relationship between Articles 101 and 102 TFEU (ex. Arts. 81 and 82 TEC) and national competition law. It states that when the competition authorities of Member States or national courts apply national competition law within the meaning of Article 101 and 102 TFEU, which may effect the trade between Member States, they shall also apply Articles 101 and 102 TFEU.[30] Thus, the HCA and the courts must apply Community competition law in each case in which they apply (parallel) national competition law to all agreements that may affect trade between Member States.

The (national) Competition Act applies to behaviour of natural persons, legal entities and business associations without legal personality and it covers the behaviour of an undertaking exhibited abroad, but potentially affecting the Hungarian market.[31] Agreements made between competitors diminish the risk of competition and restrict competition. However, Article 3(2) Regulation 1/2003 prohibits that the application of national competition law leads to the prohibition of certain agreements which do not restrict competition. Member States shall also not adopt and/or apply stricter national laws which prohibit or sanction unilateral conduct engaged in by undertakings. Therefore, a comparison between the European legislation and Hungarian law on Articles 101 and 102 TFEU is given below to indicate possible differences and similarities in the implementation of the law.

With regard to the HCA, Article 5 Regulation 1/2003 provides that the competition authority has the power to apply Articles 101 and 102 TFEU in individual cases. It can make the following decisions: requiring that an infringement be brought to and end, and/or ordering interim measures, and/or accepting commitments and /or imposing fines. Additionally, Chapter IV ('Cooperation') provides information on the cooperation between the national authorities and the European Commission. The Competition Act refers to this cooperation in Article 91/B:

> The Hungarian Competition Authority shall cooperate, in a manner specified by Regulation No 1/2003 (. . .).

30 See introduction Chapter 3.

31 Art. 1(1) Competition Act.

Table 1 Comparison Legislation (101 and 102)

Article 101 TFEU	Article 11 Hungarian Competition Act
1. The following shall be prohibited as incompatible with the internal market: all agreements between undertakings, decisions by associations of undertakings and concerted practices which may affect trade between Member States and which have as their object or effect the prevention, restriction or distortion of competition within the internal market, and in particular those which: (a) directly or indirectly fix purchase or selling prices or any other trading conditions; (b) limit or control production, markets, technical development, or investment; (c) share markets or sources of supply; (d) apply dissimilar conditions to equivalent transactions with other trading parties, thereby placing them at a competitive disadvantage; (e) make the conclusion of contracts subject to acceptance by the other parties of supplementary obligations which, by their nature or according to commercial usage, have no connection with the subject of such contracts. 2. Any agreements or decisions prohibited pursuant to this Article shall be automatically void. 3. The provisions of paragraph 1 may, however, be declared inapplicable in the case of: – any agreement or category of agreements between undertakings, – any decision or category of decisions by associations of undertakings, – any concerted practice or category of concerted practices, which contributes to improving the production or distribution of goods or to promoting technical or economic progress, while allowing consumers a fair share	1. Agreements or concerted practices between undertakings and decisions by social organisations of undertakings, public corporations, associations or other similar organisations (hereinafter together: agreements), which have as their object or potential or actual effect the prevention, restriction or distortion of competition, shall be prohibited. Agreements concluded between undertakings, which are not independent of each other do not qualify as such kind of agreements. 2 This prohibition applies, in particular, to a) the direct or indirect fixing of purchase or selling prices or other business terms and conditions; b) the limitation or control of production, distribution, technical development or investment; c) the allocation of sources of supply, or the restriction of their choice as well as the exclusion of a specified group of consumers or trading parties from purchasing certain goods; d) the allocation of markets, exclusion from sales, or restriction of the choice of marketing possibilities; e) **Repealed by Act LXVIII of 2005; no longer in force as of 1 November 2005**. f) the hindering of market entry; g) cases, where, given transactions of the same value or character, there is discrimination between trading parties, including the application of prices, periods of payment, discriminatory selling or purchase terms and conditions or methods placing certain trading parties at a competitive disadvantage;

of the resulting benefit, and which does not:
(a) impose on the undertakings concerned restrictions which are not indispensable to the attainment of these objectives;
(b) afford such undertakings the possibility of eliminating competition in respect of a substantial part of the products in question.

h) making the conclusion of contracts subject to the acceptance of obligations, which, by their nature or according to commercial usage do not belong to the subject of such contracts.

Article 102 TFEU

Any abuse by one or more undertakings of a dominant position within the internal market or in a substantial part of it shall be prohibited as incompatible with the internal market in so far as it may affect trade between Member States. Such abuse may, in particular, consist in:
(a) directly or indirectly imposing unfair purchase or selling prices or other unfair trading conditions;
(b) limiting production, markets or technical development to the prejudice of consumers;
(c) applying dissimilar conditions to equivalent transactions with other trading parties, thereby placing them at a competitive disadvantage;
(d) making the conclusion of contracts subject to acceptance by the other parties of supplementary obligations which, by their nature or according to commercial usage, have no connection with the subject of such contracts.

Article 22 Hungarian Competition Act

1 A dominant position shall be deemed to be held on the relevant market (Article 14) by persons who are able to pursue their economic activities to a large extent independently of other market participants substantially without the need to take into account the market reactions of their suppliers, competitors, customers and other trading parties when deciding their market conduct.
2 In assessing whether a dominant position exists, the following factors shall be considered, in particular:
a) the costs and risks of entry to and exit from the relevant market, and the technical, economic and legal conditions that have to be met; dominant position
b) the property status, financial strength and profitability of the undertaking or the group of undertakings (Article 15(2)), and the trends in their development;
c) the structure of the relevant market, the comparative market shares, the conduct of market participants and the economic influence of the undertaking or the group of undertakings on the development of the market joint dominance
3 Dominant positions may be held by individual undertakings or group of undertakings or jointly by more than one undertaking or more than one group of undertakings.

See also Article 21 for a list of examples of abuse.

In order to ensure an efficient division of work and an effective and consistent application of the EU competition rules, the European Competition Network (hereafter: ECN) was formed. Council Regulation 1/2003 and the joint statement of the European Council and the European Commission on the functioning of the ECN set out the principles of the network. Regulation 1/2003 created a system of parallel competence in which the Commission and the national competition authorities (hereafter: NCAs) both act in the public interest and cooperate closely in order to protect competition. The ECN is set out to be a forum for discussion and cooperation with regard to the application and enforcement of EC competition law and policy. More details on the system were presented in the Commission Notice on cooperation within the Network of Competition Authorities.[32]

One of the subjects mentioned in the Commission Notice and in Article 12 of the Commission Regulation is cooperation with regard to sharing and the exchange of information. Member States have the power to provide one another with and use evidence on any matter of factor or of law including confidential information. In this respect the Hungarian Competition Act, for instance, states in Article 58(3) that documents may be made available on request to a foreign authority and that the HCA may enter into cooperation agreements with foreign competition authorities in order to ensure parties to perform their duties.

Further, Article 6 1/2003 declares that national courts have the power to apply Articles 101 and 102 TFEU. Additionally, Article 15 of the Regulation provides for rules for the cooperation between the national courts and the European Commission. For instance, the court of a Member State can ask the Commission to transmit information, or the Commission can submit written observations to the national court. Another important provision is Article 16 1/2003. When national courts rule on practices, decisions or agreements under Articles 101 or 102 TFEU, which are already subject to a Commission decision, the court cannot take decisions contrary to this decision. This Article ensures the uniform application of Community competition law.

This dual competition law enforcement by the HCA and the Commission and the (sometimes) dual applicability of law(s) does not apply in the case of concentrations.[33] When the conditions as mentioned in Article 1 of the Merger Regulation are met, the concentration will have a 'community dimension'. The concentrations within this scope shall then be appraised in accordance with the objectives of this Regulation and the provision on the common market.[34] Referral from and to the competition authorities of Member States is possible and provided for

32 Commission Notice on Cooperation within the Network of Competition Authorities, Notice no. 2004/C 101/03.

33 Regulation no. 139/2004 of 20 January 2004 on the control of concentrations between undertakings (hereafter: Merger Regulation).

34 Art. 2 Merger Regulation.

in the Merger Regulation (Arts. 9 and 22). Article 91/A of the Competition Act states that:

> In carrying out the control of concentrations between undertakings which are covered by the European Community law the provisions of this Act shall apply when this is provided by Regulation no/ 139/2004. In such cases (. . .) of the provisions of this Chapter, those of Article 91/E and 91/G are applicable.

4. Enforcement

4.1 The Hungarian Competition Authority

Article 1(2) Competition Act states that in any proceeding for the application of Article 101 and 102 TFEU the HCA or a Hungarian Court may proceed. The procedural rules laid down in Regulation 1/2003 are applicable.

The Hungarian Competition Authority is an independent institution operating under the direct control of the Parliament of Hungary. Part II, Chapter VII, Article 33 Competition Act describes the Hungarian Competition Authority as "a public, budgetary institution which constitutes a separate chapter in the central budget, the sums of total expenditure and total income of which may be reduced only by Parliament". Unless explicitly provided by the Act, "the responsibilities concerning supervision of competition, as defined in the Competition Act and the Act on Price Setting, are performed by the Hungarian Competition Authority".[35] Additionally, all the duties of the HCA must be prescribed by law.[36] Article 33 of the Competition Act also explicitly states that duties assigned to competition authorities of a Member State by competition rules of the European Union are carried out by the HCA.[37] The Act on Trade, for example, extends the scope of duties and competence of the HCA.

4.1.1 The General Structure of the HCA

The HCA is headed by a President.[38] The duties of the President are, amongst others, to issue notices which describe the basic principles of the law enforcement practice of the Hungarian Competition Authority, to provide opinions on draft municipality regulations and to report on experience gained in the course of his activities.[39] The staff of the HCA consists of civil servants performing investigations or duties aimed at promoting investigations which are appointed by the President of the HCA.[40] The General Secretary "leads, under the direction of the

35 Art. 33(2) Competition Act.
36 *Ibid.*
37 Art. 33(3) Competition Act.
38 Art. 35(1) Competition Act.
39 Art. 36 Competition Act.
40 Art. 39 Competition Act.

President, the organisation of the Hungarian Competition Authority and is categorised as 'bureauhead-investigator'.[41]

4.1.2 The Competition Council

Hungary also has a competition council which is a panel assigned to deliberate on different matters and to perform investigations. The council consists of a Chair and several members.[42] It is a partially independent section of the HCA, the members enjoy a quasi judicial position.[43] It performs duties defined by the Competition Act.[44] The Chair, for example, organises the activities of the competition council, supervises compliance with procedural deadlines and ensures publication of the resolutions of the competition council.[45]

4.2 Proceedings

Article 45 of the Competition Act states:

> The Hungarian Competition Authority shall have power to proceed in all competition supervision cases except for those in relation to which the courts have jurisdiction (Article 86).

This jurisdictional power covers the territory of the country.[46] Supervision proceedings consist of the procedures of the investigation, the procedure of the competition council, post-investigation and enforcement.[47]

4.2.1 Proceedings with the HCA

On infringements of Articles 8, 10, 11, 21 or 24 of the Competition Act, any person may make a complaint or an informal complaint to the HCA.[48] A complaint can be made by the submission to the HCA of a properly completed form issued by this organ.[49] The investigator may collect data needed for the assessment of the complaint and hold hearings.[50] In order to protect the complainant, he may request non-disclosure of his identity.[51] Within two months of receipt of the complaint, the investigator shall issue an order to (1) open an investigation pursuant to Article 70(1), (2) state that the conditions for opening of an investigation are

41 Art. 36/A Competition Act.
42 Art. 37 Competition Act.
43 T. Toth, 'Hungary', *in* I. Kokkoris, *Competition Cases from the European Union. The Ultimate Guide to Leading Cases from the EU, Member States and Efta*, London, Thomson Reuters 2010, pp. 623-666.
44 Art. 37 Competition Act.
45 Art. 37(2) Competition Act.
46 Art. 46 Competition Act.
47 Art. 47 Competition Act.
48 Art. 43/G Competition Act.
49 Art. 43/H Competition Act.
50 Art. 43/H(4) Competition Act.
51 Art. 43/H(5) Competition Act.

not fulfilled or (3) refer the complaint to another authority.[52] When an investigation is not opened, the complainant may seek legal remedy within eight days after the order. The legal remedy shall be considered by the Budapest Metropolitan Court. The Court can oblige the investigator to order the opening of an investigation within thirty days.[53]

Complaining documents, other than the complaints in the meaning of those mentioned above, are treated as informal complaints.[54] In these cases, the HCA is not empowered to proceed and must refer the informal complaint within ten days to the body which has the power to proceed.[55] The informal complaint shall be assessed within twenty-two working days of the date of receipt. When the complaint is well founded, the investigator shall decide on taking the necessary measure and notify the complainant on his resolution.[56]

An investigator of the HCA may also open a case on its own motion (*ex officio*), under the condition that the HCA "has the power to proceed in the case and the proceeding is necessary to safeguard the public interest".[57] The control of concentrations of undertakings belongs to the exclusive competence of the HCA.

4.3 National Courts

Article 1(1) Competition Act states that in any proceeding for the application of Article 101 and 102 TFEU, the HCA or a Hungarian Court may proceed. During these proceedings the procedural rules laid down in Regulation 1/2003 are applicable. The second Chapter of the Competition Act, relating to unfair competition, is enforced by the Hungarian courts. Other infringements are usually, in first instance, enforced by the HCA trough supervision proceedings.

4.3.1 Legal Remedy against Orders Made in the Course of the Proceeding

A complainant can seek legal remedies against the orders made by an investigator (Art. 82) The application for a legal remedy shall first be assessed by the competition council proceeding in the case apart from the trial. The council can affirm, amend or annul the order of the investigator and at the same time order the investigator to proceed. The council may also order the investigator to proceed.[58] An application for a separate legal remedy against an order made by the competition council proceeding shall be considered by the Budapest Metropolitan Court "pursuant to the rules applying for the judicial review of orders made in the courts of public administration."[59]

52 Art. 43/H(8) Competition Act.
53 Art. 43/H(11) Competition Act.
54 Art. 43/I(1) Competition Act.
55 Art. 43/I(2) Competition Act.
56 Art. 43/I(3)-(6) Competition Act.
57 Art. 70 Competition Act.
58 Arti. 82(2) Competition Act.
59 Art. 82(3) Competition Act.

4.3.2 Administrative Lawsuits

Another option is the 'administrative lawsuit':

> In cases where an action is brought in order to get the decision reached in competition supervision proceedings reviewed by the court, the statement of claim shall be, within 30 days (. . .) submitted to the competition council or taken to the post as registered mail.[60]

The council refers the case to the court within thirty days of receipt of the statement of claim.[61] In these proceedings the Code of Civil Procedures is applicable.[62]

4.3.3 Litigation Initiated by the HCA

Litigation can also be initiated by the HCA itself.[63] When the HCA, for instance, finds that a resolution of an authority violates the freedom of competition it can request the authority to amend or withdraw the resolution. When an authority does not comply within twenty-two working days the HCA may seek a court review on the matter, except when law excludes a court review. The claim can only be lodged until one year after the entry into force (the 'time bar'). The procedural provisions applying for administrative lawsuits are applicable *mutatis mutandis*.[64]

The jurisdiction of the Hungarian court(s) is laid down in Article 86 Competition Act. The country court (also: the Budapest Metropolitan Court) has "the power to hear and decide cases conducted against violations of the provisions contained in Article 2-7".[65] These Articles include the prohibition of unfair competition. In the claim the interested party may demand the following actions: the establishment of the violation, the termination of the violation and the prohibition of continued violations, that the infringer makes amends by making an announcement and/or that enough publicity is given to such announcement, the termination of the infringing state of affairs/restitution of the situation and depriving of the goods produced or distributed, damaged, and lastly that the infringer supplies information about whom participated in the production and distribution of the goods.[66]

A party can also request, in addition to civil law claims, precautionary measures to be taken in accordance with the provisions laid down in the Act on Judicial Enforcement (Art. 88(5)), certain guarantees and the disclosure of information. The time bar with respect to these proceedings is six months after acquiring knowledge of the violation of competition law (Article 88) unless the conduct is performed continuously. In the last case the time bar starts to run form the date of

60 Art. 83 Competition Act.
61 Art. 83(2) Competition Act.
62 With the exceptions defined by Art. 83 Competition Act, see Art. 84 Competition Act.
63 Art. 85 Competition Act.
64 Art. 85(1) Competition Act.
65 Art. 86(1) Competition Act.
66 Art. 86 Competition Act.

termination of the conduct, but no action may be started after five years have passed.

4.3.4 Other Lawsuits under the Code of the Civil Procedures

Lawsuits with regard to unfair manipulation of business decisions (Chapter III), the prohibition of agreements restricting economic competition (Chapter IV), and the abuse of a dominant position (Chapter V) are (also) addressed in the provisions of Act III 1952 and the Code of Civil Procedures (Article 88/B). The court will notify the HCA of these types of lawsuits, and the HCA is able to submit written observations. Article 88/B(4) Competition Act contains provisions on *amicus curiae*. The aforementioned Article mainly is about the interaction between the Court and the HCA.

5. Conclusions

The research questions were (1) How is competition law regulated in Hungary?; (2) What is the relation between Hungarian competition law and European competition law?; and (3) How is competition law enforced by Hungary?

Ad (1): Competition law in Hungary is regulated by the Hungarian Competition Act. The Competition Act contains all the substantive provisions of Hungarian competition law. It also covers unfair competition and competition-related consumer protection provisions. Also of importance is additional legislation such as the European Accession Treaty, the Act CLXIV 2005 on Commerce, the Hungarian Civil Code, the Act on Business Associations, the Act on Business Advertising Activity, the Act on Price Setting, the Act on Trade, the Act on Capital Markets, the Act on Prices and the Criminal Code. Furthermore, secondary legislation legal norms, position statements and notices are of importance (see Chapter 1).

Ad (2): With Hungary's accession to the European Union, Community competition law is directly applicable to Hungarian cases relating to restrictive agreements and abuses of a dominant position that may affect the trade between member states. The Hungarian Competition Act is fully harmonised with EU law.

Ad (3): When Article 101 and 102 TFEU apply the HCA or a Hungarian Court may proceed. Responsibilities concerning supervision of competition are performed by the HCA. Hungary also has a competition council which is a panel assigned to deliberate on different matters and to perform investigations. The council consists of a Chair and several members. It is a partially independent section of the HCA.

On infringements of Articles 8, 10, 11, 21 or 24 of the Competition Act, any person may make a complaint or an informal complaint to the HCA. When an investigation is not opened, the complainant may seek legal remedy. The legal remedy shall be considered by the Budapest Metropolitan Court. An investigator of the HCA may also open a case on its own motion (*ex officio*). Another option is the administrative lawsuit initiated by a private party. Litigation can also be initiated by the HCA itself.

Annex I Figures (2009) of the HCA on the Prohibition of Unfair Manipulation of Consumer Choice and Prohibition of Unfair Commercial Practices against Consumers

	Number of Cases	**% of Cases**
Establishment of the infringement	46	90,2
Commitment	2	3,9
GVH's interventions altogether	48	94,1
Lack of infringement	3	5,9
Other	0	0,0
All cases	51	100,0
Fines imposed related to GVH intervention (million HUF)	906,8	
Number of cases ended with imposition of fines	43	

Annex II Figures (2009) of the HCA on Abuse of a Dominant Position

	Abusive	**Restrictive**	**Composite and others**	**Altogether**	**% of cases**	**Number of cases related to trade between Member States**
Establishment of the infringement	0	0	0	0	0,0	0
Commitment	1	0	0	1	100,0	0
GVH's interventions altogether	1	0	0	1	100,0	0
Lack of infringement	0	0	0	0	0,0	0
Other	0	0	0	0	0,0	0
All cases	1	0	0	1	100,0	0
% of cases	100,0	0,0	0,0	100,0		
Number of cases related to trade between Member States	0	0	0	0		
Fines imposed (million HUF)	0	0	0	0		
% of fines related to GVH interventions (million HUF)						
Number of cases ended with imposition of fines	0	0	0	0		

Annex III Figures (2009) of the HCA on Agreements Restricting Economic Competition

	Horizontal	**Vertical**	**Composite**	**Altogether**	**% of cases**	**Number of cases involv-ing trade between Member States**
Illegal agreements	3	1	2	6	85,7	2
Commitment	1	0	0	1	14.3	1
Voluntary ac-ceptance of the objections of the GVH	0	0	0	0	0,0	0
All GVH interventions	*4*	*1*	*2*	*7*	*100,0*	*3*
Individual exemption	0	0	0	0	0,0	0
Application of Block Exemption	0	0	0	0	0,0	0
Non prohibited agreement	0	0	0	0	0,0	0
Non restrictive agreement	0	0	0	0	0,0	0
Other	0	0	0	0	0,0	0
All cases	4	1	2	7	100,0	3
% of cases	57,1	14,3	28,6	100,0		
Withdrawal of block exemption	0	0	0	0		
Number of cases related to trade between Mem-ber States	2	0	1	3		
Fines imposed related to GVH intervention (million HUF)	2 986	0	2 095	5 081		
% of fines re-lated to GVH intervention	58,8	0,0	41,2	100,0		
Number of cases ended with im-position of fines	3	0	2	5		

Annex IV Figures (2009) of the HCA on Concentrations of Undertakings

	Horizontal	**Vertical**	**Composite and others**	**Altogether**	**% of cases**	**Number of cases initiated ex officio**	**% of cases initiated ex officio**
Refusal-prohibition	1	0	0	1	2,9	0	0,0
Conditional authorisation	1	0	1	2	5,9	0	0,0
Voluntary acceptance of the objections of the GVH	0	0	0	0	0,0	0	0,0
All GVH interventions	*2*	*0*	*1*	*3*	*8,8*	*0*	*0,0*
Other refusals	0	0	0	0	0,0	0	0,0
Authorisation	14	3	12	29	85,3	2	6,9
Not subject to authorization	2	0	0	2	5,9	0	0,0
Other terminations of proceedings	0	0	0	0	0,0	0	0,0
All cases	18	3	13	34	100,0	2	5,9
Decisions in the first phase	17	3	9	29			
Decisions in the second phase	1	0	4	5			
% of cases	53,0	8,8	38,2	100,0			
Lack of/ delay in notifications	3	1	1	5			
Initiated ex officio	2	0	0	2			
% of cases initiated ex officio	11,1	0,0	0,0	11,1			
Fines imposed for lack of/delay in notifications (million HUF)	28.5	5	5	38,5			
% of fines imposed for lack of/delay in notification	74,0	13,0	13,0	100,0			

Annex V Hungarian Competition Act

Chapter IV - Prohibition of Agreements Restricting Economic Competition

Article 11

(1) Agreements or concerted practices between undertakings and decisions by social organisations of undertakings, public corporations, associations or other similar organisations (hereinafter together: agreements), which have as their object or potential or actual effect the prevention, restriction or distortion of competition, shall be prohibited. Agreements concluded between undertakings, which are not independent of each other do not qualify as such kind of agreements.
(2) This prohibition applies, in particular, to
a) the direct or indirect fixing of purchase or selling prices or other business terms and conditions;
b) the limitation or control of production, distribution, technical development or investment;
c) the allocation of sources of supply, or the restriction of their choice as well as the exclusion of a specified group of consumers from purchasing certain goods;
d) the allocation of markets, exclusion from sales, or restriction of the choice of marketing possibilities;
e) [Repealed by Act LXVIII of 2005]
f) the hindering of market entry;
g) cases, where, given transactions of the same value or character, there is discrimination between trading parties, including the application of prices, periods of payment, discriminatory selling or purchase terms and conditions or methods placing certain trading parties at a competitive disadvantage;
h) making the conclusion of contracts subject to the acceptance of obligations, which, by their nature or according to commercial usage do not belong to the subject of such contracts.
(3) Legal consequences attached by this Act to the infringement of Section (1) of this Article shall be applied together with those attached by the Civil Code to contracts infringing the law.

Article 101 TFEU (ex Art. 81 TEC)

1. The following shall be prohibited as incompatible with the internal market: all agreements between undertakings, decisions by associations of undertakings and concerted practices which may affect trade between Member States and which have as their object or effect the prevention, restriction or distortion of competition within the internal market, and in particular those which:
(a) directly or indirectly fix purchase or selling prices or any other trading conditions;
(b) limit or control production, markets, technical development, or investment;
(c) share markets or sources of supply;
(d) apply dissimilar conditions to equivalent transactions with other trading parties, thereby placing them at a competitive disadvantage;

(e) make the conclusion of contracts subject to acceptance by the other parties of supplementary obligations which, by their nature or according to commercial usage, have no connection with the subject of such contracts.
2. Any agreements or decisions prohibited pursuant to this Article shall be automatically void.
3. The provisions of paragraph 1 may, however, be declared inapplicable in the case of:
– any agreement or category of agreements between undertakings,
– any decision or category of decisions by associations of undertakings,
– any concerted practice or category of concerted practices,
which contributes to improving the production or distribution of goods or to promoting technical or economic progress, while allowing consumers a fair share of the resulting benefit, and which does not:
(a) impose on the undertakings concerned restrictions which are not indispensable to the attainment of these objectives;
(b) afford such undertakings the possibility of eliminating competition in respect of a substantial part of the products in question.

Chapter V - Prohibition of Abuse of a Dominant Position

Article 21

It shall be prohibited to abuse a dominant position, particularly:
a) in business relations, including the application of standard contractual terms, to set unfair purchase or selling prices or to stipulate in any other manner unjustified advantages or to force the other party to accept disadvantageous conditions;
b) to limit production, distribution or technical development to the prejudice of consumers;
c) to refuse, without justification, to create or maintain business relations appropriate for the type of transaction;
d) to influence the business decisions of the other party in order to gain unjustified advantages;
e) to withdraw, without justification, goods from circulation or withhold them from trade prior to a price increase or with the purpose of causing a price increase or in any other manner which may possibly produce unjustified advantages or to cause competitive disadvantages;
f) to make the supply or acceptance of goods subject to the supply or acceptance of other goods, furthermore to make the conclusion of contracts subject to the acceptance of obligations which, by their nature or according to commercial usage, do not belong to the subject of such contracts;
g) in the case of transactions which are equivalent in terms of their value or character to discriminate, without justification, against trading parties including in relation to the application of prices, periods of payment, discriminatory selling or purchase terms and conditions or methods thereby placing certain trading parties at a competitive disadvantage;
h) to set extremely low prices which are not based on greater efficiency in comparison with that of competitors and which are likely to drive out competitors from the relevant market or to hinder their market entry;

i) to hinder, without justification, market entry in any other manner; or
j) to create, without justification, disadvantageous market conditions for competitors, or to influence their business decisions in order to obtain unjustified advantages.

Article 102 TFEU (ex Art. 82 TEC)

Any abuse by one or more undertakings of a dominant position within the internal market or in a substantial part of it shall be prohibited as incompatible with the internal market in so far as it may affect trade between Member States.
Such abuse may, in particular, consist in:
(a) directly or indirectly imposing unfair purchase or selling prices or other unfair trading conditions;
(b) limiting production, markets or technical development to the prejudice of consumers;
(c) applying dissimilar conditions to equivalent transactions with other trading parties, thereby placing them at a competitive disadvantage;
(d) making the conclusion of contracts subject to acceptance by the other parties of supplementary obligations which, by their nature or according to commercial usage, have no connection with the subject of such contracts.

Removing Obstacles: The Competition Law Regime of the Slovak Republic

M. DeKoninck

1. Introduction

> In 2004, the [Slovak National Competition Authority] was involved in the preparation and implementation of new legislation, which [. . .] allowed direct application of Articles 81 and 82 of the Treaty establishing the European Community [. . .] and ensured full compatibility of Slovak legislation with European law.[1]

1.1 Aligning with the European Acquis Communautaire

Like the Czech Republic, Slovakia entered the European Union in 2004.[2] Already prior to its accession the Slovak competition law regime was, as emphasised by the Slovak National Competition Authority, fully aligned with EU competition law.[3]

1.2 Outline

The following chapter sets out the competition law regime of the Slovak Republic. At first the focus is on the primary national sources of competition law. Then the enforcement of competition law within Slovakia will be discussed. This enforcement is in the hands of the Antimonopoly Office (hereafter: the Office), the Regional Court of Bratislava and the Supreme Court of the Slovak Republic.

2. The Slovak Competition Law Regime

In Slovakia the primary legal source for antitrust cases and cases relating to the abuse of a dominant position is Act No. 136/2001 on Protection of Competition – the 'Competition Act'.[4] In addition, several other Slovak Acts may be applicable when

---

1 Antimonopoly Office of the Slovak Republic, Annual Report 2010, p. 5. Available at: <www.antimon.gov.sk/files/7/2005/VS_2004.pdf>, last consulted on 16 August 2011.

2 In total, ten new Member States accessed the European Union in 2004.

3 Z. Sláviková, 'Slovakia', *in* M. Dabbah and B. Hawk, *Anti-Cartel Enforcement Worldwide*, New York: Cambridge University Press 2009, p. 1040.

4 Act No. 136/2001 on Protection of Competition and on Amendments and Supplements to Act of the Slovak National Council No. 347/1990 Coll. on Organization of Ministries and Other Central Bodies of State Administration of the Slovak Republic as amended – last amendment in 2009.

dealing with competition law, for instance the Act on Administrative Proceeding.[5] The legal basis for these Slovak competition rules can be found in Article 55(2) of the Slovak Constitution. According to this Article "the Slovak Republic protects and promotes economic competition".

2.1 *The Slovak Competition Act*

The Slovak Competition Act[6] contains the basic competition and merger control provisions and has been effective as of 1 May 2001.[7] The last amendment to this Act was made in 2009.

2.1.1 Restrictive Agreements

The general provisions on cartels – "agreements restricting competition" – laid down in the Competition Act were in conformity with European competition law already before the accession of the Slovak Republic to the EU. Article 4(1) of the Slovak Competition Act provides that:

> Agreement and concerted practice between undertakings, as well as decisions of their associations, whose objective or effect is or may be restriction of competition (hereinafter referred to as an "agreement restricting competition") are prohibited, unless this Act provides otherwise.

The Competition Act furthermore provides, in conformity with EU competition law, for a broad interpretation of an 'undertaking' and 'agreement'.[8] A 'restriction of competition' is:

> [...] any restriction placed upon an undertaking's freedom to act on a relevant market, especially the exclusion of existing or potential competitive activities, the actual or potential reduction of the scope of competitive activities, or distortion of conditions for competition.[9]

2.1.2 Abuse of a Dominant Position

The Slovak Competition Act also clearly states that the 'abuse of a dominant position in the relevant market is prohibited'.[10] Article 8(1) clarifies that a dominant position is:

---

5 Act No. 71/1967 Coll. on Administrative Proceeding.

6 Act No. 136/2001 on Protection of Competition and on Amendments and Supplements to Act of the Slovak National Council No. 347/1990 Coll. on Organization of Ministries and Other Central Bodies of State Administration of the Slovak Republic as amended.

7 T. Maretta and T. Rybár, 'Slovak Republic', National Report, available at: <http://ec.europa.eu/competition/antitrust/actionsdamages/national_reports/slovak_republic_en.pdf>, last consulted on 16 August 2011.

8 Sláviková 2009, p. 1043.

9 Art. 3(1) Slovak Competition Act.

10 Art. 8(6) Slovak Competition Act.

> [. . .] held by an undertaking or several undertakings that are not subject to substantial competition or can act independently as a result of their economic power.[11]

Like the Slovak provisions on restrictive agreements, the Slovak regulation on the abuse of a dominant position is regarded to be equivalent to Article 102 of the Treaty on the Functioning of the European Union (TFEU).[12]

2.1.3 State Aid

With Slovakia's accession to the European Union, all European state aid rules have become directly applicable in Slovakia. Only certain specific forms of aid may be exempted, for instance aid to small and medium enterprises, aid granted for training or aid for employment. In general, state aid is subjected to the approval of the European Commission on the basis of European state aid legislation.[13]

2.1.4 Private Actions for Damages

The Slovak Competition Act does not contain specific provisions relating to private actions for damages for a breach of competition law. As a result, the general provisions relating to actions for damages under the Civil[14] and Commercial[15] Code apply in these cases.[16]

2.2 An Act on Unfair Conditions in Business Relationships

In 2008 Slovakia adopted a specific Act on Unfair Conditions in Business Relationships (AUC).[17] The objective of this Act is to assure protection for small and medium-sized enterprises and consumers against the abuse of economic power by larger undertakings on the market which may create unfair business conditions. It is not the National Competition Authority which enforces the provisions of this Act but the Ministry of Agriculture and the Ministry of Economy.[18]

2.3 The Slovak Leniency Programme

The Slovak Leniency Programme was introduced in 2001 with the adoption of the Competition Act. Article 38(11) of the Competition Act provides that the Office shall not impose a fine on an undertaking which was a party to a cartel, which also

11 The abuse of a dominant position is further defined in Art. 8(2) of the Slovak Competition Act.
12 K.J. Cseres, 'The Impact of Regulation 1/2003 in the New Member States', *The Competition Law Review* July 2010, p. 154.
13 Allen&Overy, 'State Aid in Slovakia', *Bulletin* April 2005, p. 1. Available at: <www.allenovery.com/AOWeb/binaries/23767.PDF>, last consulted on 16 August 2011.
14 Act No. 40/1964 Coll. as amended.
15 Act No 513/1991 Coll. as amended.
16 T. Maretta and T. Rybár, 'Slovak Republic', National Report, available at: <http://ec.europa.eu/competition/antitrust/actionsdamages/national_reports/slovak_republic_en.pdf>, last consulted on 16 August 2011.
17 Act on Unfair Conditions in Business Relationships (AUC) of 11 April 2008.
18 Cseres 2010, p. 153.

was the first to provide, on its own incentive, decisive evidence to prove a violation of competition law or information and documents decisive to carry out an inspection.[19] Unlike EU competition law, but similarly to Czech competition law, the undertaking requesting leniency may not be the instigator of cartel.[20] When leniency has been offered, this will not provide for immunity from civil claims.

2.4 Additional Decrees

Also similar to the Czech competition law regime, is that the Slovak competition authority, the Antimonopoly Office may issue decrees. The Office has issued two decrees of importance for the application of Slovak competition law. One decree deals with the notification of a concentration.[21] The other decree lays down details for the calculation of turnover.[22] There are also several internal directives and guidelines which are not legally binding upon the parties involved but are meant to guide the Office, for instance on the method of setting of fines in case of an infringement of competition law.[23]

3. Enforcement

The enforcement of Slovak competition law is in the hands of the Antimonopoly Office of the Slovak Republic. Decisions by the Office are subject to review by the Regional Court of Bratislava and the Supreme Court of the Slovak Republic.

3.1 The Office

The Office is the central body of state administration of Slovakia for the protection and promotion of competition[24] and is seated in Bratislava.[25] The main objective of the Office is:

> [. . .] to promote and to protect the economic competition, to create conditions for its further development as well as to prevent the creation and maintenance of monopolistic or dominant position of entrepreneurs, if it precludes or restrict economic competition.[26]

---

19 Art. 38(11) Slovak Competition Act.

20 *Ibid.*

21 Decree of the Antimonopoly Office of the Slovak Republic of 21 May 2009 laying down details of particulars of a notification of concentration.

22 Decree of the Antimonopoly Office of the Slovak Republic of 21 April 2004 laying down details of the calculation of turnover.

23 Metodický pokyn o postupe pri určovaní pokút v prípadoch zneužívania dominantného postavenia a dohôd obmedzujúcich súťaž – only Slovak version availabe.

24 Art. 14(1) Slovak Competition Act.

25 Art. 14(3) Slovak Competition Act.

26 See the website of the Office: <www.antimon.gov.sk/581/activities-of-amo-sr.axd>, last consulted on 16 August 2011.

The specific powers of the Office are laid down in Part 4 of the Slovak Competition Act. The Office shall, *inter alia*: issue a decision that an undertaking's conduct or activity is prohibited; issue opinions; decide on imposing the obligation to refrain from certain conduct and the obligation to remedy the unlawful state of affairs; issue a decision that the Competition Act has been violated by a state administration authority during the performance of state administration and; ensure international relations in the area of protection of competition at the level of authorities having jurisdiction over this area.[27] If there has been a breach of the Competition Act, the Office can also impose fines.[28] The Office can impose both administrative and criminal sanctions when enforcing competition law.[29]

3.1.1 The Administrative Two Instance Procedure

The Office has three different divisions: the Division of Agreements Restricting Competition, the Division of Abuse of a Dominant Position and the Division of Concentrations. Decisions made by the divisions can be appealed to the Council of the Office. The Council may annul, amend or uphold decisions made by the separate divisions.[30]

3.1.2 A Country New to Competition Enforcement

Prior to its accession to the EU, the Slovak Republic did not have a specific "competition culture". In 2008 the Office indicated that due to the inexperience and the lack of experts it encountered several problems when enforcing competition law. The Office had to cope, amongst others, with an insufficient number of employees and insufficient training programs. The Office emphasised the importance of cooperating with other competition institutions and other EU Member States in order to create more expertise and experience.[31]

3.2 Judicial Control – The Administrative Courts

Decisions by the Council of the Office can be appealed to the Regional Court in Bratislava. The Administrative bench of the Regional Court reviews competition law issues. The Administrative bench not only reviews competition law cases but also judges on, amongst others, cases related to tax law, environmental law or social security.[32] The Supreme Court of the Slovak Republic can review the decision of the Regional Court.

---

27 Part 4 of the Slovak Competition Act.

28 Art. 38 of the Slovak Competition Act.

29 Cseres 2010, p. 168.

30 OECD, 'Questionnaire on the Challenges Facing Young Competition Authorities: Contribution from the Slovak Republic', 16 January 2009, DAF/COMP/GF/WD(2009)62, p. 5. Available at: <www.oecd.org/officialdocuments/publicdisplaydocumentpdf/?cote=DAF/COMP/GF/WD(2009)62&docLanguage=En>, last consulted on 16 August 2011.

31 *Ibid.*, p. 2.

32 *Ibid.*, p. 6.

3.3 Appeal by the Office

Earlier, the Office only had limited possibilities to appeal a decision of the Regional Court. In 2008, however, the Civil Code of Procedure was amended and now the Office "has the right to appeal against any decision of the Regional Court in Bratislava which annuls the decision of the Council of the Office".[33]

3.3.1 Criticism from the Office

In the same report of the OECD, in which the Office emphasised its own shortcomings, the Office also criticised the judicial review of competition law cases in the Slovak Republic.

> In important cases [the] court annuls the decisions of the Council of the Office, whilst most of the decisions lack the concrete identification of the failures of the Office during the proceedings and a particular legal opinion of the court. The other negative fact is unfounded and disproportionate decreases of the imposed sanctions. Lack of experience of judges in competition law and hence following outputs disable the effective enforcement of competition rules.[34]

Later in 2010, the Office emphasised in its Annual Report that judgments of courts in the Slovak Republic have long been problematic and moreover inconsistent with the European case law.

> [. . .] the effective application of the competition rules in the Slovak Republic is not ensured. Main problems of the decision-making practice of courts in the area of competition law referred to by the Office in its analysis are unusual requirements for the verdict, decisions being returned without indication of the legal opinion of the court and inconsistency of judgments with the European case law. The court often requests the Office to review cases for which it is not competent, or even makes incorrect statements.[35]

4. Conclusion

Even though it is said that Slovak competition law is fully aligned with the EU *acquis communautaire*, it seems that the Slovak Republic still faces several problems relating to the application of competition law.

Slovakia is a country (relatively) new to the enforcement of competition law and thus, prior to its accession to the EU, it did not have an extensive 'competition

33 *Ibid.*
34 *Ibid.*
35 Antimonopoly Office of the Slovak Republic, Annual Report 2010, p. 24-25. Available at: <www.antimon.gov.sk/files/26/2011/VS%20PMÚ%20SR%202010.pdf>, last consulted on 16 August 2011.

culture' with the necessary experience and experts. It is difficult for the Slovak Republic to broaden its expertise and knowledge in the field of competition law since the amount of cases relating to competition law per year is very limited. This has already been acknowledged by the Office and to improve its experience and expertise the Office intends to work closely with other competition institutions and EU Member States.

It seems that the Slovak Republic does not have a specialised Court which deals with competition law cases only. From a practical point of view, this is not unreasonable since there are only few competition law cases a year in the Slovak Republic. Still, it has been emphasised in the literature that:

> [. . .] experience shows that those countries where specialized courts existed faced fewer problems than where general courts dealt with competition cases.[36]

Furthermore, there seems to be some tension between the Slovak National Competition Authority and the national courts. The Office has openly criticised the decision-making process of the Slovak Courts in competition law cases and claims that judgements have been inconsistent, unmotivated and in contradiction with EU practice.

Annex I

Slovak Competition Act

Article 4 - Agreement restricting competition

(1) Agreement and concerted practice between undertakings, as well as decisions of their associations, whose objective or effect is or may be restriction of competition (hereinafter referred to as an "agreement restricting competition") are prohibited, unless this Act provides otherwise.

(2) For the purpose of this Act:
a) an agreement between undertakings means any verbal or written positive expression of the will of the parties thereto, as well as any other positive expression of will derived from their conduct;
b) a concerted practice between undertakings means any coördination of their activities that does not bear signs of an agreement between undertakings referred to in (a) and cannot be identified as the natural consequence of the of the behavior of another undertaking;
c) a decision by an association of undertakings is any legal act of the association's body, as well as a recommendation of the association's body.

(3) There shall be prohibited, in particular, an agreement restricting competition that involves:
a) direct or indirect fixing of prices or other trade conditions;

36 Cseres 2010, p. 173.

b) commitment to limit or control production, sales, technical development, or investments;
c) division of the market or sources of supply;
d) commitment by the parties to the agreement that different conditions relating to an identical or comparable performance will be applied to individual undertakings, which will or may disadvantage these undertakings in competition;
e) conditions stipulating that the conclusion of contracts will require the parties to accept further obligations that are not related to the subject of these contracts in terms of their nature or according to customary commercial practice; or
f) signs of collusive behavior as a result of which undertakings coordinate their behavior, especially in the process of public procurement.

(4) If the reason for prohibition is only related to part of an agreement between undertakings or decision by an association of undertakings, then only that particular part shall be deemed prohibited, provided that it follows from the content of this agreement or the content of this decision by the association that the aforementioned part can be separated from the remaining content.

(5) The Office shall assess within the same proceedings agreements restricting competition concluded between an undertaking and other undertakings which, for the purpose of such agreement restricting competition, carry out business activities at a different level of a production chain or distribution system than the said undertaking if the contents of these agreements restricting competition are identical in terms of their purpose and objective.

Article 101 TFEU (ex Art. 81 TEC)

1. The following shall be prohibited as incompatible with the internal market: all agreements between undertakings, decisions by associations of undertakings and concerted practices which may affect trade between Member States and which have as their object or effect the prevention, restriction or distortion of competition within the internal market, and in particular those which:
(a) directly or indirectly fix purchase or selling prices or any other trading conditions;
(b) limit or control production, markets, technical development, or investment;
(c) share markets or sources of supply;
(d) apply dissimilar conditions to equivalent transactions with other trading parties, thereby placing them at a competitive disadvantage;
(e) make the conclusion of contracts subject to acceptance by the other parties of supplementary obligations which, by their nature or according to commercial usage, have no connection with the subject of such contracts.
2. Any agreements or decisions prohibited pursuant to this Article shall be automatically void.
3. The provisions of paragraph 1 may, however, be declared inapplicable in the case of:
– any agreement or category of agreements between undertakings,
– any decision or category of decisions by associations of undertakings,
– any concerted practice or category of concerted practices,

which contributes to improving the production or distribution of goods or to promoting technical or economic progress, while allowing consumers a fair share of the resulting benefit, and which does not:
(a) impose on the undertakings concerned restrictions which are not indispensable to the attainment of these objectives;
(b) afford such undertakings the possibility of eliminating competition in respect of a substantial part of the products in question.

Annex II

Slovak Competition Act

Article 8 - Abuse of a Dominant Position

(1) A dominant position in the relevant market is held by an undertaking or several undertakings that are not subject to substantial competition or can act independently as a result of their economic power.

(2) Abuse of a dominant position in the relevant market shall be defined as:
a) direct or indirect enforcement of excessive prices or other unfair trade conditions;
b) a threat of restriction or an actual restriction of the production, sale or technological development of goods to the detriment of users;
c) application of different conditions for identical or comparable performance with respect to the individual undertakings, through which the respective undertakings are or may be disadvantaged in the competition;
d) tying the conclusion of a contract to the condition that the other party accepts further commitments, unrelated to the subject of the contract in terms of substance or according to customary commercial practice; or
e) temporary abuse of economic power with a view to excluding competition.

(3) Essential facility is a facility, infrastructure or part thereof, location or right, the building or acquisition of which is objectively impossible by another undertaking and without the use of which competition would or might be restricted in the relevant market.

(4) Pursuant to this Act, an owner or administrator of an essential facility is also a holder of the right if a right is the respective essential facility pursuant to paragraph 3.

(5) An undertaking that is an owner or administrator of an essential facility abuses its dominant position in the relevant market if such an undertaking refuses to provide access to it and, at the same time:
a) the essential facility permits satisfying the undertaking's requirements regarding the utilization of the essential facility, while allowing for simultaneous satisfaction of the requirements of the essential facility's owner or administrator at the time of peak demand for its services, also taking into account the fulfilment of its long-term commitments;
b) an undertaking requesting access to the essential facility with the aim of its utilization is able to ensure adherence to the respective qualitative and quantitative

parameters of the essential facility resulting from its operational requirements, or if the undertaking requesting the utilization of an essential facility represented by a right is able to ensure adherence to all requirements concerning the aforementioned right as stipulated in special legislation; 5)
c) an undertaking requesting access to the essential facility is capable of providing the essential facility's owner or administrator with adequate payment.
(6) Abuse of a dominant position in the relevant market is prohibited.

5) For example, Act No. 55/1997 Coll. on Trade Marks as amended, Act No. 618/2003 Coll. on Copyright and Rights Connected with Copyright (Copyright Act).

Article 102 TFEU (ex Art. 82 TEC)

Any abuse by one or more undertakings of a dominant position within the internal market or in a substantial part of it shall be prohibited as incompatible with the internal market in so far as it may affect trade between Member States.
Such abuse may, in particular, consist in:
(a) directly or indirectly imposing unfair purchase or selling prices or other unfair trading conditions;
(b) limiting production, markets or technical development to the prejudice of consumers;
(c) applying dissimilar conditions to equivalent transactions with other trading parties, thereby placing them at a competitive disadvantage;
(d) making the conclusion of contracts subject to acceptance by the other parties of supplementary obligations which, by their nature or according to commercial usage, have no connection with the subject of such contracts.

Removing Obstacles: The Competition Law Regime of the Czech Republic

M. DeKoninck

1. Introduction

> (. . .) the Czech Republic has become a member of the European Union, and its competition law and policy have become fully consistent with European law and practice.[1]

1.1 Alignment with the European Union Competition Regime

In 2004, the Czech Republic entered the European Union and since then it has drafted its competition law regime 'so that it mirrors EC competition law'.[2] As a result, the Czech competition law regime presently closely aligns with European Union competition law system.[3]

1.2 Outline

The following paper generally sets out the Czech competition law system. First, it discusses the main sources of Czech competition law. Then its focus will be on the enforcement of the Czech competition law regime which is mainly in the hands of the Office for the Protection of Economic Competition (hereinafter: OPEC) and the Czech Administrative Courts.

2. The Czech Competition Law Regime

The main sources of Czech competition law are the 'Competition Act',[4] the 'State Aid Act',[5] and the 'Act on Significant Market Power in the Sale of Agricultural and

---

1 M. Wise, 'Competition Law and Policy in the Czech Republic: An OECD peer review', *OECD* 2008a, p. 4.

2 P. Dejl, A. Löfflerová & F. Kubík, *Study on the conditions of claims for damages in case of infringement of EC competition rules - Czech Republic report*, available at: <http://ec.europa.eu/competition/antitrust/actionsdamages/national_reports/czech_republic_en.pdf>, last consulted on 4 July 2011.

3 M. Wise, 'Review of Competition Law and Policy in the Czech Republic', *OECD* 2002b, p. 20.

4 Consolidated Act on the Protection of Competition - ACT No. 143/2001 Coll. of 4 April 2001 on the Protection of Competition and on Amendment to Certain Acts (Act on the Protection of Competition) as amended by Act No. 340/2004 Coll. of 4 May 2004, Act No. 484/2004 Coll. of 5 August 2004, Act No. 127/2005 Coll. of 22 February, Act No. 361/2005 Coll. of 19 August 2005, Act No. 71/2007 Coll. of 4 April 2007, Act No. 296/2007 Coll. of 1 January 2008 and Act No. 155/2009 Coll. of 1 September 2009.

5 Act No. 215/2004 Coll., amending certain relationships within the area of state aid, and altering the Act on the promotion of research and development.

Food Products and Abuse thereof'.[6] In addition the national competition authority, the Office for the Protection of Economic Competition, may issue decrees.

2.1 The Czech Competition Act

The Czech Republic established its competition law regime by the enactment of Act. no. 63/1991 on the Protection of Economic Competition. In 2001 this Act was, in its totality, replaced by Act No. 143/2001 Coll. on the Protection of Economic Competition, also called 'the Competition Act'. This revised Act on the Protection of Economic Competition aligned Czech competition policy with EU competition policy in particular in the field of merger control, the definition of a dominant position, the block exemptions and the *de minimis* thresholds.[7] The Competition Act entered into force in July 2001 and since then the Czech Competition Act has been revised on numerous occasions.[8]

2.1.1 Prohibited Behaviour

In its country report on the Czech Republic of 2008, the Organisation for Economic Cooperation and Development (OECD) underlined that the Czech Competition Act 'now closely follows the substantive terms and enforcement methods of the EC'.[9] The Czech Competition Act prohibits:

> All agreements between undertakings, decisions by associations of undertakings and concerted practices (hereinafter referred to as "agreements") which have as their object or effect the distortion of competition shall be prohibited and null and void, unless this Act or a special act provides otherwise, or unless the Office for the Protection of Competition (hereinafter referred to as "the Office") grants an exemption from this prohibition by its implementing regulation. Agreements with insignificant impact on competition shall not be prohibited.[10]

This prohibition on restrictive agreements is substantively identical to the Community prohibition of Article 101 of the Treaty on the Functioning of the European Union (TFEU).[11]

> This Act further regulates the procedure for application of Articles 81 and 82 of the Treaty establishing the European Community (hereinafter referred to as "the Treaty")

6 Act No. 395/2009 of 9 September 2009 on Significant Market Power in the Sale of Agricultural and Food Products and Abuse thereof.

7 Wise 2002b, p. 12; Wise 2002a, p. 2.

8 The Czech Competition Act of 2001 has since then been amended by Act No. 340/2004 Coll. of 4 May 2004, Act No. 484/2004 Coll. of 5 August 2004, Act No. 127/2005 Coll. of 22 February, Act No. 361/2005 Coll. of 19 August 2005, Act No. 71/2007 Coll. of 4 April 2007, Act No. 296/2007 Coll. of 1 January 2008 and Act No. 155/2009 Coll. of 1 September 2009.

9 Wise 2008a, p. 7.

10 Art. 3(1) of the Czech Competition Act. See Annex I.

11 Wise 2002b, p. 16.

> by the authorities of the Czech Republic and certain issues of cooperation of these authorities with the Commission of the European Communities (hereinafter referred to as "the Commission") and with the authorities of other Member States of the European Community in procedure pursuant to the Council Regulation (EC) on the implementation of the rules of competition laid down in Articles 81 and 82 of the Treaty (hereinafter referred to as "the Regulation") and in the Council Regulation (EC) on the control of concentrations between undertakings (hereinafter referred to as "the Merger Regulation").[12]

The subsequent list of examples of *per se* prohibited agreements[13] also copies the European list.[14] In addition, the Czech laws relating to State aid also align with the EU rules on State aid.[15]

2.1.2 Private Actions for Damages

The Competition Act does not contain any special provisions regarding private actions for damages.[16] For this reason, the general provisions governing actions for damages apply. The legal basis for this action can be found in the Commercial Code. The Civil Procedure Act contains the procedural rules for bringing actions for damages.[17] No particular changes were made to Czech competition legislation to take into account the recommendations made by the Commission in the White Paper and Commission Staff Working Paper on Damages Actions for Breach of the EC antitrust rules. Regarding this, it should however be taken into consideration that some of these recommendations were already present in the Czech competition law regime.[18]

2.2 The Czech Leniency Programme

The first Czech Leniency Programme dates from 2001 and was applied for the first time in 2004 in a case relating to the energy drinks market.[19] Due to a lack of procedural guarantees for the applicants and several unclear rules, this programme led to very poor results.[20] In June 2007 OPEC launched its new Leniency

---

12 Art. 1(2) of the Czech Competition Act.

13 Art. 3(2) of the Czech Competition Act.

14 Wise 2002b, p. 16.

15 See further section 3.1.2 of this contribution.

16 Wise 2008a, pp. 34-35.

17 P. Dejl, A. Löfflerová & F. Kubík,, *Study on the conditions of claims for damages in case of infringement of EC competition rules - Czech Republic report*, available at: <http://ec.europa.eu/competition/antitrust/actionsdamages/national_reports/czech_republic_en.pdf>, last consulted on 4 July 2011.

18 J. Kindl, 'National Report on the Czech Republic', *Fide XXIII Congress – Linz 2008, Topic2: The Modernisation of the European Competition Law 'First Experiences with Regulation 1/2003'*, available at: <http://www.csesp.cz/dokumenty/CZ_Q2_Kindl.pdf>, last consulted on 4 July 2011. For OPEC's position to the White Paper on Damages actions for breach of the EC antitrust rules see Annex IV.

19 K.J. Cseres, 'The Impact of Regulation 1/2003 in the New Member States', *The Competition Law Review* July 2010, p. 167.

20 OECD, 'Questionnaire on the Challenges Facing Young Competition Authorities: Contribution from the Czech Republic', 8 January 2009, DAF/COMP/GF/WD(2009)6, p. 6. Available at: <www.oecd.org/dataoecd/24/37/41956704.pdf>, last consulted on 4 July 2011.

Programme. The framework for the Czech Leniency Programme has been set out in a Notice[21] and is regarded as soft law. Nevertheless, in practice, once the conditions for the application are fulfilled, OPEC applies the programme.[22] The Czech Leniency programme was inspired by the European Union Leniency Programme and closely aligns with the EU programme. Nonetheless, there is one particular difference between the two programmes. Under the Czech Programme, an undertaking cannot apply for leniency when it initiated the cartel, coerced other undertakings to join the cartel or remain in it or had a leading role in the cartel.[23] Under EU law even the coercer, under strict conditions, may be granted leniency.[24]

2.3 Additional Decrees

As mentioned above, the Office for the Protection of Economic Competition may issue decrees. Prior to the accession of the Czech Republic to the European Union, these decrees usually reproduced the block exemption regulations of the European Commission. Currently, the Competition Act refers directly to these exemptions:

> The prohibition pursuant to Article 3(1) shall not apply to agreements that may not effect trade between Member States of the European Community pursuant to the Article 81 of the Treaty, which, however, fulfil other conditions laid down in block exemptions adopted on the basis of Article 83(1) of the Treaty in order to implement Article 81(3) of the Treaty by relevant Commission or Council Regulations (hereinafter referred to as 'the Community Block Exemptions'), or in the exemption for the agriculture sector.[25]

3. Enforcement

The principle authority for the enforcement of competition law in the Czech Republic is the Office for the Protection of Economic Competition. The decisions of OPEC are subject to judicial review by the administrative courts of the Czech Republic.

21 Leniency programme on imposition of fines in accordance with the Article 22 of the Act No. 143/2001 Coll., on the Protection of Competition and on amendment to certain Acts (Act on the Protection of Competition) (hereinafter referred to as "the Act") as amended, on prohibited agreements distorting the competition, on condition that certain additional requirements are fulfilled the parties to the cartel can be granted immunity from a fine or a reduction of a fine (hereinafter referred to as "Leniency programme").

22 A. Bányaiová & L. Bányaiová, 'Czech Republic', *in* Dabbah & Hawk 2009, p. 341.

23 See Annex III.

24 Commission Notice on Immunity from fines and reduction of fines in cartel cases, OJ (2006) C298/17. See also J. Kindl, 'National Report on the Czech Republic', *Fide XXIII Congress – Linz 2008, Topic2: The Modernisation of the European Competition Law 'First Experiences with Regulation 1/2003'*, available at: <www.csesp.cz/dokumenty/CZ_Q2_Kindl.pdf>, last consulted on 4 July 2011.

25 Art. 4 of the Czech Competition Act.

3.1 The Czech Competition Authority

The national competition authority of the Czech Republic has its headquarters in Brno and is active since July 1991. In order to reinforce the Office's independent decision-making position, the headquarters is in Brno where OPEC is separated from the governmental institutions in Prague.[26] Even though OPEC used to be part of the government as a Ministry of Economic Competition, there is nowadays no doubt about its decision-making independence.[27] The general mission of OPEC is "to ensure that market behaviour is in compliance with competition rules and benefits the consumers".[28] OPEC:

> guides the competitors to behave in compliance with the principles of competition law; interferes with practices distorting competition, e.g. cartel agreements, abuse of dominant position, etc.; offers businesses the possibility to remedy their illegal conduct which has not resulted in a significant impact on the market so far.[29]

Within OPEC, the *Manufacturing and Services Department* has the competence to take action and make decisions in case of agreements distorting competition[30] and abuse of a dominant position in first instance proceedings. OPEC's *Cartel Department* is competent to deal with the detection of *horizontal* agreements concluded among mutual competitors in the market. The Cartel Department is also in charge of the Leniency Programme. OPEC also has a *Merger Department* which mainly deals with the assessment of the impact of concentrations between undertakings on competition and the supervision of the fulfilment of obligations and commitments laid down in OPEC's decisions.[31]

3.1.1 OPEC and State Aid

OPEC coordinates and monitors State aid in order to ensure compliance with the European Community rules on State aid. OPEC is, however, not responsible for the enforcement relating to State aid. With the Czech Republic's accession to the European Union in 2004, this enforcement responsibility for State aid matters was shifted to the European Commission.[32]

3.2 Judicial Control – The Administrative Courts

The decisions of OPEC are subject to judicial review by the administrative courts of the Czech Republic. In first instance the Regional Court addresses the case.

26 Wise 2002b, p. 12. The Administrative Court, the Regional Court and the Supreme Court are also established in Brno.

27 Wise 2008a, p. 29; Wise 2002b, p. 49.

28 Website of OPEC <www.compet.cz/en/about-the-office/commission-and-competency/>, last consulted on 4 July 2011.

29 Website of OPEC <www.compet.cz/en/about-the-office/commission-and-competency/> last consulted on 4 July 2011.

30 This does not include horizontal agreements which are subject to investigation by the Cartel Department.

31 Website of OPEC, <www.compet.cz/en/competition/#c120>, last consulted on 4 July 2011.

32 Wise 2008a, p. 29.

Appeal lies to the Supreme Administrative Court.[33] In addition, when the case involves the breach of a fundamental constitutional right, the Czech Constitutional Court may review the case.

Like Slovakia, the Czech Republic is a 'relatively' new Member State of the EU and a somewhat small jurisdiction. As a result, the country's case law related to European competition law has been rather limited. The Czech Republic also does not have a specific court specialised in the area of competition law.[34] In the literature it has been emphasised that:

> [. . .] experience shows that those countries where specialized courts existed faced fewer problems than where general courts dealt with competition cases.[35]

Nevertheless, considering the limited case law relating to article 101 and article 102 TFEU per year, approximately six cases per year,[36] it seems unpractical to establish a specialised court dealing only with competition law cases. Still, at the Regional Court in Brno it is always the same bench that decides on competition law cases. Therefore, even though there is no specialised court, since the same judges deal with competition law cases, the judges of the specific bench have the possibility to gain experience with competition law. When the case is appealed at the Supreme Administrative Court it may, however, be referred to several non-specialised benches.

3.2.1 OPEC and the Courts

OPEC also gave its opinion on the system of two level, non-specialised and partly decentralised jurisdiction. OPEC underlined that:

> Due to the complexity and low frequency of competition cases some specialisation might be necessary. However, at the same time, if the specialisation is too intensive (so that there is only one senate deciding on all competition cases), there might be a risk of dominance of a single approach without any real possibility to seek remedy'. In such cases there is certain risk of subjective point of view of an individual judge, which is in some cases hardly separable. [. . .] In addition, we think that at least at upper instance, the competition cases should be distributed among more senates in order to prevent possible monopolisation of thinking in competition issues.[37]

33 Act No. 150/122 on Judicial Administrative Proceedings.

34 J. Kindl and M. Petr, 'National Report on the Czech Republic', *Fide Congress – Madrid 2010 Topic 2: The Judicial Application of European Competition law*, available at: <www.csesp.cz/dokumenty/FIDE_2010-Q2-Czech%20Republic.pdf>, last consulted on 4 July 2011. The Czech Republic, unlike Slovakia, did however have a certain 'competition culture' before its accession to the European Union.

35 K.J. Cseres, 'The Impact of Regulation 1/2003 in the New Member States', *The Competition Law Review* July 2010, p. 173.

36 *Ibid.*, p. 166.

37 OECD, 'Questionnaire on the Challenges Facing Young Competition Authorities: Contribution from the Czech Republic', 8 January 2009, DAF/COMP/GF/WD(2009)6, p. 11. Available at: <www.oecd.org/dataoecd/24/37/41956704.pdf>, last consulted on 4 July 2011.

Even though the National Competition Authority seems to support the current organisation of the Czech judicial system, OPEC did underline that it takes relatively long for the court to finally decide on cases, which may frustrate the enforcement of competition law.[38]

3.2.2 Parallel Application of Competition Law

In 2007 the Regional Court overruled OPEC's decision in two cases on the ground that the application of both European competition law and national competition law, in relation to the same infringement, is a violation of the *ne bis in idem* principle. The Supreme Administrative Court, however, overturned the judgement by the Regional Court reasoning that the court had misinterpreted the principle.[39]

In 2009, the Regional Court once again decided that in a specific case the parallel application of both national competition law and European competition law in relation to the same infringement would be a violation of the *ne bis in idem* principle. On appeal, the Supreme Court, also once again, overruled the Regional Court's decision.[40] As a reaction to the judgments of the Supreme Court the Regional Court has decided to refer the case to Court of Justice of the European Union. In its reference for a preliminary ruling the Regional Court asked the following questions:

> Must Article 11(6) of Council Regulation (EC) No 1/2003 in conjunction with Article 3(1) thereof and recital 17 in the preamble thereto, with point 51 of the Commission Notice on cooperation within the Network of Competition Authorities, with the principle *ne bis in idem* under Article 50 of the Charter of Fundamental Rights of the European Union, and with the general principles of European law be interpreted as meaning that if the Commission brings proceedings after 1.5.2004 for infringement of Article 81 EC and makes a decision in that case:
> a) the Competition Authorities of the Member States are automatically relieved of their competence to deal with that conduct from that time onwards?
> b) the Competition Authorities of the Member States are relieved of their competence to apply to that conduct the provisions of domestic law containing parallel legislation to Article 81 EC (now Article 101 of the Treaty on the Functioning of the European Union)?[41]

38 OPEC did also emphasise that this 'seems to be an obvious phenomenon, occurring in many countries'.

39 Decision of the Regional Court Brno, 22 October 2007, Case No. 62 Ca 8/2007-171, *RWE Transgas* and decision of the Regional Court Brno, 1 November 2007, No. 62 Ca 4/2007-115, *Tupperware*. Decision of the Supreme Administrative Court, 31 October 2008, Case 5 Afs 8/2008 – 328, *RWE Transgas* and decision of the Supreme Administrative Court, 3 December 2008, Case 7 Afs7/2008-200, *Tupperware*.

40 Decision of the Supreme Administrative Court, 10 April 2009, No. 2 Afs 93/2008-920, *Toshiba*. For a summary of the case see: <www.juradmin.eu/en/jurisprudence/jurifast/jurifast_en.php?PHPSESSID=gp5pnv5b9r5goqgutekq64p7u3&page=detail&id=699>.

41 Reference for a preliminary ruling lodged on 11 January 2010, Case C-17/10, *Toshiba*.

4. Conclusion

The Czech competition regime has developed significantly since the accession of the Czech Republic to the European Union. As underlined above, it is clear that the Czech competition regime now closely aligns with the EU competition policy regarding prohibited cartels, unlawful State aid and the Leniency Programme. The enforcement responsibility for State aid matters has moreover been shifted to the European Commission. Currently the system seems to function well but it may become problematic that at the appeal level there is no specific court specialized in (EU) competition law issues. Still, as emphasised by OPEC, specialised courts at the same time increase the risk of monopolisation of thinking in competition issues.

Annex I

Czech Competition Act

Section II - Agreements Distorting Competition

Article 3

(1) All agreements between undertakings, decisions by associations of undertakings and concerted practices (hereinafter referred to as "agreements") which have as their object or effect the distortion of competition shall be prohibited and null and void, unless this Act or a special act provides otherwise, or unless the Office for the Protection of Competition (hereinafter referred to as "the Office") grants an exemption from this prohibition by its implementing regulation. Agreements with insignificant impact on competition shall not be prohibited.
(2) Particular agreements shall be prohibited within the meaning of paragraph 1, which have as their object or effect the distortion of competition due to containing provisions on:
a) direct or indirect fixing of prices or other business terms and conditions,
b) limitation or control of production, sales, research and development or investments,
c) division of markets or sources of supply,
d) making the conclusion of a contract subject to acceptance of further performance, which by its nature or according to commercial usage and fair business practices has no connection with the object of such contracts,
e) application of dissimilar conditions to identical or equivalent transactions with other undertakings, thereby placing them at a competitive disadvantage,
f) obligation of the parties to the agreement to refrain from trading or other economic co-operation with undertakings not being party to the agreement, or to otherwise harm such undertakings (group boycott).

(3) If the reason for prohibition relates only to a part of the agreement, only that particular part thereof shall be prohibited and null and void. Provided that it may be inferred from the nature, contents or purpose of the agreement, or the circumstances in which the agreement was concluded that such part may not be severed from its remaining content, the whole such agreement shall be prohibited and null and void.
(4) The prohibition pursuant to paragraph 1 shall not apply to agreements, which
a) contribute to improving the production or distribution of goods or to promoting technical or economic progress while allowing consumers a fair share of the resulting benefit,
b) do not impose on the undertakings restrictions which are not indispensable to the attainment of the objectives pursuant to letter a),
c) do not afford the undertakings the possibility of eliminating competition in respect to a substantial part of the market of goods, the supply or purchase which constitutes the objective of the agreement.

Article 101 TFEU (ex Art. 81 TEC)

1. The following shall be prohibited as incompatible with the internal market: all agreements between undertakings, decisions by associations of undertakings and concerted practices which may affect trade between Member States and which have as their object or effect the prevention, restriction or distortion of competition within the internal market, and in particular those which:
(a) directly or indirectly fix purchase or selling prices or any other trading conditions;
(b) limit or control production, markets, technical development, or investment;
(c) share markets or sources of supply;
(d) apply dissimilar conditions to equivalent transactions with other trading parties, thereby placing them at a competitive disadvantage;
(e) make the conclusion of contracts subject to acceptance by the other parties of supplementary obligations which, by their nature or according to commercial usage, have no connection with the subject of such contracts.
2. Any agreements or decisions prohibited pursuant to this Article shall be automatically void.
3. The provisions of paragraph 1 may, however, be declared inapplicable in the case of:
– any agreement or category of agreements between undertakings,
– any decision or category of decisions by associations of undertakings,
– any concerted practice or category of concerted practices,
which contributes to improving the production or distribution of goods or to promoting technical or economic progress, while allowing consumers a fair share of the resulting benefit, and which does not:
(a) impose on the undertakings concerned restrictions which are not indispensable to the attainment of these objectives;
(b) afford such undertakings the possibility of eliminating competition in respect of a substantial part of the products in question.

Annex II

Czech Competition Act

Section III - Dominant Position and its Abuse

Article 10

(1) One or more undertakings jointly (joint dominance) shall be deemed to have a dominant position in the relevant market, if their market power enables them to behave independently to a significant extent of other undertakings or consumers.
(2) The Office shall assess the market power pursuant to paragraph 1 above on the basis of the amount of ascertained volume of sales or purchases in the relevant market for the goods in question (market share), achieved by the relevant undertaking or undertakings in joint dominant position during the period examined pursuant to this Act. Also on the basis of other indices, in particular the economic and financial power of the undertakings, legal or other obstacles for other undertakings to enter into the market, the level of vertical integration of undertakings, market structure and size of the market shares of their immediate competitors.
(3) Unless proven otherwise by means of the indices pursuant to paragraph 2 above, an undertaking or undertakings in joint dominance shall be deemed not to be in a dominant position, if its/their share in the relevant market achieved during the examined period does not exceed 40%.

Article 11

(1) Abuse of dominant position to the detriment of other undertakings or consumers shall be prohibited. Abuse of dominant position shall consist particularly of:
a) direct or indirect enforcement of unfair conditions in agreements with other participants in the market, especially enforcement of performance, which is at the time of conclusion of contract conspicuously inadequate to the counter-performance provided,
b) making the conclusion of contracts subject to acceptance by the other party of supplementary performance, which by its nature or according to commercial usage has no connection with the object of such contracts,
c) application of dissimilar conditions to identical or equivalent transactions with other trading parties, thereby placing them at a competitive disadvantage,
d) termination or limitation of production, sales or research and development to the prejudice of consumers,
e) consistent offer and sale of goods for unfairly low prices, which results or may result in distortion of competition,
f) refusal to grant other undertakings access for a reasonable reimbursement, to own transmission grids or similar distribution networks or other infrastructure facilities, which are owned or used on other legal grounds by the undertaking in

dominant position, provided other undertakings are unable for legal or other reasons to operate in the same market as the dominant undertakings without being able to jointly use such facilities, and such dominant undertakings fail to prove, that such joint use is unfeasible for operational or other reasons or that they cannot be reasonably requested to enable such use. The same also applies in due proportion to the refusal of access for a reasonable reimbursement, of other undertakings to the use of intellectual property or access to networks owned or used on other legal grounds by the undertaking in a dominant position, provided such use is necessary for participating in competition in the same market as the dominant undertakings or in any other market,

(2) If the Office finds within the framework of proceedings concerning the matters pursuant to paragraph 1 that abuse of a dominant position has been committed, it shall declare such fact in a decision and it shall by this decision prohibit such action for the future.

(3) Instead of a decision pursuant to paragraph 2, the Office shall decide on the termination of the proceedings on condition that the parties to the proceedings jointly proposed commitments in favour of restorating effective competition sufficient for the protection of competition, the harmful situation is eliminated by their fulfilment, and abuse of dominant position did not result in substantial distortion of competition. In such decision the Office may lay down conditions and obligations necessary to secure fulfilment of these commitments. Should the Office find such commitments insufficient, it shall communicate the reasons to the parties to the proceedings in writing and it shall continue with the proceedings.

(4) The parties to the proceedings may propose the commitments pursuant to paragraph 3 to the Office in writing within 15 days following the day, on which the Office delivered to them its the statement of objections. Any proposal made after this period shall be taken into account by the Office only in cases worthy of special attention. The parties to the proceedings are bound by their proposal vis-à-vis the Office and vis-à-vis each other, or vis-à-vis third parties, and following the proposal, not to perform the agreement in its original wording until the decision of the Office pursuant to paragraph 3 is issued.

(5)Following the termination of the proceedings pursuant to paragraph 3, the Office may reopen the proceedings pursuant to paragraph 2, where

a) there has been a substantial change in circumstances on which the decision pursuant to paragraph 3 was based,

b) the undertakings act contrary to the commitments pursuant to paragraph 3, or

c) the decision was issued on the basis of incorrect or incomplete documents, data or information.

Article 102 TFEU (ex Art. 82 TEC)

Any abuse by one or more undertakings of a dominant position within the internal market or in a substantial part of it shall be prohibited as incompatible with the internal market in so far as it may affect trade between Member States.

Such abuse may, in particular, consist in:
(a) directly or indirectly imposing unfair purchase or selling prices or other unfair trading conditions;
(b) limiting production, markets or technical development to the prejudice of consumers;
(c) applying dissimilar conditions to equivalent transactions with other trading parties, thereby placing them at a competitive disadvantage;
(d) making the conclusion of contracts subject to acceptance by the other parties of supplementary obligations which, by their nature or according to commercial usage, have no connection with the subject of such contracts.

Annex III

Czech Leniency programme

1.3. Common conditions attached to Leniency programme

1.3.1. In order to qualify for Leniency programme, the applicant must satisfy the following conditions:
a) The Applicant must cooperate genuinely, helpfully, fully and on a continuous basis from the time of its application with the Office until the conclusion of the administrative proceeding. This includes especially:

- Providing the Office promptly with all relevant information and evidence that comes into the applicant's possession or under its control;
- Providing the Office only with complete and exact, not misguiding information,
- Remaining at the disposal of the Office to reply promptly to any requests that, in the Office's view, may contribute to the establishment of relevant facts on this subject;
- making current and, to the extent possible, former employees, directors and members of statutory bodies available for the interviews with the Office;
- not destroying, falsifying or concealing relevant information or evidence which falls within the scope of alleged cartel agreement; and
- not disclosing the fact or any of the content of the leniency application before the Office has initiated administrative proceeding on this subject.

b) The applicant ended its involvement in the alleged cartel agreement immediately following its application
c) At a time when contemplating making Leniency application the applicant must not have destroyed, falsified or concealed evidence relevant to alleged cartel or disclosed its intention to submit application or a part of intended application, except having done this to any other competition authority.
d) The applicant didn't initiate concluding of the cartel, didn't take steps to coerce other undertakings to join the cartel or to remain in it or didn't have a leading role in the alleged cartel.

Annex IV The Position of the Office for the Protection of Competition of the Czech Republic to the White Paper on Damages actions for breach of the EC antitrust rules

I. Introduction

1. The White Paper on Damages actions for breach of the EC antitrust rules issued by the European Commission on 2 April 2008 (hereinafter referred to as the "White Paper") presents a variety of measures to be adopted in order to facilitate the enforcement of the victims' right to damages in competition matters. These measures are in detail described in the Commission staff working paper accompanying the White Paper (hereinafter referred to as the "Working Paper").
2. The Office for the Protection of Competition of the Czech Republic (hereinafter referred to as the "Office") welcomes the proposals contained in the White Paper and endorses the Commission's view on the need of adopting certain measures, which would help to foster development of private enforcement within the European Union. On the basis of discussion about the White Paper in the Czech Republic, the Office encourages the Commission to adopt binding legal instruments (directives or even regulations) guaranteeing minimal standards and harmonised redress mechanism for damages claims throughout the European Union in order to overcome existing obstacles dissuading the potential claimants.
3. Nonetheless, as will be in detail described below, the Office would like to recommend clarification of particular proposals contained in the White Paper, especially with regard to the *inter partes* access to evidence and collective redress, which would necessitate significant changes of the Czech Civil Procedure Act[42] and the Competition Act,[43] eventually the Commercial Code.[44] Since the civil proceedings are generally based on very formal and strict rules in the Czech Republic, the Office expects a thorough discussion concerning any legislative proposals on these issues and it might be extremely difficult to implement the measures contained in the White Paper if they would not be explicitly and precisely specified at the European level.
4. The Office strongly supports the private enforcement of competition law in the Czech Republic. Recently, a proposal of amendment of the Competition Act prepared by the Office has been submitted to the Czech Government (hereinafter referred to as the "Amendment of the Competition Act"). It is inspired by the regulation of unfair competition, designed to

42 Civil Procedure Act No. 99/1963 Coll., as amended.
43 Competition Act No. 143/2001 Coll., as amended.
44 Commercial Code No. 513/1991 Coll., as amended.

protect consumer's rights, and suggests that the same regulation should be adopted for infringements of the Competition Act (or European Competition Law). Individuals injured by anticompetitive behaviour should be able to bring an action claiming cease and desist orders or removal of effects of the infringement, and to ask for damage and recovery of unjust enrichment. Also the associations of undertakings or consumers should be empowered to bring "representative" claims for cease and desist orders (but not for recovery of damages). Should an individual consumer file an action, the burden of proof should be reversed as far as the infringement is concerned; nevertheless, even the consumers would still be bound to prove that they sustained damage as a result of the infringement and the amount they are claiming.

II. Standing: indirect purchasers and collective redress

5. The White Paper suggests explicitly granting standing to sue damages to indirect purchasers and presents two complementary systems of collective redress, namely representative action for damages brought by qualified entities on behalf of victims and an opt-in collective action combining two or more claims from individuals or businesses.

6. There is no special legal regulation concerning the standing of indirect purchasers and representative or collective actions in the Czech Republic. Those injured by infringement of competition law can bring an action in civil procedure to the regional court, the applicable rules being the same for stand-alone and follow-on actions. If one action is brought in a single matter, other victims can join the legal proceeding as interpleaders. The Office is aware of the fact that this general regulation might not be suitable for recovery of damages caused especially to the consumers or small-sized undertakings.

(A) Indirect Purchasers

7. There is a general rule in the Czech law that *anybody* harmed by unlawful behaviour shall have a right to claim damages suffered by it. The Office therefore fully supports the standing of indirect purchasers and regards it as necessary for equitable private enforcement.

(B) Collective redress

8. The Office fully appreciates the fact that establishing some form of collective redress is necessary. As mentioned above, the Office has so far proposed the Amendment of Competition Act, on the basis of which the legal entities qualified to defend consumers' and competitors' interests should be empowered to bring claims for cease and desist orders; suing for damages by these entities could be the next step in legislative efforts of the Office.

(i) Representative actions

9. A representative action could be according to the White Paper brought by qualified entities on behalf of identified or identifiable victims, who are not themselves parties to the proceedings but are represented by this entity. Represented victims should be informed that an action is about to be brought or have been brought. Qualified entities could be designated "generally" in advance or certified according to national law on an *ad hoc* basis to bring the representation action to protect the interests of its members in relation to a particular infringement of competition law.

10. The Office supports this proposition; we would nonetheless welcome further clarification on certain points.

11. Firstly, the Office believes it is necessary to stipulate which individuals are to be represented, especially in cases when the action is brought on behalf of merely "identifiable" individuals – the term "rather restricted cases" mentioned in the White Paper needs to be clarified. The Office would welcome an "opt-out" system stipulating the obligation of representative bodies to inform the "representable" victims that the action is about to be brought, what consequences it has for them and how they could express their position, including their willingness not to be represented.

12. Secondly, as far as the quantification of damages and their distribution is concerned, the Office would welcome more detailed rules. Because of the loosely defined notion of "victims" who are to be represented, it would probably not be able to quantify the damages exactly, which could cause application problems to Czech courts; the same would be true for the amount allocated to each of the represented individuals. The Office is therefore of an opinion that there should be some minimal standard rules for distribution of damages, including conditions for who should be entitled to decide and for which purposes it would be possible to use the money awarded to the representative entity.

(ii) Opt-in collective actions

13. The White Paper proposes a system of opt-in collective actions, whereby individual claims could be joined in one single action. The proceedings should be initiated upon express intention of the victims to do so. The damages should correspond to the harm suffered by them. Individual victims should not be deprived of their right to bring an individual action for damages.

14. With regard to complete lack of experience with collective actions in the Czech Republic, the Office is not convinced that the opt-in system would be sufficient to stimulate individuals to combine their claims. The Office therefore encourages the Commission to reconsider the possibility of collective actions being based on the opt-out principle.

(iii) The interrelationship between available types of action

15. The proposed means of collective redress should not deprive individuals of their right to bring their claims on their own. The White Paper stresses the

importance of safeguards preventing overcompensation, i.e. that the same harm should not be compensated several times, through the various means of action available. Nonetheless, no concrete proposals are contained in the White Paper in this regard.

16. The Office believes that such measures should be explicitly specified, especially with regard to implementation of these measures on national level.

III. *Access to evidence: disclosure inter partes*

17. The White Paper proposes a minimum level of disclosure *inter partes* in order to overcome obstacles caused by potential claimants by the information asymmetry among parties in competition matters. The central role is entrusted to the courts, which should be empower to order the defendant to disclose precise categories of relevant evidence provided the legal conditions on part of the plaintiff are fulfilled. Regarding specification of facts and means of evidence, member states should alleviate their requirements if they are very strict. The adequate protection should be given to confidential information, corporate statements of leniency applicants and the results of investigations of competition authorities. Courts should have the power to impose effective sanctions to prevent destruction of relevant evidence or refusal to comply with the disclosure order.

18. The *inter partes* disclosure is unknown in Czech legal order. According to the Czech Civil Procedure Act, the claimants are obliged to precisely specify relevant facts supporting their claim and individually identified evidence proving it, together with a clear-cut demand for relief. The judge is entitled to order the defendant or third parties to submit to the court the evidence. There are no legal measures alleviating the burden of proof, although the proposed Amendment of Competition Act should reverse the burden of proof in case of consumers.

19. The Office admits that current legal framework in the Czech Republic may pose serious obstacles to potential plaintiffs. Strict legal requirements imposed on parties having burden of proof in civil proceedings and unequal access to evidence dissuades victims from private enforcement actions in competition matters. The Office therefore supports the proposal of *inter partes* disclosure, contained in the White Paper.

(A) *Conditions for obtaining a disclosure order by the court and its scope*

(i) *Sufficient fact pleading*

20. The plaintiffs must put forward plausible grounds demonstrating that they suffered some harm through infringement of competition law caused by the defendant; it must be admitted that the claimants cannot be expected to demonstrate any elevated degree of certainty proving their claims are well founded. The claimant would thus only have to assert general facts and propose less precisely identified evidence.

21. The Office considers this condition to be crucial in order to prevent unfounded or even abusive claims. Since the *inter partes* disclosure would be a completely new legal instrument in the Czech legal order, the Office would however need further clarification of the proposed measures, especially the minimal standard of pleading the plaintiff would be required to make, the timing of the disclosure request (whether it could be made only at the beginning of the proceedings or even later) and possible remedies in case the court rejected the request. It might also be considered whether the court should not be allowed to order the disclosure upon its own motion under certain conditions.

(ii) Inability of to claimant to get access to relevant evidence by other means

22. The claimants must also show that they are unable to produce the requested evidence by other means, despite making all efforts that can reasonably be expected from them. Similarly to the submission made above, the Office would welcome clarification of minimal procedural rules related to proving this condition and the extent of the claimants' obligations.

(iii) Specification of categories of evidence to be disclosed

23. Specification of sufficiently precise categories information, evidence or other means of evidence relevant to the claim is the third condition for the court to issue a disclosure order. From the point of view of the Office, the term "categories of evidence" requires further clarification, as well as their "sufficiently precise" specification.

(iv) Judicial control of relevance, necessity and proportionality of disclosure measure

24. The fourth condition requires that information about to be disclosed support the allegations of claimants (relevance), that there is no available equally suitable but less onerous measure which could have equivalent results (necessity) and that legitimate interests of the other parties should not be manifestly out of proportion to the objective of disclosure measure (proportionality).

25. The Office considers the judicial control in terms proposed as suitable to safeguard protection against unmeritorious claims. Should the Commission decide to turn the White Paper into some form of legally binding measures, the Office would encourage it to specify these terms in a way similar to the text contained in paragraphs 108 to 109 of the Working Paper.

(B) Further issues related to the scope of the disclosure order

26. The White Paper proposes that disclosure order should include all types of evidence that are admissible in the Member State concerned and that are under the control of defendants or third parties. With regard to disclosure and protection of confidential information the court should assess these conflicting interests from the point of view of proportionality. Disclosure of corporate statements submitted to a competition authority as part of a leniency application should be treated specifically; leniency applicants should be protected

against court disclosure orders to submit these documents. The protection from disclosure should be also granted to certain pieces or categories of evidence during a specified period of time if the competition authority shows the disclosure would jeopardise an ongoing antitrust investigation. On the other hand, unfavourable evidence should not be protected from disclosure.

27. The Office considers these rules governing the extent of disclosure as crucial for the effectiveness of the proposed systems. The Office encourages the Commission to specify these terms in the forthcoming legislative measures in a way similar to paragraphs 116 -120 of the Working Paper directly to the legislative text and specify more clearly what is to be meant by "adequate" protection. Minimal rules governing the process of assessment whether the information is really confidential should also be considered.

28. With regard to the "investigative privilege" of competition authorities the Office also suggests adopting specific rules on sharing information among the competition authorities and the courts.

(C) Potential addressees of disclosure orders and their right to be heard

29. The paragraphs 121 to 127of the Working Paper deal with different means of assessing the proportionality of disclosure by courts depending on potential addressees of the disclosure orders. Judges should take into account whether required evidence is in possession of the defendant, third party that may be a co-infringer or a non involved third party. Special protection should be given to such third parties who could be ordered to disclose only if the evidence is not available from parties of the law suit. They are entitled to have reimbursed any costs they incurred in relation with the disclosure order. As for public authorities, they should not be normally ordered to disclose any documents.

30. The right to be heard should be awarded to all potential addressees provided that there is no particular urgency. The Office puts forward that the right to be heard should guaranteed unless there were some clearly defined exceptional circumstances. Moreover, the individuals ordered to disclose should have the right of appeal against the court's order.

(D) Refusal to submit evidence and destruction thereof

31. In case that the party obliged to do so refuses to disclose evidence regardless of the court's order or it destroys it, the White Paper proposes that the courts should be provided with the power to choose from a range of sufficiently deterrent sanctions, including drawing adverse inferences from it. Whether sanctions would be imposed in individual cases should only depend on the discretion of courts.

32. Apart from the sanctions that clearly are necessary for the *inter partes* disclosure to be workable, the Offices proposes that there should be set up a supervisory system of compliance with the court orders and the position of judges during this process should be specified. Some undertakings under

investigation refuse to submit to the Office requested evidence even though the Office possesses very far reaching investigative and enforcement powers – without very strong and efficient supervisory and enforcement mechanism, the Office doubts that the system could work in countries where there is no experience with *inter pates* disclosure.

33. In this regard, the Office also encourages the Commission to Commission to consider the possibility of introducing presumptions of infringement of competition law for undertakings that would not submit the documents required.

IV. Binding effect of NCA decisions

34. Final decisions adopted by competition authorities or review courts finding an infringement of article 81 or 82 EC, which are related to the same agreements, decisions or practices of the identical infringers, should be legally binding on national courts in actions for damages. However, national courts can (or have to), in case of serious doubts, seek clarification on the interpretation of article 81 or 82 EC by the question for preliminary ruling to the Court of Justice pursuant to Article 234 EC.

35. Decisions of the Office are already binding for Czech courts, and so are the decisions of the Commission. The Office shares the view of the Commission that "*...there are no reasons to introduce a distinction of the effects of NCA decisions based on their origin.*" The Office therefore strongly supports this proposal.

36. Exceptions to the binding effect of NCA decisions analogous to the public order principle in Article 34 of Regulation 44/2001 seem to be reasonable and guaranteeing protection of interests of parties concerned.

37. The Office would however welcome a further clarification of what is to be meant by "*final judgement upholding the decision*". For example in the Czech Republic, decisions of the Office are reviewed by the Regional court; its judgement is binding and immediately effective, but it can still be cancelled by the Supreme Administrative Court, whose decisions are in turn reviewed by the Constitutional Court, not to mention the European Court of Human Rights. It is not clear from the White Paper at which level should the decision of competition authorities start to have binding effects.

V. Fault requirement

38. The White Paper sets out standards for proving fault with regard to the harm caused by the infringer. Since the Czech law does not require fault to be proven in order to claim damages, these proposals are not applicable. The Office nonetheless supports these proposals and it would even suggest to reconsider whether there should be at all the necessity to prove fault.

VI. Damages

39. The guiding principle for determination of damages suggested in the White Paper is the full compensation of the real value of the loss suffered by victims,

including actual loss, loss of profit and respective interest. However, if the national law sets out exemplary or punitive damages for infringement of national competition law, the victims are entitled to be awarded the same level of damages level in case EC law is infringed. The Office agrees that the *acquis communautaire* on the definition of damages should be codified as a minimum standard.

40. To ensure effective antitrust damages actions the Commission further intends to issue non-binding guidance for quantification of damages which should show calculation methods and could include simplified rules on estimating the loss suffered.

41. The Office fully supports such guidelines. Since there is a rule in the Czech law (albeit not often used in practice) that the judges can in exceptionally difficult cases only estimate the damages (i.e. the precise calculation and proof thereof is not required), the Office further suggests that similar rule could be set as a binding measure in the private enforcement as well.

VII. *Passing-on of overcharges*

42. As far as the passing on is concerned, the White Paper firstly proposes that defendants should be entitled to rely on the passing-on defence against a claim for compensation of the overcharge. The Office fully supports this proposal, which is in its opinion fully in line with the compensatory nature of private enforcement.

43. The White Paper further suggests to ease the burden of proof for indirect purchasers by enabling them to rely on a rebuttable presumption that the overcharge that the defendant illegally imposed on the direct purchaser has been passed on in its entirety down to their level. They are however still required to show to what extent the overcharge caused them harm. The Office supports the view of the Commission that the likelihood that the defendant would face multiple litigations on different levels of distribution is much lower than the likelihood of non-compensation of the indirect purchaser (and thus unjust enrichment of the infringer) due to the fact that the indirect purchaser was not able to bring sufficient evidence of the passing-on and its extent.

44. The last suggestion of the Commission as regards the passing-on is dealing with the cases in which purchasers at different levels in the distribution chain brought joint, parallel or consecutive actions. In the view of the Office the main principles for preventing under- or over-compensation in such cases should be specified directly in the forthcoming legal text. Mechanisms for informing about judgements in these matters should be established, for in the Czech Republic, there are no mechanisms under which claimants could gain knowledge about earlier judgments issued by the courts in damages actions.

VIII. *Limitation periods*

45. Setting out rules on calculating limitation periods in cases of continuous or repeated infringements as well as such rules concerning cases where victims are

not aware of the infringement and the harm it caused them is proposed by the Commission. The limitation periods should not start to run before the day, on which the infringement ended (in a case of a continuous or repeated infringement) and the victim of the infringement could be reasonably expected to have knowledge of it. These rules are already included in the Czech law.

46. There is also suggested to establish a new limitation period of at least two years which should start to run on the day that the appeal period against an infringement decision of a competition authority has elapsed or the review court has upheld its decision. Such a rule might strongly facilitate bringing of follow on suites and the Office encourages it to be established.

IX. *Costs of damages actions*

47. The White Paper encourages the Member States to reconsider their rules on costs associated with bringing actions for damages and the recovery thereof to facilitate meritorious litigation, namely in cases when claimant's financial situation is significantly weaker then that of defendant and when high costs prevent meritorious claims being brought due to the uncertainty of the outcome. Commission suggests that there should be a possibility of providing courts with power to issue cost orders derogating from the general cost rules, preferably upfront in the proceeding, which would guarantee that the unsuccessful party will not have to bear all costs incurred by the other party. These principles should cover also the court fees.

48. As civil procedure before courts in the Czech Republic is very strict and formal, the Office would welcome binding and more specific rules dealing with the allocation of costs directly in the forthcoming legal text. The only reason when the Czech court shall not have to award reimbursement of costs of proceedings (fully or in part) in situations "eligible for special concern"; this derogation from the "loser pays" principle is however not often applied by Czech courts.

49. Decisions on costs are typically an integral part of judgments on the merits in the Czech Republic. Therefore, the parties get knowledge about the amount of costs they are to carry only when they receive the judgement. The Office believes this might dissuade potential claimants and therefore supports the Commission's proposal to shift the decision on the distribution of costs to initial stages of the proceedings.

50. As far as the court fees are concerned, the basic amount constitutes 4 % of the amount sued according to the Czech law. There are exemptions for certain categories of claimants and claims from having to pay the court fees, they do however not apply for the antitrust damage actions. The requirement of the White Paper to set the fees in an "appropriate manner" is not sufficiently precise and the Office would welcome further clarification on this issue.

51. The White Paper finally suggests that there should be rules favouring settlements negotiations both before initiation of court proceedings and in the course of them. There is no effective mechanism in the Czech law in this regard. Due to its lack of experience, the Office would welcome further

clarification of rules governing the settlements procedure and encourages the Commission to set them in a binding legal instrument.

X. *Interaction between leniency programmes and actions for damages*

52. The measures which the Commission suggests in relation to the issue of interaction between leniency programmes and actions for damages are based on the principle that all leniency applications for immunity and for a reduction of fines submitted under the EC and national leniency programmes should be protected against disclosure. The protection of them should not depend on the fact whether the decision by the competition authority was already taken or not. The Office fully supports these propositions.

53. On the other hand, the Office does not support the idea of limiting the immunity applicant's civil liability to his direct and indirect contractual partners. The Office perceives the mere immunity or reduction of fines within public enforcement as sufficient to motivate undertakings to file leniency applications.

The Croatian Competition Law Regime from a European Perspective

M. DeKoninck

1. Introduction

The European Commission is looking forward to welcoming Croatia as the 28th EU Member State as soon as possible.[1]

1.1 Alignment with the European Acquis Communautaire

The EU and Croatia have entered the final phase of the accession negotiations.[2] In the process of fully aligning Croatian law with the European *acquis communautaire* difficult issues still remain to be tackled, in particular in the field of competition law. This chapter discusses the Croatian competition law regime from a European perspective; it focuses in particular on the extent to which the Croatian competition regime currently has been aligned with the Community *acquis*.

1.2 Outline

The following chapter first discusses the accession and negotiation process between the EU and Croatia. Then, the current Croatian competition law regime will be set out. This chapter addresses issues which have come to the surface during the process of aligning Croatian competition law with the European *acquis communautaire*. Afterwards, focus is on the enforcement of Croatian competition law and the issues which need to be tackled in this area to ensure full alignment with the Community *acquis*.

2. Croatian Competition Law and the EU

In 2003, the Republic of Croatia applied for European Union Membership and in June 2004 the European Council granted Croatia the official status of candidate country for EU Membership.[3]

1 Statement by EU Commission President Barroso following a meeting with Prime Minister of Croatia Kosor, 7 April 2011, Zagreb, <www.europa-eu-un.org/articles/en/article_10904_en.htm>, last consulted on 2 May 2011.

2 This contribution was written in the preparatory phase leading up to the conference. The accession negotiations have now been closed and the Accession Treaty of the EU with Croatia was signed on 9 December 2011. The country will become the 28th Member State of the European Union on 1 July 2013 subject to ratification of the Treaty by the EU Member States.

3 *Croatia: Commission recommends opening of accession negotiations*, Brussels, 20 April 2004, IP/04/507; *The Stabilisation and Association Agreement with Croatia enters into force today*, Brussels, 1 February 2005, IP/05/122.

2.1 The Stabilisation and Association Agreement

In order to pave to way towards EU Membership, Croatia had already in 2001 committed to the Stabilisation and Association Agreement (hereafter: SAA). On the basis of this agreement a competition regime is to be applied in trade relations between the Community and Croatia based on the EU criteria for agreements between undertakings, abuses of dominant position, public undertakings and undertakings with special or exclusive rights and State aid.[4] In February 2005, the SAA entered into force and later that year the accession negotiations between the EU and Croatia were opened.[5]

With the SAA Croatia has agreed to ensure the approximation of Croatian legislation to the Community *acquis*.[6] Croatia will, moreover, directly apply "the criteria arising from the application of the competition rules applicable in the Community" and "interpretative instruments adopted by the Community institutions".[7]

2.2 Croatia: the 28th EU Member State?

Important progress has been made since 2004 and the EU and Croatia have entered the final phase of the accession negotiations with 28 out of 35 negotiating chapters provisionally closed.[8] The European Commission (hereafter: the Commission) has emphasised that it is looking forward to welcoming Croatia as the 28th EU Member State as soon as possible.[9]

Nevertheless, the Commission emphasised that still difficult issues remain to be tackled. One of the main challenges is competition policy; significant efforts are still required to fully align the Croatian competition law regime with the EU *acquis communautaire*.[10]

---

4 Commission Opinion [COM(2004) 257 final] p. 67.

5 Commission Report [COM(2008) 674 final – SEC(2008) 2694].

6 Arts. 5 and 69 of the *Stabilisation and Association Agreement between the European Communities and their Member States, of the one part, and the Republic of Croatia, of the other part*, 28 January 2005, OJ L 26/3.

7 Art. 70(2) of the *Stabilisation and Association Agreement between the European Communities and their Member States, of the one part, and the Republic of Croatia, of the other part*, 28 January 2005, OJ L 26/3, see Annex I; B. Porobija, 'The Republic of Croatia', *in* M. Dabbah and B. Hawk, *Anti-Cartel Enforcement Worldwide*, 2009, p. 289; Evaluation of the Commission: <europa.eu/legislation_summaries/competition/international_dimension_and_enlargement/e12114_en.htm>, last consulted on 2 May 2011.

8 'Croatia on the Way to EU Membership: Challenges and Expectations' - Speech by EU Commission Vice-President Reding, 3 March 2011, Zagreb, <www.europa-eu-un.org/articles/en/article_10754_en.htm>, last consulted on 2 May 2011.

9 Statement by EU Commission President Barroso following a meeting with Prime Minister of Croatia Kosor, 7 April 2011, Zagreb, <www.europa-eu-un.org/articles/en/article_10904_en.htm>, last consulted on 2 May 2011.

10 Speech by EU Commission President Barroso at the Croatian Parliament, 7 April 2011, Zagreb, <www.europa-eu-un.org/articles/en/article_10930_en.htm>, last consulted on 2 May 2011; 'Croatia on the Way to EU Membership: Challenges and Expectations' - Speech by EU Commission Vice-President Reding, 3 March 2011, Zagreb, <www.europa-eu-un.org/articles/en/article_10754_en.htm>, last consulted on 2 May 2011; Commission Report [COM (2009) 533 – SEC (2009) 1333]; Commission Report [COM (2008) 674 final – SEC(2008) 2694]; Commission

3. Croatian Competition Legislation

The primary sources of Croatian competition law are the Competition Act and the State Aid Act.[11] In addition there are several bylaws and other subordinate regulations which regulate the areas concerned in more detail, for instance the regulation on the definition of relevant market (OG 51/2001), the regulation on agreements of minor importance (OG 51/2004) and the guide on the procedure for the assessment of concentrations.[12]

3.1 The Croatian Competition Act

The Croatian Competition Act is effective from 2003[13] and has recently been amended by the Competition Act of 2009 which entered into force on 1 October 2010.[14] Croatian competition law has been modelled on EU competition law and contains the main principles of the Community competition rules. The Act "lays down the competition rules and establishes the competition regime, regulates the powers, duties, internal organisation and proceedings carried out by the competent authority entrusted with the enforcement of this Act."[15] Croatian competition legislation contains provisions on both the prohibition of restrictive agreements and the abuse of a dominant position.[16]

3.1.1 Prohibited Agreements

The Croatian Competition Act does not specifically refer to cartels but uses the term 'prohibited agreements'.[17] These prohibited agreements are defined as: "all agreements between two or more independent undertakings, decisions by associations of undertakings and concerted practices, which have as their object or effect the distortion of competition in the relevant market."[18] Any such agreement, not exempted by Article 10 of the Competition Act on block exemptions, shall be void.[19] Croatian competition law currently acknowledges block exemptions for certain categories of horizontal agreements (OG 158/2004), vertical agreements (OG 51/2004), technology transfer agreements (OG 2/2005), distribution and servicing of motor vehicles agreements (OG 105/2004), technology transfer agreements (OG 2/2005) and insurance agreements (OG 54/2005).[20]

Report [COM (2007) 663 final – SEC(2007) 1431]; Commission Report [COM (2006) 649 final – SEC(2006) 1385]; Commission Report [COM (2005) 561 final – SEC(2005) 1424]; Commission Opinion [COM (2004) 257 final]; Porobija 2009, p. 289.

11 State Aid Act (OG 140/05).

12 Croatian Competition Agency, *Annual Plan 2010-2011*, Zagreb, 25 February 2010, p. 2.

13 Competition Act 2003 (OG 122/03).

14 Competition Act 2009 (OG 79/09).

15 Art. 1 Competition Act 2009 (OG 79/09).

16 Commission Opinion [COM (2004) 257 final], Chapter 6; see Annex II.

17 Art. 8 Competition Act 2009 (OG 79/09); see Annex II; Porobija 2009, p. 290.

18 Art. 8 Competition Act 2009 (OG 79/09); see Annex II.

19 Art. 8(4) Competition Act 2009 (OG 79/09); see Annex II.

20 The CCA website; <www.aztn.hr/trzisno-natjecanje/29/croatian-legislation/>; Porobija 2009 p. 291.

3.2 The Croatian State Aid Act

The Croatian State Aid Act sets out "general conditions and rules for the authorisation, monitoring the implementation and recovery of State aid for the purpose of the implementation of the international commitments undertaken by the Republic of Croatia, arising under the Stabilisation and Association Agreement between the Republic of Croatia and the European Communities and their Member States".[21]

3.3 Croatia and the Acquis Communautaire

The process of alignment of the Croatian competition regime with the Community *acquis* has progressed significantly since 2004. Important changes to Croatian competition law have, in particular, been introduced with the adoption of the Competition Act of 2009. The Act of 2009, amongst others, introduced a leniency policy.[22]

According to the Commission, Croatian competition law is now *generally* in line with the main Community principles on anti-competitive agreements, abuse of a dominant position, merger control and State aid.[23] In its latest progress report on Croatia the Commission concluded that in the field of competition law: "Overall, a reasonable level of alignment has been achieved."[24]

Nevertheless, as mentioned above, both the Council and the Commission have emphasised that still significant efforts are required to *fully align* the Croatian competition law regime with the European *acquis communautaire*.[25] It is especially needed to supplement the legislative framework in the area of State aid.[26] According to the Commission: "particular attention should be paid to State aid for the steel industry and to shipbuilding and tax aid, since these are key elements in the accession negotiations".[27]

21 Art. 1 State Aid Act (OG 140/05), see Annex III.

22 Commission Report [COM (2009) 533 – SEC (2009) 1333]; see Annex IV.

23 Commission Report [COM (2009) 533 – SEC (2009) 1333]; Commission Report [COM(2008) 674 final – SEC(2008) 2694]; Commission Report [COM(2007) 663 final – SEC(2007) 1431]; Commission Report [COM(2006) 649 final – SEC(2006) 1385]; Commission Report [COM(2005) 561 final – SEC(2005) 1424]; Commission Opinion [COM(2004) 257 final].

24 Commission Report [COM (2009) 533 – SEC (2009) 1333], p. 36.

25 Commission Report [COM (2009) 533 – SEC (2009) 1333]; Commission Report [COM (2008) 674 final – SEC(2008) 2694]; Commission Report [COM (2007) 663 final – SEC(2007) 1431]; Commission Report [COM (2006) 649 final – SEC(2006) 1385]; Commission Report [COM (2005) 561 final – SEC(2005) 1424]; Commission Opinion [COM (2004) 257 final]; Porobija, 2009, p. 289.

26 Council Decision of 12 February 2008 on the principles, priorities and conditions contained in the Accession Partnership with Croatia and repealing Decision 2006/145/EC, (2008/119/EC) – L42/51; Commission Report [COM (2009) 533 – SEC (2009) 1333], p. 34.

27 Evaluation of the Commission: <http://europa.eu/legislation_summaries/competition/international_dimension_and_enlargement/e12114_en.htm>, last consulted on 2 May 2011.

4. Enforcement

The principle authority for the enforcement of competition law in Croatia is the Croatian Competition Agency (CCA).[28] The decisions of the CCA are subject to the judicial control of the Administrative Court of the Republic of Croatia.[29]

4.1 The National Competition Authority – CCA

The CCA, which is seated in Zagreb, has been operative since 1997 and acts as an independent entity and performs its activities autonomously.[30] In line with the SAA, the CCA "applies the competition rules applicable in the EU and interpretative instruments adopted by the EU institutions".[31] In June 2009, the Commission underlined that:

> The Croatian Competition Agency must strengthen its administrative capacities. To do this it needs additional resources, including both a larger budget and personnel trained in competition law. The Competition Agency must also ensure full independence in decision-making and significantly improve its enforcement record, particularly as regards economic and legal assessment. Efforts should focus on preventing the most serious distortions of competition and introducing a new system of fines that acts as an effective deterrent.[32]

The Agency's deterrent effect and enforcement policy has been strengthened with the introduction of the 2009 Competition Act. Under the 2009 Competition Act infringements of competition rules are no longer treated as minor offences, instead they are considered *sui generis* violations and the CCA is empowered to impose fines.[33] The new Competition Act also enables the CCA to conduct a leniency programme.[34] This leniency programme "provides for the reduction of or immunity from fines for cartel members who are first to come forward and submit compelling evidence which contributes to the disclosure of the cartel".[35]

4.1.1 The CCA Structure

The managing body of the CCA is the Competition Council.[36] The Competition Council consists of five members and has a president which "represents and

28 Art. 6 Competition Act 2009 (OG 79/09).
29 Art. 67 Competition Act 2009 (OG 79/09).
30 Commission Opinion [COM(2004) 257 final], p. 68; This is in conformity with Art. 70(3) *Stabilisation and Association Agreement between the European Communities and their Member States, of the one part, and the Republic of Croatia, of the other part*, 28 January 2005, OJ L 26/3.
31 See the CCA website: <www.aztn.hr/o-nama/22/legal-powers/>, last consulted on 2 May 2011.
32 Evaluation of the Commission: <http://europa.eu/legislation_summaries/competition/international_dimension_and_enlargement/e12114_en.htm>, last consulted on 2 May 2011.
33 Commission Report [COM (2009) 533 – SEC (2009) 1333], p. 35; Croatian Competition Agency, *Annual Plan 2010-2011*, Zagreb, 25 February 2010, p. 7.
34 See Annex IV.
35 Commission Report [COM (2009) 533 – SEC (2009) 1333], p. 35; see the CCA website: <www.aztn.hr/trzisno-natjecanje/29/croatian-legislation/>, last consulted on 2 May 2011.
36 Art. 27 Competition Act 2009 (OG 79/09).

speaks for the Agency and manages its activities".[37] The members of the Council are appointed by the Croatian Parliament on the proposal of the Government of the Republic of Croatia with a five-year term of office. The Council is supported by expert staff who, amongst others, carry out investigations, establish distortion of competition and work on competition advocacy.[38]

4.2 Judicial Control – The Administrative Court

The decisions of the CCA are subject to the judicial control of the Administrative Court of the Republic of Croatia.[39] Previously, the system of control of the decisions of the CCA has been criticised heavily. The standard duration of the proceedings (three years) was regarded to be too long and the Administrative Court has not been found to be a suitable judicial forum to exercise the judicial control of the decisions adopted by the CCA.[40] The Commission also emphasised that improvements had to be made to the Croatian judicial system "to enable it to handle appeals against decisions of the Agency efficiently and in line with European legislation".[41]

With the adoption of the 2009 Competition Act several changes to the judicial system have been introduced. Article 67 of the 2009 Competition Act indicates the specific grounds for challenging the CCA's decisions; (1) misapplication or erroneous application of substantive provisions of competition law; (2) manifest errors in application of procedural provisions; (3) incorrect or incomplete facts of the case; (4) inappropriate fine and other issues contained in the decisions of the Agency.[42] In addition, with the adoption of the 2009 Competition Act, the Administrative Court of Croatia now reviews both the legality and the merits of the decisions of the CCA and it also decides on the level of fines imposed by the CCA for infringements of competition rules.[43] Also, all actions brought before the Administrative Court of the Republic of Croatia pursuant to the Competition Act are now regarded as 'urgent'.[44]

37 Art. 27(1) Competition Act 2009 (OG 79/09), for further information on the structure of the CCA; see Annex V.

38 See the CCA website: <www.aztn.hr/o-nama/33/expert-staff/>, last consulted on 2 May 2011.

39 Art. 67 Competition Act 2009 (OG 79/09); see Annex VI.

40 Porobija 2009, p. 302.

41 Evaluation of the Commission: <http://europa.eu/legislation_summaries/competition/international_dimension_and_enlargement/e12114_en.htm>, last consulted on 2 May 2011; Council Decision of 12 February 2008 on the principles, priorities and conditions contained in the Accession Partnership with Croatia and repealing Decision 2006/145/EC, (2008/119/EC) – OJ L 42/51.

42 Art. 67 Competition Act 2009 (OG 79/09), see Annex VI.

43 The CCA website: <www.aztn.hr/trzisno-natjecanje/29/croatian-legislation/>, last consulted on 2 May 2011.

44 Art. 69(1) Competition Act 2009 (OG 79/09); see Annex VI.

Time will eventually tell whether these procedural changes have enabled the Croatian judicial system to handle appeals against the decisions of the CCA "efficiently and in line with EU legislation".[45]

5. Conclusion

Croatian competition law is, generally, in line with the main Community principles on anti-competitive agreements, abuse of a dominant position, merger control and State aid. With the adoption of the 2009 Competition Act, several changes to the Croatian competition law regime have been introduced. The CCA is now empowered to impose fines and to conduct a leniency programme. In addition, several adjustments have been made to the process of judicial control.
Nevertheless, in order to achieve the status of the 28th EU Member State, efforts are still required to *fully* align the Croatian competition law regime with the European *acquis communautaire*, in particular in the area of State aid since this is considered to be one of the key elements in the accession negotiations. Also, it remains to be seen whether the amendments to the judicial procedure have made the procedure truly efficient and in line with EU law.

Annex I

Article 70 SAA - Competition and other economic provisions

1. The following are incompatible with the proper functioning of the Agreement, in so far as they may affect trade between the Community and Croatia:
(i) all agreements between undertakings, decisions by associations of undertakings and concerted practices between undertakings which have as their object or effect the prevention, restriction or distortion of competition;
(ii) abuse by one or more undertakings of a dominant position in the territories of the Community or of Croatia as a whole or in a substantial part thereof;
(iii) any State aid which distorts or threatens to distort competition by favouring certain undertakings or certain products.

45 Evaluation of the Commission: <http://europa.eu/legislation_summaries/competition/international_dimension_and_enlargement/e12114_en.htm>, last consulted on 2 May 2011; Council Decision of 12 February 2008 on the principles, priorities and conditions contained in the Accession Partnership with Croatia and repealing Decision 2006/145/EC, (2008/119/EC) – OJ L 42/51.

Annex II

Article 8 Competition Act - Prohibited agreements

(1) There shall be prohibited all agreements between two or more independent undertakings, decisions by associations of undertakings and concerted practices, which have as their object or effect the distortion of competition in the relevant market, and in particular those which:
1. directly or indirectly fix purchase or selling prices or any other trading conditions;
2. limit or control production, markets, technical development or investment;
3. share markets or sources of supply;
4. apply dissimilar conditions to equivalent transactions with other undertakings, thereby placing them at a competitive disadvantage;
5. make the conclusion of contracts subject to acceptance by the other parties of supplementary obligations which, by their nature or according to commercial usage, have no connection with the subject of such contracts.
(2) Within the meaning of paragraph (1) of this Article agreements particularly refer to contracts, particular provisions thereof, implicit oral or explicitly written down arrangements between undertakings, concerted practices resulting form such arrangements, decisions by undertakings or associations of undertakings, general terms of business and other acts of undertakings which are or may constitute a part of these agreements and similar, notwithstanding the fact if they are concluded between undertakings operating at the same level of the production or distribution chain (horizontal agreements) or between undertakings who do not operate at the same level of the production or distribution chain (vertical agreements).
(3) By way of derogation from paragraph (1) hereof, certain categories of agreements shall be granted exemption from general prohibition under paragraph (1) of this Article and consequently shall not be prohibited if they, throughout their duration, cumulatively comply with the following conditions:
1. they contribute to improving the production or distribution of goods and/or services, or to promoting technical or economic progress,
2. while allowing consumers a fair share of the resulting benefit,
3. they do not impose on the undertakings concerned restrictions which are not indispensable to the attainment of those objectives, and
4. they do not afford such undertakings the possibility of eliminating competition in respect of a substantial part of goods and/or services in question.
(4) Agreements that prevent, restrict or distort competition within the meaning of paragraph (1) of this Article, and which do not fulfil the conditions of paragraph (3) of this Article, and agreements to which Article 10 of this Act does not apply shall be *ex lege* void.
(5) Undertakings – parties to the agreement bear the burden of proof of demonstrating that the conditions referred to in paragraph (3) of this Article apply.

Article 101 TFEU (ex Art. 81 TEC)

1. The following shall be prohibited as incompatible with the internal market: all agreements between undertakings, decisions by associations of undertakings and

concerted practices which may affect trade between Member States and which have as their object or effect the prevention, restriction or distortion of competition within the internal market, and in particular those which:
(a) directly or indirectly fix purchase or selling prices or any other trading conditions;
(b) limit or control production, markets, technical development, or investment;
(c) share markets or sources of supply;
(d) apply dissimilar conditions to equivalent transactions with other trading parties, thereby placing them at a competitive disadvantage;
(e) make the conclusion of contracts subject to acceptance by the other parties of supplementary obligations which, by their nature or according to commercial usage, have no connection with the subject of such contracts.
2. Any agreements or decisions prohibited pursuant to this Article shall be automatically void.
3. The provisions of paragraph 1 may, however, be declared inapplicable in the case of:
– any agreement or category of agreements between undertakings,
– any decision or category of decisions by associations of undertakings,
– any concerted practice or category of concerted practices,
which contributes to improving the production or distribution of goods or to promoting technical or economic progress, while allowing consumers a fair share of the resulting benefit, and which does not:
(a) impose on the undertakings concerned restrictions which are not indispensable to the attainment of these objectives;
(b) afford such undertakings the possibility of eliminating competition in respect of a substantial part of the products in question.

Article 12 Competition Act - Dominant position

(1) An undertaking can be presumed to be in a dominant position when, due to its market power, it can act in the relevant market to a considerable extent independently of it's actual or potential competitors, consumers, buyers or suppliers and this is particularly the case when an undertaking:
1. has no significant competitors in the relevant market, and/or
2. holds a significant market power in relation to its actual or potential competitors, and particularly relating to the following:
– its market share and a period of time in which this market position has been held, and/or,
– its financial power, and/or,
– access to sources of supply or to the market itself, and/or,
– connected undertakings, and/or,
– legal or factual barriers for other undertakings to enter the market, and/or,
– the capability to dictate market conditions considering its supply or demand, and/or,
– the capacity of foreclosure against competitors by redirecting them to other undertakings.
(2) Within the meaning of this Act an undertaking which holds more than 40% of the market share in the relevant market may hold a dominant position.

(3) Two or more legally independent economic entities may hold a joint dominant position if they act to a considerable extent independently of their competitors and/or customers and/or consumers on the relevant market.

Article 13 Competition Act - Abuse of a dominant position

(1) Any abuse by one or more undertakings of a dominant position in the relevant market shall be prohibited, particularly involving the behaviour which consists of:
1. directly or indirectly imposing unfair purchase or selling prices or other unfair trading conditions;
2. limiting production, markets or technical development to the prejudice of consumers;
3. applying dissimilar conditions to equivalent transactions with other undertakings, thereby placing them at a competitive disadvantage;
4. making the conclusion of contracts subject to acceptance by the other parties of supplementary obligations which, by their nature or according to commercial usage, have no connection with the subject of such contract.

Article 102 TFEU (ex Art. 82 TEC)

Any abuse by one or more undertakings of a dominant position within the internal market or in a substantial part of it shall be prohibited as incompatible with the internal market in so far as it may affect trade between Member States.
Such abuse may, in particular, consist in:
(a) directly or indirectly imposing unfair purchase or selling prices or other unfair trading conditions;
(b) limiting production, markets or technical development to the prejudice of consumers;
(c) applying dissimilar conditions to equivalent transactions with other trading parties, thereby placing them at a competitive disadvantage;
(d) making the conclusion of contracts subject to acceptance by the other parties of supplementary obligations which, by their nature or according to commercial usage, have no connection with the subject of such contracts.

Annex III

Article 3 Competition Act - Definition of State Aid

(1) Within the meaning of this Act, state aid shall mean any actual and potential expenditures or decreased revenue of the state granted in any form whatsoever by the aid provider, which distorts or threatens to distort competition by favouring certain aid beneficiaries, insofar as it may affect the international commitments undertaken by the Republic of Croatia referred to in Article 1 hereof.
(2) Within the meaning of this Act, state aid scheme (hereinafter: aid scheme) shall mean any legal document on the basis of which, without any additional implementing measures required, individual aid may be granted to ex ante unspecified aid beneficiaries, and any legal document on the basis of which state aid which is not linked to a particular project may be awarded to one or more aid beneficiaries for an indefinite period of time and/or in an indefinite amount.

(3) Within the meaning of this Act, individual state aid (hereinafter: individual aid) referred to under paragraph (1) hereof shall mean any state aid which is not granted under the aid scheme, and any state aid granted under the aid scheme which is subject to additional authorisation.

Article 107 TFEU (ex Art. 87 TEC)

1. Save as otherwise provided in the Treaties, any aid granted by a Member State or through State resources in any form whatsoever which distorts or threatens to distort competition by favouring certain undertakings or the production of certain goods shall, in so far as it affects trade between Member States, be incompatible with the internal market.
2. The following shall be compatible with the internal market:
(a) aid having a social character, granted to individual consumers, provided that such aid is granted without discrimination related to the origin of the products concerned;
(b) aid to make good the damage caused by natural disasters or exceptional occurrences;
(c) aid granted to the economy of certain areas of the Federal Republic of Germany affected by the division of Germany, in so far as such aid is required in order to compensate for the economic disadvantages caused by that division. Five years after the entry into force of the Treaty of Lisbon, the Council, acting on a proposal from the Commission, may adopt a decision repealing this point.
3. The following may be considered to be compatible with the internal market:
(a) aid to promote the economic development of areas where the standard of living is abnormally low or where there is serious underemployment, and of the regions referred to in Article 349, in view of their structural, economic and social situation;
(b) aid to promote the execution of an important project of common European interest or to remedy a serious disturbance in the economy of a Member State;
(c) aid to facilitate the development of certain economic activities or of certain economic areas, where such aid does not adversely affect trading conditions to an extent contrary to the common interest;
(d) aid to promote culture and heritage conservation where such aid does not affect trading conditions and competition in the Union to an extent that is contrary to the common interest;
(e) such other categories of aid as may be specified by decision of the Council on a proposal from the Commission.

Annex IV

Article 65 Competition Act - Reduction of or immunity from fines

(1) With the view to disclosing the most severe infringements of the provisions of this Act, the Agency may grant immunity from fine to a cartel member who first comes forward and informs the Agency on the existence of a cartel and supplies evidence which will enable the Agency to initiate the proceeding in connection

with the alleged cartel, or to the first cartel member who submits information and evidence which will enable the Agency to find the infringement of this Act in connection with the alleged cartel in the previously initiated proceedings where the Agency had no sufficient evidence to adopt a decision, i.e. to detect the existence of a cartel.

(2) Immunity from fine under paragraph (1) of this Article may not be granted to the undertaking who was the originator (leader) or instigator of the cartel.

(3) Undertakings disclosing their participation in a cartel that do not meet the conditions for immunity from paragraph (1) of this Article may be eligible to benefit from a reduction of the fine, if they provide the Agency with evidence which represents significant added value with respect to the evidence already in the Agency's possession and which substantially contribute to the closure of the proceeding concerned.

(4) Upon the proposal of the Agency, the Government of the Republic of Croatia shall further develop the criteria for the immunity from and reduction of fines referred to under paragraphs (1) and (2) this Article in line with the criteria arising form the application of competition rules in the Community and within the meaning of Article 74 of this Act.

(5) The imposition of fines under the provisions of this Act is without prejudice to criminal liability of the person who was imposed the fine pursuant to this Act.

Annex V The Structure of the CCA

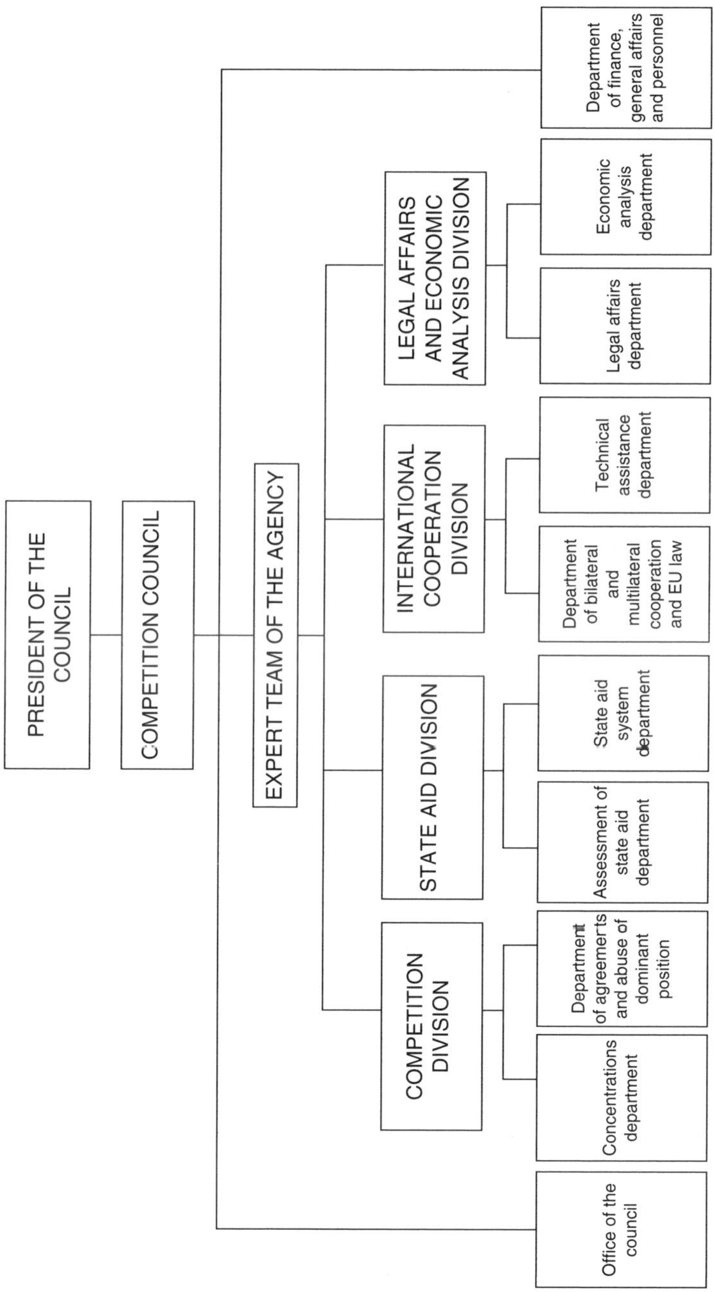

Annex VI

Competition Act 2003

Article 58 - Court Protection

Against the decisions of the Agency referred to in Article 57 of this Act, no appeal is allowed, but the injured party may file an administrative dispute before the Administrative Court of the Republic of Croatia.

Competition Act 2009

Article 67 - Court review

(1) Against the decisions of the Agency which establish the infringements of this Act and impose fines, and against the decisions by which the proceeding is terminated on the account of dealing with the preliminary issue, no appeal is allowed but the injured party may bring a claim before the Administrative Court of the Republic of Croatia within 30 days from the receipt of the decision. The claim shall be decided over by a panel of 3 judges concerning the following points of the decision concerned:
1. misapplication or erroneous application of substantive provisions of competition law;
2. manifest errors in application of procedural provisions;
3. incorrect or incomplete facts of the case;
4. inappropriate fine and other issues contained in the decisions of the Agency.

(2) Against the procedural orders adopted by the Agency during the proceedings, no appeal is allowed but the injured party may bring a claim before the Administrative Court of the Republic of Croatia.
(3) By way of derogation from paragraph (2) of this Article, against the procedural order by which the proceedings are initiated (Article 39), the procedural order on the basis of which the Agency decides to initiate one single procedure against two or more independent undertakings in the case where rights and/or obligations are based on the same or similar facts of the case and on the same legal basis, the procedural order on the basis of which the request for access to files or a part thereof has been denied (Article 47) and the procedural order by which the Agency joins two or more new notifications of a concentration previously notified by one and the same undertaking and conducts a joint assessment proceeding (Article 21 paragraph (7)) no appeal and no claim at the Administrative Court of the Republic of Croatia is allowed.
(4) The claim referred to under paragraph (1) of this Article postpones the enforcement of the decision of the Agency.
(5) Against the decision of the Agency establishing an infringement of this Act and imposing a fine for the committed infringement referred to under paragraph (1) hereof a claim may be filed by the injured party to the proceedings, whereas against the decision of the Agency establishing that no infringement of competition rules within the meaning of this Act has been committed a claim may be filed also by a person who filed the initiative and the person who has been granted the

same procedural rights which are enjoyed by the person who filed the initiative as referred to in Article 36 paragraphs (3) and (4).

Competition Act 2009

Article 68

(1) The panel of judges of the Administrative Court of the Republic of Croatia shall discuss and decide on the basis of the facts presented in evidence during the proceedings.
(2) The plaintiff may not present new facts in evidence but he/she may propose new evidence relating to the facts which had been presented in evidence during the proceeding.
(3) New facts may be presented only under the condition that the plaintiff provides evidence that he/she did not have or could not have had knowledge of these facts during the proceeding.

Competition Act 2009

Article 69

(1) All actions brought before the Administrative Court of the Republic of Croatia pursuant to this Act are urgent.
(2) Damages claims relating to the infringements of this Act shall fall under the competence of the relevant commercial courts.